PRESIDENT RONALD REAGAN

THE QUEST FOR PEACE,
THE CAUSE OF FREEDOM

PRESIDENT RONALD REAGAN

THE QUEST FOR PEACE, THE CAUSE OF FREEDOM

SELECTED SPEECHES ON THE UNITED STATES AND THE WORLD

Fredonia Books
Amsterdam, The Netherlands

The Quest for Peace, the Cause of Freedom

by
Ronald Reagan

ISBN: 1-4101-0837-6

Copyright © 2005 by Fredonia Books

Reprinted from the 1988 edition

Fredonia Books
Amsterdam, The Netherlands
http://www.fredoniabooks.com

PRESIDENT RONALD REAGAN:

THE QUEST FOR PEACE, THE CAUSE OF FREEDOM

SELECTED SPEECHES ON THE UNITED STATES AND THE WORLD

Table of Contents

Introduction   9

PART I: PRESIDENT REAGAN'S VISION OF AMERICA   13

Televised Address Prior to the 1964 Presidential Election
October 27, 1964   14

Televised Address on the Eve of the 1980 Presidential Election
November 3, 1980   25

First Inaugural Address
January 20, 1981   33

Commencement Address at the University of Notre Dame
May 17, 1981   39

Radio Address on Domestic Social Issues
January 22, 1983   46

Remarks to the National Association of Evangelicals
March 8, 1983   49

Message for Independence Day
July 3, 1983   58

Second Inaugural Address
January 21, 1985   61

Address on the Explosion of the Space Shuttle *Challenger*
January 28, 1986   67

Remarks at the Memorial Service for the Crew of the *Challenger*
January 31, 1986   69

Address on the State of the Union
February 4, 1986   73

Proclamation Establishing Law Day U.S.A.
April 16, 1986   81

PART II: INTERNATIONAL ISSUES 85

Address to the Permanent Council of the Organization of American States
February 24, 1982 86

Remarks to the Conference on Free Elections
November 4, 1982 95

Radio Address to the Nation and Peoples of Other Countries
September 24, 1983 98

Announcement of the Central America Democracy, Peace and Development Initiative
February 3, 1984 102

Address to the Center for Strategic and International Studies, Georgetown University
April 6, 1984 104

Address to the 39th Session, United Nations General Assembly
September 24, 1984 116

Address on Establishing International Human Rights Day
December 10,1984 127

Announcement of a Peace Proposal for Central America
April 4, 1985 132

Address to the 42nd Session, United Nations General Assembly
September 21, 1987 135

Ronald Reagan: A Pictorial Biography 145

PART III: DEFENSE POLICY AND ARMS REDUCTION 171

Address to the United Nations Second Special Session on Disarmament
June 17, 1982 172

Televised Address on Strategic Arms Reduction and Nuclear Deterrence
November 22, 1982 180

Televised Address on National Security
February 26, 1986 188

PART IV: THE UNITED STATES AND EUROPE   197

Address to the British Parliament
June 8, 1982 198

Address to the Irish Parliament
June 4, 1984 208

Remarks to Veterans at Pointe du Hoc, Normandy
June 6, 1984 219

Statement on the 40th Anniversary of the Yalta Conference
February 5, 1985 224

Remarks at the Bergen-Belsen Concentration Camp
May 5, 1985 226

Address to the European Parliament
May 8, 1985 229

Televised Address to Western Europe prior to the Venice Economic Summit
June 5, 1987 240

Remarks at the Brandenburg Gate, West Berlin
June 12, 1987 247

Televised Worldnet Address to Europe
November 4, 1987 253

PART V: THE UNITED STATES AND THE SOVIET UNION   263

Address to the 40th Session, United Nations General Assembly
October 24, 1985 264

Report to the U.S. Congress on the Geneva Summit
November 21, 1985 273

Televised-New Year's Day Address to the Soviet People
January 1, 1986 279

**Address to the Soviet and American Peoples Following the
Signing of the INF Treaty**
December 8, 1987 282

Introduction

I have been giving speeches for more than 40 years—as a radio announcer, an actor and head of the Screen Actors Guild, as governor of the state of California, and as President of the United States. In that time, I have spoken before groups of five or less gathered in a living room—and to hundreds of millions of people around the world via satellite television.

My audiences have been as varied as their size—factory workers and business executives, students and farmers, homemakers and heads of state. I have spoken to crowds of cheering supporters throughout the country and, yes, to crowds filled with political opponents who booed when I spoke. (I like the cheering better, but disagreement and boos come with the territory when one is running for office in a democracy.)

Abroad, I have tried to convey the message of a strong America, dedicated to the quest for peace and the cause of freedom, in speeches before the British Parliament in London and the Brandenburg Gate in West Berlin, in the halls of the United Nations and to the citizens of such countries as Brazil, Mexico and Costa Rica; China, South Korea and Japan; Italy, Spain and France. And by means of radio and television, I have sought to communicate with the peoples of the Soviet Union and other nations across the barriers of distance, language and political ideology.

Whatever the occasion for the speeches presented here, which span seven years of my presidency, I have always tried to speak plainly about the enduring values upon which this nation was founded: faith in God, commitment to democracy, the quest for peace, limited government, reliance on the free enterprise system, and an unyielding belief in human freedom as the essential key to human achievement and the progress of mankind. I believe as fervently in these core values today as I did when I spoke to the nation on the eve of the 1980 presidential election, and years earlier, in 1964, when I first spoke nationally on behalf of another candidate for President, my good friend Barry Goldwater.

I have sometimes been accused of being overly optimistic in my speeches about America and the future, but I make no apologies. Faith and freedom are not wishful thinking, but, quite simply, the most powerful forces in the world today. Democracy, freedom, economic opportunity—these are not uniquely American concepts, but ideas that lift the hearts and compel the allegiance of peoples throughout the world. And they are the lodestars that have guided my presidency.

Achievement, after all, can only be built on aspiration and hope, not pessimism. Seven years ago, when I first took office as President, who would have believed that we could sign an agreement with the Soviets not only to stop building additional nuclear weapons, but indeed to eliminate some of them? Yet, last year we took that important step with the signing of the INF Treaty. This truly historic treaty eliminates—for the first time—an entire class of U.S. and Soviet nuclear weapons.

Realism is essential, but democracy rests upon the rock of hope, the belief in a future of greater freedom and opportunity for succeeding generations. When the children of the world turn their faces to the light, let them see a sunrise. We owe them no less.

I offer this collection of speeches as the expression of my belief in the values at work in the United States and the world today, and of my vision of a world of peace, democracy and individual freedom that millions of men and women are striving daily to build.

As I so often end my speeches—thank you and God bless you.

Ronald Reagan
PRESIDENT OF THE UNITED STATES OF AMERICA

The White House
Washington, D C.
May 1988

PART I

President Reagan's Vision of America

A Time for Choosing

TELEVISED ADDRESS

OCTOBER 27, 1964

(This televised address in support of the 1964
Republican Party presidential candidate, Barry Goldwater,
brought Ronald Reagan national political attention
In 1966 Mr. Reagan was elected governor of
the state of California.)

I am going to talk of contro-
versial things. I make no apology for this. I have been talking
on this subject for 10 years, obviously under the administration of both parties. I mention this only because it seems
impossible to legitimately debate the issues of the day without being subjected to name-calling and the application of
labels. Those who deplore use of the terms "pink" and "leftist"
are themselves guilty of branding all who oppose their liberalism as right-wing extremists. How long can we afford the luxury of this family fight when we are at war with the most dangerous enemy ever known to man?

If we lose that war, and in so doing lose our freedom, it
has been said history will record with the greatest astonish-
ment that those who had the most to lose did the least to
prevent its happening. The guns are silent in this war, but
frontiers fall while those who should be warriors prefer neu-

trality. Not too long ago, two friends of mine were talking to a Cuban refugee. He was a businessman who had escaped from Castro. In the midst of his tale of horrible experiences, one of my friends turned to the other and said, "We don't know how lucky we are." The Cuban stopped and said, "How lucky you are? I had some place to escape to." And in that sentence he told the entire story. If freedom is lost here, there is no place to escape to.

Government and Freedom

It's time we asked ourselves if we still know the freedoms intended for us by the Founding Fathers. James Madison said, "We base all our experiments on the capacity of mankind for self-government." This idea, that government was beholden to the people, that it had no other source of power except the sovereign people, is still the newest, most unique idea in all the long history of man's relation to man. For almost two centuries we have proved man's capacity for self-government, but today we are told we must choose between a left and right or, as others suggest, a third alternative, a kind of safe middle ground. I suggest to you there is no left or right, only an up or down. Up to the maximum of individual freedom consistent with law and order, or down to the ant heap of totalitarianism and, regardless of their humanitarian purpose, those who would sacrifice freedom for security have, whether they know it or not, chosen this downward path. Plutarch warned, "The real destroyer of the liberties of the people is he who spreads among them bounties, donations and benefits."

Today there is an increasing number who can't see a fat man standing beside a thin one without automatically coming to the conclusion the fat man got that way by taking advantage of the thin one. So they would seek the answer to all the problems of human need through government. Howard K. Smith of television fame has written, "The profit motive is outmoded. It must be replaced by the incentives of the welfare state." He says, "The distribution of goods must be effected by a planned economy."

Another articulate spokesman for the welfare state defines liberalism as meeting the material needs of the masses through the full power of centralized government. I for one find it disturbing when a representative refers to the free men and women of this country as the masses, but beyond this, the full power of centralized government was the very thing the Founding Fathers sought to minimize. They knew you don't control things, you can't control the economy, without controlling people. So we have come to a time for choosing. Either we accept the responsibility for our own destiny, or we abandon the American Revolution and confess that an intellectual belief in a far-distant capital can plan our lives for us better than we can plan them ourselves.

Already the hour is late. Government has laid its hand on health, housing, farming, industry, commerce, education, and, to an ever-increasing degree, interferes with the people's right to know. Government tends to grow; government programs take on weight and momentum, as public servants say, always with the best of intentions, "What greater service we could render if only we had a little more money and a little more power." But the truth is that outside of its legitimate function, government does nothing as well or as economically as the private sector of the economy.

Farming

What better example do we have of this than government's involvement in the farm economy over the last 30 years? One-fourth of farming has seen a steady decline in the per capita consumption of everything it produces. That one-fourth is regulated and subsidized by government.

In contrast, the three-fourths of farming unregulated and unsubsidized has seen a 21 percent increase in the per capita consumption of all its produce. Since 1955 the cost of the farm program has nearly doubled. Direct payment to farmers is eight times as great as it was nine years ago, but farm income remains unchanged while [the] farm surplus is bigger. In that same period we have seen a decline of five million in the farm population, but an increase in the number of Department of Agriculture employees.

There is now one such employee for every 30 farms in the United States, and still they can't figure how 66 shiploads of grain headed for Austria could disappear without a trace, and Billy Sol Estes* never left shore. Three years ago, the government put into effect a program to curb the over-production of feed grain. Now, $2,500 million later, the corn crop is 100 million bushels bigger than before the program started. And the cost of the program prorates out to $43 for every dollar bushel of corn we don't grow. Nor is this the only example of the price we pay for government meddling. Some government programs with the passage of time take on a sacrosanct quality.

TVA

One such considered above criticism, sacred as motherhood, is TVA (Tennessee Valley Authority). This program started as a flood-control project; the Tennessee Valley was periodically ravaged by destructive floods. The Army Engineers set out to solve this problem. They said that it was possible that once in 500 years there could be a total capacity flood that would inundate some 240,000 hectares. Well, the Engineers fixed that. They made a permanent lake which inundated a half million hectares. This solved the problem of the floods, but the annual interest on the TVA debt is five times as great as the annual flood damage they

*Corrupt agricultural financier

sought to correct.

Of course, you will point out that TVA gets electric power from the impounded waters, and this is true, but today 85 percent of TVA's electricity is generated in coal-burning steam plants. Now, perhaps you'll charge that I'm overlooking the navigable waterway that was created, providing cheap barge traffic, but the bulk of the freight barged on that waterway is coal being shipped to the TVA steam plants, and the cost of maintaining that channel each year would pay for shipping all of the coal by rail, and there would be money left over.

One last argument remains: The prosperity produced by such large programs of government spending. Certainly there are few areas where more spending has taken place. The Labor Department lists 50 percent of the 169 counties in the Tennessee Valley as permanent areas of poverty, distress and unemployment.

Housing

Meanwhile, back in the city, under urban renewal, the assault on freedom carries on. Private property rights have become so diluted that public interest is anything a few planners decide it should be. In Cleveland, Ohio, to get a project underway, city officials reclassified 84 buildings as substandard in spite of the fact their own inspectors had previously pronounced these buildings sound. The owners stood by and watched $26 million worth of property destroyed by the "headache" ball [wrecker's ball]. Senate Bill 628 says, "Any property, be it home or commercial structure, can be declared slum or blighted and the owner has no recourse at law. The Law Division of the Library of Congress and the General Accounting Office have said that the Courts will have to rule against the owner."

In one key eastern city, a man owning a blighted area sold his property to urban renewal for several million dollars. At the same time, he submitted his own plan for the rebuilding of this area and the government sold him back his own property for 22 percent of what they paid. Now the government announces, "We are going to build subsidized housing in the thousands where we have been building in the hundreds." At the same time, FHA (Federal Housing Administration) and the Veterans Administration reveal they are holding 120,000 housing units reclaimed from mortgage foreclosure, mostly because the low down payments and the easy terms brought the owners to a point where they realized the unpaid balance on the homes amounted to a sum greater than the homes were worth, so they just walked out the front door, possibly to take up residence in newer subsidized housing, again with little or no down payment and easy terms.

Some of the foreclosed homes have already been bulldozed into the earth; others, it has been announced, will be refurbished and put on sale for down payments as low as $100 and 35 years to pay. This will give the bulldozers a second crack.

Welfare

It is in the area of social welfare that government has found its most fertile growing bed. So many of us accept our responsibility for those less fortunate. We are susceptible to humanitarian appeals.

Federal welfare spending is today 10 times greater than it was in the dark depths of the Depression [1930s]. Federal, state and local welfare combined spend $45,000 million a year. Now the government has announced that 20 percent, some 9.3 million families, are poverty stricken on the basis that they have less than a $3,000 a year income.

If this present welfare spending was prorated equally among these poverty-stricken families, we could give each family more than $4,500 a year. Actually, direct aid to the poor averages less than $600 per family. There must be some administrative overhead somewhere. Now, are we to believe that another multimillion dollar program added to the half a hundred programs and the $45,000 million, will, through some magic, end poverty? For three decades we have tried to solve unemployment by government planning, without success. The more the plans fail, the more the planners plan.

The latest is the Area Redevelopment Agency, and in two years less than one-half of one percent of the unemployed could attribute new jobs to this agency, and the cost to the taxpayer for each job found was $5,000. But beyond the great bureaucratic waste, what are we doing to the people we seek to help?

Recently a judge told me of an incident in his court. A fairly young woman with six children, pregnant with her seventh, came to him for a divorce. Under his questioning it became apparent her husband did not share this desire. Then the whole story came out. Her husband was a laborer earning $250 a month. By divorcing him she could get a $100 raise. She was eligible for $350 a month from the Aid to Dependent Children Program. She had been talked into divorce by two friends who had already done this very thing. But any time we question the schemes of the do-gooders, we are denounced as being opposed to their humanitarian goal. It seems impossible to legitimately debate their solutions with the assumption that all of us share the desire to help those less fortunate. They tell us we are always against, never for anything. Well, it isn't so much that liberals are ignorant. It's just that they know so much that isn't so.

Social Security

We are for a provision that destitution should not follow unemployment by reason of old age. For that reason we have accepted Social Security as a step toward meeting that problem. However, we are against the irresponsibility of those who charge that any criticism or suggested improvement of the program means we want to end payment to those who depend on Social Security for their livelihood.

We have been told in millions of pieces of literature and press releases that Social Security is an insurance program; but the executives of Social Security appeared before the Supreme Court in the case of *Nestor v. Fleming* and proved to the Court's satisfaction that it is not insurance but is a welfare program, and Social Security dues are a tax for the general use of the government. Well, it can't be both, insurance and welfare. Later, appearing before a congressional committee, they admitted that Social Security is today $298,000 million in the red. This fiscal irresponsibility has already caught up with us.

Faced with a bankruptcy, we find that today a young man in his early 20s, going to work at less than an average salary, will, with his employer, pay into Social Security an amount which could provide the young man with a retirement insurance policy guaranteeing $220 a month at age 65, and the government promises him $127.

Now, are we so lacking in business sense that we cannot put this program on a sound actuarial basis, so that those who do depend on it won't come to the cupboard and find it bare? And at the same time, can't we introduce voluntary features, so that those who can make better provision for themselves are allowed to do so? Incidentally, we might also allow participants in Social Security to name their own beneficiaries, which they cannot do in the present program. These are not insurmountable problems.

Plans for Old and Young

We have today 30 million workers protected by industrial and union pension funds that are soundly financed by some $70,000 million invested in corporate securities and income-earning real estate. I think we are for telling our senior citizens that no one in this country should be denied medical care for lack of funds, but we are against forcing all citizens into a compulsory government program regardless of need. Now the government has turned its attention to our young people, and suggests that it can solve the problem of school dropouts and juvenile delinquency through some kind of revival of the old CCC [Civilian Conservation Corps, 1930s] camps. The suggested plan prorates out to a cost of $4,700 a year for each young person we want to help. We can send them to Harvard for $2,700 a year. Of course, don't get me wrong—I'm not suggesting Harvard as the answer to juvenile delinquency.

Foreign Aid

We are for an international organization where the nations of the world can legitimately seek peace. We are against subordinating American interests to an organization so structurally unsound that a two-thirds majority can be mustered in the U.N. General Assembly among nations representing less than 10 percent of the world population.

Is there not something of hypocrisy in assailing our allies for so-called vestiges of colonialism while we engage in a conspiracy of silence about peoples enslaved by the Soviets in the satellite nations? We are for aiding our allies by sharing our material blessings with those nations which share our fundamental beliefs. We are against doling out money, government to government, which ends up financing socialism all over the world.

We set out to help 19 war-ravaged countries at the end of World War II. We are now helping 107. We have spent $146,000 million. Some of that money bought a $2 million yacht for Haile Selassie [of Ethiopia]. We bought dress suits for undertakers. We bought 1,000 TV sets, with 58-centimeter screens, for a country where there is no electricity.... When Congress moved to cut foreign aid, they were told that if they cut it one dollar they endangered national security, and then Senator Harry Byrd revealed that since its inception foreign aid has rarely spent its allotted budget. It has today $21,000 million in unexpended funds.

Some time ago, Dr. Howard Kershner was speaking to the prime minister of Lebanon. The prime minister told him proudly that his little country balanced its budget each year. It had no public debt, no inflation, a modest tax rate, and had increased its gold holdings from $70 million to $120 million. When he finished, Dr. Kershner said, "Mr. Prime Minister, my country hasn't balanced its budget 28 out of the last 40 years. My country's debt is greater than the combined debt of all the nations of the world. We have inflation, we have a tax rate that takes from the private sector a percentage of income greater than any civilized nation has ever taken and survived. We have lost gold at such a rate that the solvency of our currency is in danger. Do you think that my country should continue to give your country millions of dollars each year?" The prime minister smiled and said, "No, but if you are foolish enough to do it, we are going to keep on taking the money."

And so we built a model stock farm in Lebanon, and we built nine stalls for each bull. I find something peculiarly appropriate in that. We have in our vaults $15,000 million in gold. We don't own an ounce. Foreign dollar claims against that gold total $27,000 million. In the last six years, 52 nations have bought $7,000 million worth of our gold and all 52 are receiving foreign aid.

Size and Cost of Government

Because no government ever voluntarily reduces itself in size, government programs, once launched, never go out of existence. A government agency is the nearest thing to eternal life we'll ever see on this earth. The *United States Government Manual* takes 25 pages to list by name every congressman and senator, and all the agencies controlled by Congress. It then lists the agencies coming under the Executive Branch, and this requires 520 pages.

Since the beginning of the century our gross national product has increased 33 times. In the same period, the cost of federal government has increased 234 times and, while the work force is only one-and-a-half times greater, federal employees number nine times as many. There are now two and a half million federal employees. No one knows what they all do. One congressman found out what one of them does. This man sits at a desk in Washington. Documents come to him each morning. He reads them, initials them, and passes them on to the proper agency. One day a document arrived he wasn't supposed to read, but he read it, initialed it, and passed it on. Twenty-four hours later it arrived back at his desk with a memo attached that said, "You weren't supposed to read this. Erase your initials, and initial the erasure."

While the federal government is the great offender, the idea filters down. During a period in California when our population has increased 90 percent, the cost of state government has gone up 862 percent and the number of employees 500 percent. Governments, state and local, now employ one out of six of the nation's work force. If the rate of increase of the last three years continues, by 1970 one-fourth of the total work force will be employed by government. Already we have a permanent structure so big and complex it is virtually beyond the control of Congress and the comprehension of the people, and tyranny inevitably follows when this permanent structure usurps the policymaking function that belongs to elected officials.

One example of this occurred when Congress was debating whether to lend the United Nations $100 million. While they debated, the State Department gave the United Nations $217 million and the United Nations used part of that money to pay the delinquent dues of Castro's Cuba.

Rights by Dispensation

Under bureaucratic regulations adopted with no regard to the wish of the people, we have lost much of our Constitutional freedom. For example, federal agents can invade a man's property without a warrant, can impose a fine without a formal hearing, let alone a trial by jury, and can seize and sell his property at auction to enforce payment of that fine.

An Ohio deputy fire marshal sentenced a man to prison after a secret proceeding in which the accused was not allowed to have a lawyer present. The Supreme Court upheld that sentence, ruling that it was an administrative investigation of incidents damaging to the economy. Somewhere a perversion has taken place. Our natural inalienable rights are now presumed to be a dispensation of government, divisible by a vote of the majority. The greatest good for the greatest number is a high-sounding phrase but contrary to the very basis of our nation, unless it is accompanied by recognition that we have certain rights which cannot be infringed upon, even if the individual stands outvoted by all of his fellow citizens. Without this recognition, majority rule is nothing more than mob rule.

It is time we realized that socialism can come without overt seizure of property or nationalization of private business. It matters little that you hold the title to your property or business if government can dictate policy and procedure, and holds life and death power over your business. The machinery of this power already exists. Lowell Mason, former anti-trust law enforcer for the Federal Trade Commission, has written, "American business is being harassed, bled and even black-jacked under a preposterous crazy quilt system of laws." There are so many that the government literally can find some charge to bring against any concern it chooses to prosecute. Are we safe in our books and records?

The natural gas producers have just been handed a 428-page questionnaire by the Federal Power Commission. It weighs 10 pounds. One firm has estimated it will take 70,000 accountant man hours to fill out this questionnaire, and it must be done in quadruplicate. The Power Commission says it must have it to determine whether a proper price is being charged for gas. The National Labor Relations Board ruled that a business firm could not discontinue its shipping department even though it was more efficient and economical to subcontract this work out.

The Supreme Court has ruled the government has the right to tell a citizen what he can grow on his own land for his own use. The Secretary of Agriculture has asked for the right to imprison farmers who violate their planting quotas. One business firm has been informed by the Internal Revenue Service that it cannot take a tax deduction for its institutional advertising because this advertising espoused views not in the public interest.

A child's prayer in a school cafeteria endangers religious freedom, but people of the Amish religion in the state of Ohio, who cannot participate in Social Security because of their religious beliefs, have had their livestock seized and sold at auction to enforce payment of Social Security dues.

We approach a point of no return when government becomes so huge and entrenched that we fear the consequences of upheaval and just go along with it. The federal government accounts for one-fifth of the industrial capacity of the nation, one-fourth of all construction, holds or guarantees one-third of all mortgages, owns one-third of the land, and engages in some 19,000 businesses covering half a hundred different lines. The Defense Department runs 269 supermarkets. They do a gross business of $730 million a year, and lose $150 million. The government spends $11 million an hour every hour of the 24, and pretends we had a tax cut while it pursues a policy of planned inflation that will more than wipe out any benefit with depreciation of our purchasing power.

We need true tax reform that will at least make a start toward restoring for our children the American dream that wealth is denied to no one, that each individual has the right to fly as high as his strength and ability will take him. The economist Sumner Schlicter has said, "If a visitor from Mars looked at our tax policy, he would conclude it had been designed by a communist spy to make free enterprise unworkable." But we cannot have such reform while our tax policy is engineered by people who view the tax as a means of achieving changes in our social structure. Senator Joseph Clark says the tax issue is a class issue, and the government must use the tax to redistribute the wealth and earnings downward.

Taxes

On January 15th in the White House, the President [Lyndon Johnson] told a group of citizens they were going to take all the money they thought was being unnecessarily spent, "take it from the haves and give it to the have-nots who need it so much." When Karl Marx said this he put it: "...from each according to his ability, to each according to his need."

Have we the courage and the will to face up to the immorality and discrimination of the progressive surtax, and demand a return to traditional proportionate taxation? Many decades ago the Scottish economist, John Ramsey McCulloch, said, "The moment you abandon the cardinal principle of exacting from all individuals the same proportion of their income or their property, you are at sea without a rudder or compass and there is no amount of injustice or folly you may not commit." No nation has survived the tax burden that reached one-third of its national income.

Today in our country the tax collector's share is 37 cents of every dollar earned. Freedom has never been so fragile, so close to slipping from our grasp. I wish I could give you some magic formula, but each of us must find his own role. One man in Virginia found what he could do, and dozens of business firms have followed his lead. Concerned because his 200 employees seemed unworried about government extravagance, he conceived the idea of taking all of their withholding out of only the fourth paycheck each month. For three paydays his employees received their full salary. On the fourth payday all withholding was taken. He has one employee who owes him $4.70 each fourth payday. It took only one month to produce 200 conservatives.

Are you willing to spend time studying the issues, making yourself aware, and then conveying that information to family and friends? Will you resist the temptation to get a government handout for your community? Realize that the doctor's fight against socialized medicine is your fight. We can't socialize the doctors without socializing the patients. Recognize that government invasion of public power is eventually an assault upon your own business....If some among you fear taking a stand because you are afraid of reprisals from customers, clients, or even government, recognize that you are just feeding the crocodile hoping he'll eat you last.

Appeasement or Courage

If all of this seems like a great deal of trouble, think what's at stake. We are faced with the most evil enemy mankind has known in his long climb from the swamp to the stars. There can be no security anywhere in the free world if there is not fiscal and economic stability within the United States. Those who ask us to trade our freedom for the soup kitchen of the welfare state are architects of a policy of accommodation. They tell us that by avoiding a direct confrontation with the enemy, he will learn to love us and give up his evil ways. All who oppose this idea are blanket-indicted as war-mongers. Well, let us set one thing straight, there is no argument with regard to peace and war. It is cheap demagoguery to suggest that anyone would want to send other people's sons to war. The only argument is with regard to the best way to avoid war. There is only one sure way—surrender.

The spectre our well-meaning liberal friends refuse to face is that their policy of accommodation is appeasement, and appeasement does not give you a choice between peace and war, only between fight or surrender. We are told that the problem is too complex for a simple answer. They are wrong. There is no easy answer, but there is a simple answer. We must have the courage to do what we know is morally right, and this policy of accommodation asks us to accept the greatest possible immorality. We are being asked to buy our safety from the threat of the bomb by selling into permanent slavery our fellow human beings enslaved behind the Iron Curtain, to tell them to give up their hope of freedom because we are ready to make a deal with their slave masters.

Alexander Hamilton warned us that a nation that can prefer disgrace to danger is prepared for a master and deserves one. Admittedly there is a risk in any course we follow. Choosing the high road cannot eliminate that risk. Already some of the architects of accommodation have hinted what their decision will be if their plan fails and we are faced with the final ultimatum. The English commentator Kenneth Tynan has put it that he would rather live on his knees than die on his feet. Some of our own have said, "Better Red than dead." If we are to believe that nothing is worth the dying, when did this begin? Should Moses have told the children of Israel to live in slavery rather than dare the wilderness? Should Christ have refused the Cross? Should the patriots at Concord Bridge* have refused to fire the shot heard round the world? Are we to believe that all the martyrs of history died in vain?

You and I have a rendezvous with destiny. We can preserve for our children this the last best hope of man on earth, or we can sentence them to take the first step into a thousand years of darkness. If we fail, at least let our children and our children's children say of us we justified our brief moment here. We did all that could be done. □

*Site where first shot of the American Revolution was fired

A Vision for America

TELEVISED ADDRESS ON THE EVE OF THE PRESIDENTIAL ELECTION

NOVEMBER 3, 1980

A child born this year will begin his or her adult life in what will be the 21st century. What kind of country, what kind of legacy, will we leave to these young men and women who will live out America's third century as a nation?

In thinking about these questions, many Americans seem to be wondering, searching...feeling frustrated and perhaps even a little afraid.

Many of us are unhappy about our worsening economic problems, about the constant crisis atmosphere in our foreign policy, about our diminishing prestige around the globe, about the weakness in our economy and national security that jeopardizes world peace, about our lack of strong, straightforward leadership.

And many Americans today, just as they did 200 years ago, feel burdened, stifled and sometimes even oppressed by government that has grown too large, too bureaucratic, too wasteful, too unresponsive, too uncaring about people and their problems.

Americans, who have always known that excessive bureaucracy is the enemy of excellence and compassion, want a change in public life—a change that makes government work for people. They seek a vision of a better America, a vision of a society that frees the energies and ingenuity of our people while it extends compassion to the lonely, the desperate and the forgotten.

-25-

I believe we can embark on a new age of reform in this country and an era of national renewal. An era that will reorder the relationship between citizen and government, that will make government again responsive to people, that will revitalize the values of family, work and neighborhood, and that will restore our private and independent social institutions. These institutions always have served as both buffer and bridge between the individual and the state—and these institutions, not government, are the real sources of our economic and social progress as a people.

That's why I've said throughout this campaign that we must control and limit the growth of federal spending, that we must reduce tax rates to stimulate work and savings and investment. That's why I've said we can relieve labor and business of burdensome, unnecessary regulations and still maintain high standards of environmental and occupational safety. That's why I've said we can reduce the cost of government by eliminating millions and millions lost to waste and fraud in the federal bureaucracy—a problem that is now an unrelenting national scandal. And because we are a federation of sovereign states, we can restore the health and vitality of state and local governments by returning to them control over programs best run at those levels of government closer to the people. We can fight corruption while we work to bring into our government women and men of competence and high integrity.

This last pledge is particularly important. No person who understands the American presidency can possibly hope to make every decision or tend to every detail in the national government. But he can promise to bring to government the best leaders in this nation and put them to work for the American people.

During the past three months, many of these leaders have been working—as part of our transition process—on ways to reform the federal bureaucracy to make it truly a partnership between people and government.

With their help and guidance, some of the reforms I will seek to implement, if elected, are:

— A new structuring of the presidential Cabinet that will make Cabinet officers the managers of the national administration—not captives of the bureaucracy or special interests in the departments they are supposed to direct.

— Businesslike revisions of federal auditing and management procedures. Such revisions are long overdue and will ultimately save millions and millions in wasted tax dollars.

— Appointment of a special ombudsman to work with labor and industry groups to strengthen needed federal regulations while eliminating those that are burdensome and unnecessarily costly.

— We would seek to put the Social Security system back on a sound financial footing so there can never be any question about its strength.

— The appointment of special panels of top law enforcement experts to deal with the menacing problems of organized crime, drug abuse and the corruption of public officials.

I realize these reforms provide an ambitious agenda for our nation in the next four years. But I believe each of these objectives can be achieved.

In accomplishing these goals, it will be imperative to establish a close working relationship with the new Congress. No objective will be more important to me, if I am elected President, than that of opening a new era of cooperation between the executive and legislative branches of government.

Standards of Decency and Excellence

These are much more than promises made in an election campaign. When I first entered office as governor of California, that state—which, if it were a nation, would be the seventh greatest economic power in the world—faced many of the same problems that confront our nation today.

We brought into California government the best leaders from the private and public sectors. We cut the rate of government spending and provided millions and millions in tax relief to our citizens. We brought the state back from bankruptcy by working closely with the legislature in constructing a welfare program that put cheaters off the rolls, reducing them by some 350,000, while it increased benefits to the truly needy. The Urban Institute, a Washington nonprofit scholarly foundation, recently referred to this program as a "major policy success."

That's why I am confident we can effect the reforms I have mentioned—reforms that will get government off our backs, out of our pockets and up to the standards of decency and excellence envisioned by the Founding Fathers.

But beyond even these reforms—as important as they are—there is something more, much more, that needs to be said tonight.

That's why I want to talk with you...about America, about us, you and me.

Not so long ago, we emerged from a world war. Turning homeward at last, we built a grand prosperity and hoped—from our own success and plenty—to help others less fortunate.

Our peace was a tense and bitter one, but in those days the center seemed to hold.

Then came the hard years: riots and assassinations, domestic strife over the Vietnam War and, in the last four years, drift and disaster in Washington.

It all seems a long way from a time when politics was a national passion and sometimes even fun.

American Heroes

A popular novel of the '60s ended prophetically with its description of a "kindly, pleasant, greening land about to learn whether history still has a place for a nation so strangely composed of great ideals and uneasy compromise as she."

That is really the question before us tonight. For the first time in our memory many Americans are asking: Does history still have a place for America, for her people, for her great ideals? There are some who answer "no," that our energy is spent, our days of greatness at an end, that a great national malaise is upon us.

They say we must cut our expectations, conserve and withdraw, that we must tell our children...not to dream as we once dreamed.

Last year I lost a friend who was more than a symbol of the Hollywood dream industry; to millions he was a symbol of our country itself. And when he died, the headlines seemed to convey all the doubt about America, all the nostalgia for a seemingly lost past.

"The *Last* American Hero," said one headline, "Mr. America dies," said another.

Well, I knew John Wayne well, and no one would have been angrier at being called the "*last* American hero."

Just before his death, he said in his own blunt way, "Just give the American people a good cause, and there's nothing they can't lick." Duke Wayne did not believe that our country was ready for the dust bin of history and, if we'll just think about it, we too will know it isn't.

Have we forgotten that night several years ago, when we waited through the long hours watching our TV screens for that first plane to land at Clark Field in the Philippines bearing our men who had been prisoners of the North Vietnamese? Finally the moment came. What would we see when that plane door opened? Those men had been imprisoned and tortured by savage captors for years—as many as 10 in some cases. The door opened, and we had our answer—Admiral Jeremiah Denton came down the ramp, saluted our country's flag, thanked us for bringing them home and said, "God Bless America."

I was governor of California at the time, and Nancy and I were privileged to have many of the returned POWs in our home on four different occasions. We heard stories of incredible heroism and unbelievable horror told without bitterness or attempt at embellishment. We saw two men meet in our home, hear each other's name and throw their arms around each other—they were the closest of friends, knew every detail of each other's life, but they were seeing each other face to face for the first time in their lives, there in our home. Their friendship had been built up over the years, tapping in code on the wall that divided their solitary confinement cells.

One night after such an evening had ended, I asked Nancy, "Where did we find such men?" The answer came to me as quickly as I had asked the question: We found them where we've always found them. In our shops, on our farms, on our city streets, in our villages and towns. They are just the product of the freest society the world has ever known.

There were astronauts Virgil Grissom, Ed White and Roger Chaffee who died as other Americans have died in opening new frontiers. Their courage was remembered when later the message came back to

Earth from other astronauts—"The eagle has landed." Man had set foot on the moon.

These were not the deeds of men who set out be heroes. In many ways, they were ordinary Americans whose spontaneous response to time and circumstance gave us a glimpse into the soul of this country and the enduring vigor of her people.

City on a Hill

Do not mistake me. No reasonable man who sees the world as it is, who views the deterioration of our economy, the waning of our relationships with our allies, the growth of Soviet might and the sufferings of our recent past could underestimate the difficulties before us.

But I wonder if those who doubt America have forgotten that just as in the lives of individuals, so too in the lives of nations: It is always when things seem most unbearable that we must have faith that America's trials have meaning beyond our own understanding.

Since her beginning America has held fast to this hope of divine providence, this vision of "man *with* God."

It is true that world peace is jeopardized by those who view man—not as a noble being—but as an accident of nature, without soul, and important only to the extent he can serve an all powerful state.

But it is our spiritual commitment—more than all the military might in the world—that will win our struggle for peace.

It is not "bombs and rockets" but belief and resolve—it is humility before God that is ultimately the source of America's strength as a nation.

Our people always have held fast to this belief, this vision, since our first days as a nation.

I know I have told before of the moment in 1630 when the tiny ship *Arabella* bearing settlers to the New World lay off the Massachusetts coast. To the little bank of settlers gathered on the deck, John Winthrop said: "We shall be a city upon a hill. The eyes of all people are upon us, so that if we shall deal falsely with our God in this work we have undertaken and so cause him to withdraw his present help from us, we shall be made a story and a byword through the world."

Well, America became more than "a story," or a "byword"—more than a sterile footnote in history. I have quoted John Winthrop's words more than once this year—for I believe that Americans in 1980 are every bit as committed to that vision of a shining "city on a hill" as were those long-ago settlers.

We celebrated our 200th anniversary as a nation a short time ago. Fireworks exploded over Boston harbor, Arthur Fiedler [of the Boston Pops Orchestra] conducted, thousands cheered and waved Old Glory.

These were not just images of a bicentennial; they were reminders of our birthright of freedom—and of a generous, fervent patriotism that burns in America. A patriotism that shows itself sometimes in very unexpected places. Remember "baseball's designated patriot"—Rick

Monday—an outfielder for the Chicago Cubs who on April 25, 1976, at Dodger Stadium grabbed our flag from two demonstrators who were trying to burn it in center field. As he came off the field to the dugout, carrying the flag, thousands stood and cheered and then found themselves singing "God Bless America."

During this last year, I have had a chance to meet and talk with Americans in every corner of the United States.

I find no national malaise, I find nothing wrong with the American people. Oh, they are frustrated, even angry at what has been done to this blessed land. But more than anything they are sturdy and robust as they have always been.

Any nation that sees softness in our prosperity or disunity—in our sometimes noisy arguments with each other—let such nations not make the mistakes others have made. Let them understand that we will put aside in a moment the fruits of our prosperity and the luxury of our disagreements if the cause is a safe and peaceful future for our children.

Peace with Freedom

Let it always be clear that we have no dreams of empire, that we seek no manifest destiny, that we understand the limitations of any one nation's power.

But let it also be clear that we do not shirk history's call; that America is not turned inward but outward—toward others. Let it be clear that we have not lessened our commitment to peace or to the hope that someday all of the people of the world will enjoy lives of decency, lives with a degree of freedom, with a measure of dignity.

Together, tonight, let us say what so many long to hear: that America is still united, still strong, still compassionate, still clinging fast to the dream of peace and freedom, still willing to stand by those who are persecuted or alone.

For those who seek the right to self-determination without interference from foreign powers, tonight let us speak for them.

For those who suffer from social or religious discrimination;

For those who are victims of police states or government-induced torture or terror;

For those who are persecuted;

For all the countries and peoples of the world who seek only to live in harmony with each other, tonight let us speak for them.

And to our allies—who regard us with such constant puzzlement and profound affection—we must also speak tonight.

To our Canadian neighbors who so recently rescued Americans in Teheran, to the people of Great Britain to whom ties of blood, language and culture bind so closely, to the people of France who midwifed our birth as a nation, to the people of Germany and Japan with whom we bound up the wounds of war, to the people of Ireland and Italy and all the ethnic communities whose national heritages have enriched this nation and become our own, to the people of Israel with whom we enjoy the closest of friendships, to the people of Latin America, Australia, the Philippines, Taiwan, Korea—to all our allies great and small, we say tonight: At last the sleeping giant stirs and is filled with a resolve—a resolve that we will win together our struggle for world peace—our struggle for the human spirit.

And to the people of Africa, we say that we seek a lasting, just and close relationship.

To the people of China, with whom we have begun the first important steps to friendship—let it be known to them that we mean for that friendship to bring our peoples closer together.

To the people of Russia—if only we could speak to them without their government intervening, they would know our willingness to build an enduring peace.

Tonight, my fellow Americans, we have reached deep into our national past—remembered the words and deeds of great men who have gone before us.

Worthy of Ourselves

But before I close, I want to leave with you a speech by a man not so well remembered in history, but those words, spoken on the eve of our struggle for independence, should uplift and inspire now as surely as they did in 1775. Joseph Warren, a Boston doctor, left us these words before giving his life at Bunker Hill: "Our country is in danger, but not to be despaired of...on you depend the fortunes of America—you are to decide the important question, on which rests the happiness and liberty of millions yet unborn. Act worthy of yourselves."

Tomorrow morning, you will be making a choice between different visions of the future. Your decision is a uniquely personal one. It belongs to no one but you. It will be critical in determining the path we will follow in the years ahead.

If you feel that Mr. Carter has faithfully served America with the kind of competence and distinction which deserve four more years in office, then you should vote for him. If he has given you the kind of leadership you are looking for, if he instills in you pride for our country and a sense of optimism about our future, then he should be reelected.

But consider these questions as well when you finally make your decision:

Are you more confident that our economy will create productive work for our society or are you less confident? Do you feel you can keep the job you have or gain a job if you don't have one?

Are you satisfied that inflation at the highest rates in 33 years was the best that we could do? Are interest rates at 14.5 percent something you are prepared to live with?

Are you pleased with the ability of young people to buy a home? Of the elderly to live their remaining years in happiness? Of our youngsters to take pride in the world we have built for them?

Is our nation stronger and more capable of leading the world toward peace and freedom or is it weaker?

Is there more stability in the world or less?

Are you convinced that we have earned the respect of the world and our allies, or has America's position across the globe diminished?

Are you personally more secure in your life? Is your family more secure? Is America safer in the world?

And, most importantly—quite simply—the basic question of our lives: Are you happier today than when Mr. Carter became President of the United States?

I cannot answer those questions for you. Only you can.

It is autumn now in Washington, and the residents there say that more than ever during the past few years, Americans are coming to visit their capital—some say because economic conditions rule out more expensive vacations elsewhere; some say an election year has heightened interest in the workings of the national government.

Others say something different: In a time when our values, when our place in history, is so seriously questioned, they say Americans want their sons and daughters to see what is still for them, and for so many other millions in the world, a city offering the "last best hope of man on Earth!"

You can see them—these Washington visitors—looking for the famous as they walk through Congressional hallways; see them as they return silent and tight-lipped to tour buses that brought them for a walk through rows of white crosses in Arlington Cemetery; you can see them as they look up at a towering statue of Jefferson or out from the top of the Washington Monument; or as they read the words inscribed at the Lincoln Memorial: "Let us bind up the nation's wounds."

These visitors to that city on the Potomac do not come as white or black, red or yellow; they are not Jews or Christians, conservatives or liberals, or Democrats or Republicans. They are Americans awed by what has gone before, proud of what for them is still...a shining city on a hill.

At this very moment, some young American, coming up along the Virginia or Maryland shores of the Potomac, is seeing for the first time the lights that glow on the great halls of our government and the monuments to the memory of our great men.

Let us resolve tonight that young Americans will always see those Potomac lights; that they will always find there a city of hope in a country that is free. And let us resolve they will say of our day and of our generation that we did keep faith with our God, that we did act "worthy of ourselves," that we did protect and pass on lovingly that shining city on a hill. □

An Era of National Renewal

INAUGURAL ADDRESS

WASHINGTON, D.C.
JANUARY 20, 1981

T o a few of us here today this is a solemn and most momentous occasion, and yet in the history of our nation it is a commonplace occurrence. The orderly transfer of authority as called for in the Constitution routinely takes place, as it has for almost two centuries, and few of us stop to think how unique we really are. In the eyes of many in the world, this every-four-year ceremony we accept as normal is nothing less than a miracle.

President [Carter], I want our fellow citizens to know how much you did to carry on this tradition. By your gracious cooperation in the transition process, you have shown a watching world that we are a united people pledged to maintaining a political system which guarantees individual liberty to a greater degree than any other, and I thank you and your people for all your help in maintaining the continuity which is the bulwark of our Republic.

Economic Challenge

The business of our nation goes forward. These United States are confronted with an economic affliction of great proportions. We suffer from the longest and one of the worst sustained inflations in our national history. It distorts our economic decisions, penalizes thrift, and crushes the struggling young and the fixed-income elderly alike. It threatens to shatter the lives of millions of our people.

Idle industries have cast workers into unemployment, human misery and personal indignity. Those who do work are denied a fair return for their labor by a tax system which penalizes successful achievement and keeps us from maintaining full productivity.

But great as our tax burden is, it has not kept pace with public spending. For decades we have piled deficit upon deficit, mortgaging our future and our children's future for the temporary convenience of the present. To continue this long trend is to guarantee tremendous social, cultural, political and economic upheavals.

You and I, as individuals, can, by borrowing, live beyond our means, but for only a limited period of time. Why, then, should we think that collectively, as a nation, we're not bound by that same limitation? We must act today in order to preserve tomorrow. And let there be no misunderstanding: We are going to begin to act, beginning today.

The economic ills we suffer have come upon us over several decades. They will not go away in days, weeks or months, but they will go away. They will go away because we as Americans have the capacity now, as we've had in the past, to do whatever needs to be done to preserve this last and greatest bastion of freedom.

Curbing Excessive Government

In this present crisis, government is not the solution to our problem; government is the problem. From time to time we've been tempted to believe that society has become too complex to be managed by self-rule, that government by an elite group is superior to government for, by, and of the people. Well, if no one among us is capable of governing himself, then who among us has the capacity to govern someone else? All of us together, in and out of government, must bear the burden. The solutions we seek must be equitable, with no one group singled out to pay a higher price.

We hear much of special interest groups. Well, our concern must be for a special interest group that has been too long neglected. It knows no sectional boundaries or ethnic and racial divisions, and it crosses political party lines. It is made up of men and women who raise our food, patrol our streets, man our mines and factories, teach our children, keep our homes, and heal us when we're sick—professionals, industrialists, shopkeepers, clerks, cabbies and truck drivers. They are, in short, "We the people," this breed called Americans.

This administration's objective will be a healthy, vigorous, growing economy that provides equal opportunities for all Americans, with no barriers born of bigotry or discrimination. Putting America back to work means putting all Americans back to work. Ending inflation means freeing all Americans from the terror of runaway living costs. All must share in the productive work of this "new beginning," and all must share in the bounty of a revived economy. With the idealism and fair play which are the core of our system and our strength, we can have a strong and prosperous America, at peace with itself and the world.

So, as we begin, let us take inventory. We are a nation that has a government—not the other way around. And this makes us special among the nations of the Earth. Our government has no power except that granted it by the people. It is time to check and reverse the growth of government, which shows signs of having grown beyond the consent of the governed.

It is my intention to curb the size and influence of the federal establishment and to demand recognition of the distinction between the powers granted to the federal government and those reserved to the states or to the people. All of us need to be reminded that the federal government did not create the states; the states created the federal government.

Now, so there will be no misunderstanding, it's not my intention to do away with government. It is rather to make it work—work with us, not over us; to stand by our side, not ride on our back. Government can and must provide opportunity, not smother it; foster productivity, not stifle it.

If we look to the answer as to why for so many years we achieved so much, prospered as no other people on Earth, it was because here in this land we unleashed the energy and individual genius of man to a greater extent than has ever been done before. Freedom and the dignity of the individual have been more available and assured here than in any other place on Earth. The price for this freedom at times has been high, but we have never been unwilling to pay that price.

It is no coincidence that our present troubles parallel and are proportionate to the intervention and intrusion in our lives that result from unnecessary and excessive growth of government. It is time for us to realize that we're too great a nation to limit ourselves to small dreams. We're not, as some would have us believe, doomed to an inevitable decline. I do not believe in a fate that will fall on us no matter what we do. I do believe in a fate that will fall on us if we do do nothing. So, with all the creative energy at our command, let us begin an era of national renewal. Let us renew our determination, our courage and our strength. Let us renew our faith and our hope.

Values Sustain National Life

We have every right to dream heroic dreams. Those who say that we're in a time when there are not heroes, they just don't know where to look. You can see heroes every day going in and out of factory gates. Others, a handful in number, produce enough food to feed all of us and then the world beyond. You meet heroes across a counter, and they're on both sides of that counter. There are entrepreneurs with faith in themselves and faith in an idea who create new jobs, new wealth and opportunity. They're individuals and families whose taxes support the government and whose voluntary gifts support church, charity, culture, art and education. Their patriotism is quiet, but deep. Their values sustain our national life.

Now, I have used the words "they" and "their" in speaking of these heroes. I could say "you" and "your," because I'm addressing the heroes of whom I speak—you, the citizens of this blessed land. Your dreams, your hopes, your goals are going to be the dreams, the hopes, and the goals of this administration, so help me God.

We shall reflect the compassion that is so much a part of your makeup. How can we love our country and not love our countrymen; and loving them, reach out a hand when they fall, heal them when they're sick, and provide opportunity to make them self-sufficient so they will be equal in fact and not just in theory?

Can we solve the problems confronting us? Well, the answer is an unequivocal and emphatic "yes." To paraphrase Winston Churchill, I did not take the oath I've just taken with the intention of presiding over the dissolution of the world's strongest economy.

In the days ahead I will propose removing the roadblocks that have slowed our economy and reduced productivity. Steps will be taken aimed at restoring the balance between the various levels of government. Progress may be slow, measured in inches and feet, not miles, but we will progress. It is time to reawaken this industrial giant, to get government back within its means, and to lighten our punitive tax burden. These will be our first priorities, and on these principles there will be no compromise.

On the eve of our struggle for independence, a man who might have been one of the greatest among the Founding Fathers, Dr. Joseph Warren, president of the Massachusetts Congress, said to his fellow Americans, "Our country is in danger, but not to be despaired of....On you depend the fortunes of America. You are to decide the important questions upon which rests the happiness and the liberty of millions yet unborn. Act worthy of yourselves."

Exemplar of Freedom, Beacon of Hope

I believe we, the Americans of today, are ready to act worthy of ourselves, ready to do what must be done to ensure happiness and liberty for ourselves, our children and our children's children. And as we renew ourselves here in our own land, we will be seen as having greater strength throughout the world. We will again be the exemplar of freedom and a beacon of hope for those who do not now have freedom.

To those neighbors and allies who share our freedom, we will strengthen our historic ties and assure them of our support and firm commitment. We will match loyalty with loyalty. We will strive for mutually beneficial relations. We will not use our friendship to impose on their sovereignty, for our own sovereignty is not for sale.

As for the enemies of freedom, those who are potential adversaries, they will be reminded that peace is the highest aspiration of the American people. We will negotiate for it, sacrifice for it; we will not surrender for it, now or ever.

Our forbearance should never be misunderstood. Our reluctance for conflict should not be misjudged as a failure of will. When action is required to preserve our national security, we will act. We will maintain sufficient strength to prevail if need be, knowing if that we do so we have the best chance of never having to use that strength.

Above all, we must realize that no arsenal or no weapon in the arsenals of the world is so formidable as the will and moral courage of free men and women. It is a weapon our adversaries in today's world do not have. It is a weapon we as Americans do have. Let that be understood by those who practice terrorism and prey upon their neighbors.

I'm told that tens of thousands of prayer meetings are being held on this day, and for that I'm deeply grateful. We are a nation under God, and I believe God intended for us to be free. It would be fitting and good, I think, if on each Inaugural Day in future years it should be declared a day of prayer.

This is the first time in our history that this ceremony has been held, as you're been told, on this west front of the Capitol. Standing here, one faces a magnificent vista, opening up on this city's special beauty and history. At the end of this open mall are those shrines to the giants on whose shoulders we stand.

Directly in front of me, the monument to a monumental man, George Washington, father of our country. A man of humility who came to greatness reluctantly. He led America out of revolutionary victory into infant nationhood. Off to one side, the stately memorial to Thomas Jefferson. The Declaration of Independence flames with his eloquence. And then, beyond the Reflecting Pool, the dignified columns of the Lincoln Memorial. Whoever would understand in his heart the meaning of America will find it in the life of Abraham Lincoln.

Beyond those monuments to heroism is the Potomac River, and on the far shore the sloping hills of Arlington National Cemetery, with its row upon row of simple white markers bearing crosses or Stars of David. They add up to only a tiny fraction of the price that has been paid for our freedom.

Each one of those markers is a monument to the kind of hero I spoke of earlier. Their lives ended in places called Belleau Wood, The Argonne, Omaha Beach, Salerno, and halfway around the world on Guadalcanal, Tarawa, Pork Chop Hill, the Chosin Reservoir,* and in a hundred rice paddies and jungles of a place called Vietnam.

Our Best Effort

Under one such marker lies a young man, Martin Treptow, who left his job in a small town barbershop in 1917 to go to France with the famed Rainbow Division. There, on the western front, he was killed trying to carry a message between battalions under heavy artillery fire.

*Battlefields of World War I, World War II and the Korean War

We're told that on his body was found a diary. On the flyleaf under the heading, "My Pledge," he had written these words: "America must win this war. Therefore I will work, I will save, I will sacrifice, I will endure, I will fight cheerfully and do my utmost, as if the issue of the whole struggle depended on me alone."

The crisis we are facing today does not require of us the kind of sacrifice that Martin Treptow and so many thousands of others were called upon to make. It does require, however, our best effort and our willingness to believe in ourselves and to believe in our capacity to perform great deeds, to believe that together with God's help we can and will resolve the problems which now confront us.

And after all, why shouldn't we believe that? We are Americans.

God bless you, and thank you.   □

Legacy for Tomorrow

COMMENCEMENT ADDRESS AT THE UNIVERSITY OF NOTRE DAME

SOUTH BEND, INDIANA
MAY 17, 1981

Nancy and I are greatly honored to share this day with you, and our pleasure has been more than doubled because I am also sharing the platform with a longtime and very dear friend, Pat O'Brien.*

Pat and I haven't been able to see much of each other lately, so I haven't had a chance to tell him that there is now another tie that binds us together. Until a few weeks ago I knew very little about my father's ancestry. He had been orphaned at age six. But now I've learned that his grandfather, my great-grandfather, left Ireland to come to America, leaving his home in Ballyporeen, a village in County Tipperary in Ireland, and I have learned that Ballyporeen is the ancestral home of the O'Briens.

Memories of Notre Dame

Now, if I don't watch out, this may turn out to be less of a commencement than a warm bath in nostalgic memories. Growing up in Illinois, I was influenced by a sports legend so national in scope, it was almost mystical. It is difficult to explain to anyone who didn't live in those times. The legend was based on a combination of three elements: a game, football; a university, Notre Dame; and a man, Knute Rockne.**

*Well-known American actor
** 1888-1931. Famous Notre Dame football coach

-39-

There has been nothing like it before or since.

My first time to ever see Notre Dame was to come here as a sports announcer to broadcast a football game. You won or I wouldn't have mentioned it.

A number of years later I returned here in the company of Pat O'Brien and a galaxy of Hollywood stars for the world premiere of "Knute Rockne—All American"* in which I was privileged to play George Gipp.** I've always suspected that there might have been many actors in Hollywood who could have played the part better, but no one could have wanted to play it more than I did. And I was given the part largely because the star of that picture, Pat O'Brien, kindly and generously held out a helping hand to a beginning young actor.

Having come from the world of sports, I'd been trying to write a story about Knute Rockne. I must confess that I had someone in mind to play the Gipper.*** On one of my sports broadcasts before going to Hollywood, I had told the story of his career and tragic death. I didn't have very many words on paper when I learned that the studio that employed me was already preparing a story treatment for that film. And that brings me to the theme of my remarks.

I'm the fifth President of the United States to address a Notre Dame commencement. The temptation is great to use this forum as an address on a great international or national issue that has nothing to do with this occasion. Indeed, this is somewhat traditional. So, I wasn't surprised when I read in several reputable journals that I was going to deliver an address on foreign policy or on the economy. I'm not going to talk about either.

But, by the same token, I'll try not to belabor you with some of the standard rhetoric that is beloved of graduation speakers. For example, I'm not going to tell you that "you know more today than you've ever known before or that you will ever know again." The other standby is, "When I was 14, I didn't think my father knew anything. By the time I was 21, I was amazed at how much the old gentleman had learned in seven years." And then, of course, the traditional and the standby is that "a university like this is a storehouse of knowledge because the freshmen bring so much in and the seniors take so little away."

You members of the graduating class of 1981 are what behaviorists call achievers. And while you will look back with warm pleasure on your memories of these years that brought you to where you are today, you are also looking at the future that seems uncertain to most of you, but which offers great expectations.

Take pride in this day. Thank your parents, as one on your behalf has already done here. Thank those who've been of help to you over the last four years. And do a little celebrating; you're entitled. This is your

---

* 1940 motion picture An "all American" is one of the best college football players in the country
** 1895-1920 Outstanding Notre Dame football player under Rockne Played especially brilliantly against Army teams from West Point, Notre Dame's arch rival Died of pneumonia Rockne always claimed that Gipp's dying words were "win one for the Gipper"
*** Nickname for Gipp, today, a nickname for President Reagan

day, and whatever I say should take cognizance of that fact. It is a milestone in life, and it marks a time of change.

Winston Churchill, during the darkest period of the "Battle of Britain" in World War II, said: "When great causes are on the move in the world...we learn we are spirits, not animals, and that something is going on in space and time, and beyond space and time, which, whether we like it or not, spells duty."

Now, I'm going to mention again that movie that Pat and I and Notre Dame were in, because it says something about America. First, Knute Rockne as a boy came to America with his parents from Norway. And in the few years it took him to grow up to college age, he became so American that here at Notre Dame, he became an All American in a game that is still, to this day, uniquely American.

As a coach, he did more than teach young men how to play a game. He believed truly that the noblest work of man was building the character of man. And maybe that's why he was a living legend. No man connected with football has ever achieved the stature or occupied the singular niche in the nation that he carved out for himself, not just in a sport, but in our entire social structure.

Now, today I hear very often, "Win one for the Gipper," spoken in a humorous vein. Lately I've been hearing it by Congressmen who are supportive of the programs that I've introduced. But let's look at the significance of that story. Rockne could have used Gipp's dying words to win a game any time. But eight years went by following the death of George Gipp before Rock revealed those dying words, his deathbed wish.

And then he told the story at halftime to a team that was losing, and one of the only teams he had ever coached that was torn by dissension and jealousy and factionalism. The seniors on that team were about to close out their football careers without learning or experiencing any of the real values that a game has to impart. None of them had known George Gipp. They were children when he played for Notre Dame. It was to this team that Rockne told the story and so inspired them that they rose above their personal animosities. For someone they had never known, they joined together in a common cause and attained the unattainable.

We were told when we were making the picture of one line that was spoken by a player during that game. We were actually afraid to put it in the picture. The man who carried the ball over for the winning touchdown was injured on the play. We were told that as he was lifted on the stretcher and carried off the field he was heard to say, "That's the last one I can get for you, Gipper."

Now, it's only a game. And maybe to hear it now, afterward—and this is what we feared—it might sound maudlin and not the way it was intended. But is there anything wrong with young people having an experience, feeling something so deeply, thinking of someone else to the point that they can give so completely of themselves? There will come times in the lives of all of us when we'll be faced with causes bigger than ourselves, and they won't be on a playing field.

Inalienable Rights

This nation was born when a band of men, the Founding Fathers, a group so unique we've never seen their like since, rose to such selfless heights. Lawyers, tradesmen, merchants, farmers—56 men—achieved security and standing in life but valued freedom more. They pledged their lives, their fortunes and their sacred honor. Sixteen of them gave their lives. Most gave their fortunes. All preserved their sacred honor.

They gave us more than a nation. They brought to all mankind for the first time the concept that man was born free, that each of us has inalienable rights—ours by the grace of God—and that government was created by us for our convenience, having only the powers that we choose to give it. This is the heritage that you're about to claim as you come out to join the society made up of those who have preceded you by a few years, or some of us by a great many.

This experiment in man's relation to man is a few years into its third century. Saying that may make it sound quite old. But let's look at it from another viewpoint or perspective. A few years ago, someone figured out that if you could condense the entire history of life on Earth into a motion picture that would run for 24 hours a day, 365 days...the United States wouldn't appear on the screen until three-and-a-half seconds before midnight on December 31. And in those three-and-a-half seconds, not only would a new concept of society come into being, a golden hope for all mankind, but more than half the activity, economic activity in world history, would take place on this continent. Free to express their genius, individual Americans, men and women, in three-and-a-half seconds, would perform such miracles of invention, construction and production as the world had never seen.

Government's Legitimate Role

As you join us out there beyond the campus, you know there are great unsolved problems. Federalism, with its built in checks and balances, has been distorted. Central government has usurped powers that properly belong to local and state governments. And in so doing, in many ways that central government has begun to fail to do the things that are truly the responsibility of a central government.

All of this has led to the misuse of power and preemption of the prerogatives of people and their social institutions. You are graduating from a great private, or, if you will, independent university. Not too many years ago, such schools were relatively free from government interference. In recent years, government has spawned regulations covering virtually every facet of our lives. The independent and church-supported colleges and universities have found themselves enmeshed in that network of regulations and the costly blizzard of paperwork that government is demanding. Thirty-four congressional committees and almost 80 subcommittees have jurisdiction over 439 separate laws affecting education at the college level alone. Almost every aspect of campus life is now regulated—hiring, firing, promotions, physical plant, construction, record-keeping, fund-raising and, to some extent, curriculum and educational programs.

I hope when you leave this campus that you will do so with a feeling of obligation to your alma mater. She will need your help and support in the years to come. If ever the great independent colleges and universities like Notre Dame give way to and are replaced by tax-supported institutions, the struggle to preserve academic freedom will have been lost.

We're troubled today by economic stagnation, brought on by inflated currency and prohibitive taxes and burdensome regulations. The cost of stagnation in human terms, mostly among those least equipped to survive it, is cruel and inhuman.

Now, after those remarks, don't decide that you'd better turn your diploma back in so you can stay another year on the campus. I've just given you the bad news. The good news is that something is being done about all this because the people of America have said, "Enough already." You know, we who had preceded you had just gotten so busy that we let things get out of hand. We forgot that we were the keepers of the power, forgot to challenge the notion that the state is the principal vehicle of social change, forgot that millions of social interactions among free individuals and institutions can do more to foster economic and social progress than all the careful schemes of government planners.

Well, at last we're remembering, remembering that government has certain legitimate functions which it can perform very well, that it can be responsive to the people, that it can be humane and compassionate, but that when it undertakes tasks that are not its proper province, it can do none of them as well or as economically as the private sector.

For too long government has been fixing things that aren't broken and inventing miracle cures for unknown diseases.

Legacy for Tomorrow

We need you. We need your youth. We need your strength. We need your idealism to help us make right that which is wrong. Now, I know that in this period of your life, you have been and are critically looking at the mores and customs of the past and questioning their value. Every generation does that. May I suggest, don't discard the time-tested values upon which civilization was built simply because they're old. More important, don't let today's doomcriers and cynics persuade you that the best is past, that from here on it's all downhill. Each generation sees farther than the generation that preceded it because it stands on the shoulders of that generation. You're going to have opportunities beyond anything that we've ever known.

The people have made it plain already. They want an end to excessive government intervention in their lives and in the economy, an end to the burdensome and unnecessary regulations and a punitive tax policy that does take "from the mouth of labor the bread it has earned." They want a government that cannot only continue to send men across the vast reaches of space and bring them safely home, but that can guarantee that you and I can walk in the park of our neighborhood after dark and get safely home. And finally, they want to know that this nation has the ability to defend itself against those who would seek to pull it down.

And all of this, we the people can do. Indeed, a start has already been made. There's a task force under the leadership of the Vice President, George Bush, that is to look at those regulations I've spoken of. They have already identified hundreds of them that can be wiped out with no harm to the quality of life. And the cancellation of just those regulations will leave thousands of millions of dollars in the hands of the people for productive enterprise and research and development and the creation of jobs.

The years ahead are great ones for this country, for the cause of freedom and the spread of civilization. The West won't contain communism, it will transcend communism. It won't bother to denounce it, it will dismiss it as some bizarre chapter in human history whose last pages are even now being written.

William Faulkner, at a Nobel Prize ceremony some time back, said man "would not only endure: he will prevail" against the modern world because he will return to "the old verities and truths of the heart." And then Faulkner said of man, "He is immortal because he alone among creatures...has a soul, a spirit capable of compassion and sacrifice and endurance."

One can't say those words—compassion, sacrifice and endurance—without thinking of the irony that one who so exemplifies them, Pope John Paul II, a man of peace and goodness, an inspiration to the world, would be struck by a bullet from a man towards whom he could only feel compassion and love. It was Pope John Paul II who warned in last year's encyclical on mercy and justice against certain economic theories that use the rhetoric of class struggle to justify injustice. He said, "In the name of an alleged justice the neighbor is sometimes destroyed, killed, deprived of liberty or stripped of fundamental human rights."

For the West, for America, the time has come to dare to show to the world that our civilized ideas, our traditions, our values, are not—like the ideology and war machine of totalitarian societies—just a facade of strength. It is time for the world to know our intellectual and spiritual values are rooted in the source of all strength, a belief in a Supreme Being, and a law higher than our own.

When it's written, history of our time won't dwell long on the hardships of the recent past. But history will ask—and our answer determine the fate of freedom for a thousand years—Did a nation born of hope lose hope? Did a people forged by courage find courage wanting? Did a generation steeled by hard war and a harsh peace forsake honor at the moment of great climactic struggle for the human spirit?

If history asks such questions, it also answers them. And the answers are to be found in the heritage left by generations of Americans before us. They stand in silent witness to what the world will soon know and history someday record: that in its third century, the American nation came of age, affirmed its leadership of free men and women serving selflessly a vision of man with God, government for people, and humanity at peace.

A few years ago, an Australian Prime Minister, John Gorton said, "I wonder if anybody ever thought what the situation for the comparatively small nations in the world would be if there were not in existence the United States, if there were not this giant country prepared to make so many sacrifices." This is the noble and rich heritage rooted in great civil ideas of the West, and it is yours.

My hope today is that in the years to come—and come it shall—when it's your time to explain to another generation the meaning of the past and thereby hold out to them their promise of the future, that you'll recall the truths and traditions of which we've spoken. It is these truths and traditions that define our civilization and make up our national heritage. And now, they're yours to protect and pass on.

I have one more hope for you: when you do speak to the next generation about these things, that you will always be able to speak of an America that is strong and free, to find in your hearts an unbounded pride in this much-loved country, this once and future land, this bright and hopeful nation whose generous spirit and great ideals the word still honors.

Congratulations, and God bless you. ☐

Religious and Moral Values Hold Society Together

RADIO ADDRESS TO THE NATION ON DOMESTIC SOCIAL ISSUES

CAMP DAVID, MARYLAND
JANUARY 22, 1983

My fellow Americans:

A week ago, Graham Washington Jackson, an ex-Navy musician, died in Atlanta at the age of 79. You probably don't recognize his name, but his face became familiar to millions of Americans when President Roosevelt died in Warm Springs, Georgia, in 1945. There's a very famous, very moving photo of Chief Petty Officer Jackson, tears streaming down his face while he played "Going Home" on his accordion as FDR's body was borne away by train to Washington.

Mr. Jackson once said that as he began to play, "It seemed like every nail and every pin in the world just stuck in me." Mr. Jackson symbolized the grief of the nation back in 1945, and I just wanted his own family to know the nation hasn't forgotten their personal grief today, 38 years later.

As I'm sure Mr. Jackson's family would tell you, in times of sorrow the warmth and support of a family's ties are especially important. I've spoken a great deal about the strength and virtues of the American family. I'd like to return to that topic today, because the family will again be a top priority as we head into the new year—for the family is still the basic unit of religious and moral values that hold our society together.

In the year ahead we face serious, painful problems, like unemployment. In a few days I'll speak about the economic situation facing us, but I also want you to know we'll not ignore the moral essentials in the coming months. As many of you know, I strongly support an amendment that will permit our children to hold prayer in our schools. The amendment would allow communities to determine for themselves whether voluntary prayer should be permitted in their public schools. We didn't get that amendment through the last Congress, but I'll continue to push for it in the next Congress.

I believe that schoolchildren deserve the same right to pray that's enjoyed by the Congress and chaplains and troops in our armed services. The motto on our coinage reads, "In God We Trust." No one must ever be forced or pressured to take part in any religious exercise, but neither should the government forbid religious practice. The public expression through prayer of our faith in God is a fundamental part of our American heritage and a privilege which should not be excluded from our schools.

Tax Credits

Today, five million American kids attend private schools because of the emphasis on religious values and educational standards. The overwhelming majority of these schools are church-supported—Catholic, Protestant and Jewish. And the majority of students are from families earning less than $25,000 [a year]. In many parochial schools, the majority of students are from minority neighborhoods. In addition to private [school] tuition, these families also pay their full share of taxes to fund the public schools. I think they're entitled to some relief, since they're supporting two school systems and only using one.

Last year, as a matter of tax equity, we introduced legislation to give these families a break. We don't seek to aid the rich, but those lower- and middle-income families who are most strapped by taxes and the recession. In proposing tuition tax credits, we hope to provide greater choice and wider educational opportunity for our children. The Congress failed to pass the measure we proposed, but we're not giving up. In the coming session, we will again work to secure passage of tuition tax credits.

Protecting the Unborn

There's another issue closely identified with families, although the issue itself often splits families apart. Ten years ago today, the Supreme Court overturned the state laws protecting the lives of the unborn. Heated debate on abortion has raged ever since. On one hand, there is the argument that a woman should have control over her own person. On the other hand, there is the argument that another life is involved here—the unborn child. That's the belief which has drawn many here to Washington today to march and to pray.

I, too, have always believed that God's greatest gift is human life and that we have a duty to protect the life of an unborn child. Until someone can prove the unborn child is not a life, shouldn't we give it the benefit of the doubt and assume it is? That's why I favored legislation to end the practice of abortion on demand and why I will continue to support it in the new Congress.

Now, some of you may be thinking, "Well, he hasn't said a thing that's new." I guess that's true. Some values shouldn't change. But I want you to know there are certain family issues I'll advocate even though it's the budget and the economy that will be getting the headlines, especially in the days ahead....

Until next week at this time, thanks for listening, and God bless you. □

America's Spiritual Reawakening

REMARKS TO THE ANNUAL CONVENTION OF
THE NATIONAL ASSOCIATION OF EVANGELICALS

ORLANDO, FLORIDA
MARCH 8, 1983

Those of you in the National Association of Evangelicals are known for your spiritual and humanitarian work. And I would be especially remiss if I didn't discharge right now one personal debt of gratitude. Thank you for your prayers. Nancy and I have felt their presence many times in many ways. And believe me, for us they've made all the difference.

Prayer

The other day in the East Room of the White House at a meeting there, someone asked me whether I was aware of all the people out there who were praying for the President. And I had to say, "Yes, I am. I've felt it. I believe in intercessionary prayer." But I couldn't help but say to that questioner, after he'd asked the question that if sometimes when he was praying he got a busy signal, it was just me in there ahead of him. I think

I understand how Abraham Lincoln felt when he said, "I have been driven many time to my knees by the overwhelming conviction that I had nowhere else to go."

From the joy and the good feeling of this conference, I go to a political reception. Now, I don't know why, but that bit of scheduling reminds me of a story—which I'll share with you.

An evangelical minister and a politician arrived at Heaven's gate one day together. And St. Peter, after doing all the necessary formalities, took them in hand to show them where their quarters would be. And he took them to a small, single room with a bed, a chair, and a table and said this was for the clergyman. And the politician was a little worried about what might be in store for him. And he couldn't believe it then when St. Peter stopped in front of a beautiful mansion with lovely grounds, many servants, and told him that these would be his quarters.

And he couldn't help but ask, he said, "But wait—there's something wrong—how do I get this mansion while that good and holy man only gets a single room?" And St. Peter said, "You have to understand how things are up here. We've got thousands and thousands of clergy. You're the first politician who ever made it."

Freedom Under God

But I don't want to contribute to a stereotype. So, I tell you there are a great many God-fearing, dedicated, noble men and women in public life, present company included. And, yes, we need your help to keep us ever mindful of the ideas and the principles that brought us into the public arena. The basis of those ideals and principles is a commitment to freedom and personal liberty that, itself, is grounded in the much deeper realization that freedom prospers only where the blessings of God are avidly sought and humbly accepted.

The American experiment in democracy rests on this insight. Its discovery was the great triumph of our Founding Fathers, voiced by William Penn* when he said: "If we will not be governed by God, we must be governed by tyrants." Explaining the inalienable rights of men, Thomas Jefferson said, "The God who gave us life, gave us liberty at the same time." And it was George Washington who said that "of all the dispositions and habits which lead to political prosperity, religion and morality are indispensable supports."

And finally, that shrewdest of all observers of American democracy, Alexis de Tocqueville,** put it eloquently after he had gone on a search for the secret of America's greatness and genius, and he said: "Not until I went into the churches of America and heard her pulpits aflame with righteousness did I understand the greatness and the genius of America....America is good. And if America ever ceases to be good, America will cease to be great."

---

*1644-1718 English Quaker, founder of Pennsylvania
**1805-59 French writer, author of *Democracy in America*

Well, I'm pleased to be here today with you who are keeping America great by keeping her good. Only through your work and prayers and those of millions of others can we hope to survive this perilous century and keep alive this experiment in liberty, this last, best hope of man.

I want you to know that this administration is motivated by a political philosophy that sees the greatness of America in you—her people—and in your families, churches, neighborhoods, communities—the institutions that foster and nourish values like concern for others and respect for the rule of law under God.

Now, I don't have to tell you that this puts us in opposition to, or at least out of step with, a prevailing attitude of many who have turned to a modern-day secularism, discarding the tried and time-tested values upon which our very civilization is based. No matter how well intentioned, their value system is radically different from that of most Americans. And while they proclaim that they're freeing us from superstitions of the past, they've taken upon themselves the job of superintending us by government rule and regulation. Sometimes their voices are louder than ours, but they are not yet a majority.

Parental Rights

An example of that vocal superiority is evident in a controversy now going on in Washington. And since I'm involved, I've been waiting to hear from the parents of young America. How far are they willing to go in giving to government their prerogatives as parents?

Let me state the case as briefly and simply as I can. An organization of citizens, sincerely motivated and deeply concerned about the increase in illegitimate births and abortions involving girls well below the age of consent, sometime ago established a nationwide network of clinics to offer help to these girls and, hopefully, alleviate this situation. Now, again, let me say, I do not fault their intent. However, in their well-intentioned effort, these clinics have decided to provide advice and birth control drugs and devices to underage girls without the knowledge of their parents.

For some years now, the federal government has helped with funds to subsidize these clinics. In providing for this, the Congress decreed that every effort would be made to maximize parental participation. Nevertheless, the drugs and devices are prescribed without getting parental consent or giving notification after they've done so. Girls termed "sexually active"—and that has replaced the word "promiscuous"—are given this help in order to prevent illegitimate birth or abortion.

Well, we have ordered clinics receiving federal funds to notify the parents such help has been given. One of the nation's leading newspapers has created the term "squeal rule" in editorializing against us for doing this, and we're being criticized for violating the privacy of young people. A judge has recently granted an injunction against an enforcement of our rule. I've watched TV panel shows discuss this issue, seen columnists pontificating on our error, but no one seems to mention morality as playing a part in the subject of sex.

Traditional Values

Is all of Judeo-Christian tradition wrong? Are we to believe that something so sacred can be looked upon as a purely physical thing with no potential for emotional and psychological harm? And isn't it the parents' right to give counsel and advice to keep their children from making mistakes that may affect their entire lives?

Many of us in government would like to know what parents think about this intrusion in their family by government. We're going to fight in the courts. The right of parents and the rights of family take precedence over those of Washington-based bureaucrats and social engineers.

But the fight against parental notification is really only one example of many attempts to water down traditional values and even abrogate the original terms of American democracy. Freedom prospers when religion is vibrant and the rule of law under God is acknowledged. When our Founding Fathers passed the First Amendment, they sought to protect churches from government interference. They never intended to construct a wall of hostility between government and the concept of religious belief itself.

The evidence of this permeates our history and our government. The Declaration of Independence mentions the Supreme Being no less than four times. "In God We Trust" is engraved on our coinage. The Supreme Court opens its proceedings with a religious invocation. And the Members of Congress open their sessions with a prayer. I just happen to believe the schoolchildren of the United States are entitled to the same privileges as Supreme Court justices and congressmen.

Prayer in Public Schools

Last year, I sent the Congress a constitutional amendment to restore prayer to public schools. Already this session, there's growing bipartisan support for the amendment, and I am calling on the Congress to act speedily to pass it and to let our children pray.

Perhaps some of you read recently about the Lubbock [Texas] school case, where a judge actually ruled that it was unconstitutional for a school district to give equal treatment to religious and nonreligious student groups, even when the group meetings were being held during the students' own time. The First Amendment never intended to require government to discriminate against religious speech.

Senators [Jeremiah] Denton and [Mark] Hatfield have proposed legislation in the Congress on the whole question of prohibiting discrimination against religious forms of student speech. Such legislation could go far to restore freedom of religious speech for public school students. And I hope the Congress considers these bills quickly. And with your help, I think it's possible we could also get the constitutional amendment through the Congress this year.

More than a decade ago, a Supreme Court decision literally wiped off the books of 50 states statutes protecting the rights of unborn children. Abortion on demand now takes the lives of up to 1.5 million unborn children a year. Human life legislation ending this tragedy will some day pass the Congress, and you and I must never rest until it does. Unless and until it can be proven that the unborn child is not a living entity, then its right to life, liberty and the pursuit of happiness must be protected.

You may remember that when abortion on demand began, many, and, indeed, I'm sure many of you, warned that the practice would lead to a decline in respect for human life, that the philosophical premises used to justify abortion on demand would ultimately be used to justify other attacks on the sacredness of human life—infanticide or mercy killing. Tragically enough, those warnings proved all too true. Only last year a court permitted the death by starvation of a handicapped infant.

I have directed the Health and Human Services Department to make clear to every health care facility in the United States that the Rehabilitation Act of 1973 protects all handicapped persons against discrimination based on handicaps, including infants. And we have taken the further step of requiring that each and every recipient of federal funds who provides health care services to infants must post and keep posted in a conspicuous place a notice stating that "discriminatory failure to feed and care for handicapped infants in this facility is prohibited by federal law." It also lists a 24-hour, toll-free number so that nurses and others may report violations in time to save the infant's life.

In addition, recent legislation introduced in the Congress not only increases restrictions on publicly financed abortions, it also addresses this whole problem of infanticide. I urge the Congress to begin hearings and to adopt legislation that will protect the right of life to all children, including the disabled or handicapped.

Spiritual Awakening

Now, I'm sure that you must get discouraged at times, but you've done better than you know, perhaps. There's a great spiritual awakening in America, a renewal of the traditional values that have been the bedrock of America's goodness and greatness.

One recent survey by a Washington-based research council concluded that Americans were far more religious than the people of other nations; 95 percent of those surveyed expressed a belief in God and a huge majority believed the Ten Commandments had real meaning in their lives. And another study has found that an overwhelming majority of Americans disapproved of adultery, teenage sex, pornography, abortion and hard drugs. And this same study showed a deep reverence for the importance of family ties and religious belief.

I think the items that we've discussed here today must be a key part of the nation's political agenda. For the first time the Congress is openly and seriously debating and dealing with the prayer and abortion issues—and that's enormous progress right there. I repeat: America is in the midst of a spiritual awakening and a moral renewal. And with your Biblical keynote, I say today, "Yes, let justice roll on like a river, righteousness like a never-failing stream."

Now, obviously, much of this new political and social consensus I've talked about is based on a positive view of American history, one that takes pride in our country's accomplishments and record. But we must never forget that no government schemes are going to perfect man. We know that living in this world means dealing with what philosophers would call the phenomenology of evil or, as theologians would put it, the doctrine of sin.

There is sin and evil in the world, and we're enjoined by Scripture and the Lord Jesus to oppose it with all our might. Our nation, too, has a legacy of evil with which it must deal. The glory of this land has been its capacity for transcending the moral evils of our past. For example, the long struggle of minority citizens for equal rights, once a source of disunity and civil war, is now a point of pride for all Americans. We must never go back. There is no room for racism, anti-Semitism, or other forms of ethnic and racial hatred in this country.

I know that you've been horrified, as have I, by the resurgence of some hate groups preaching bigotry and prejudice. Use the mighty voice of your pulpits and the powerful standing of your churches to denounce and isolate these hate groups in our midst. The commandment given us is clear and simple: "Thou shalt love thy neighbor as thyself."

But whatever sad episodes exist in our past, any objective observer must hold a positive view of American history, a history that has been the story of hopes fulfilled and dreams made into reality. Especially in this century, America has kept alight the torch of freedom, but not just for ourselves but for millions of others around the world.

Marxist Doctrine

And this brings me to my final point today. During my first press conference as President, in answer to a direct question, I pointed out that, as good Marxist-Leninists, the Soviet leaders have openly and publicly declared that the only morality they recognize is that which will further their cause, which is world revolution. I think I should point out I was only quoting Lenin, their guiding spirit, who said in 1920 that they repudiate all morality that proceeds from supernatural ideas—that's their name for religion—or ideas that are outside class conceptions. Morality is entirely subordinate to the interests of class war. And everything is moral that is necessary for the annihilation of the old, exploiting

-54-

social disorder and for uniting the proletariat.

I think the refusal of many influential people to accept this elementary fact of Soviet doctrine illustrates an historical reluctance to see totalitarian powers for what they are. We saw this phenomenon in the 1930s. We see it too often today.

This doesn't mean we should isolate ourselves and refuse to seek an understanding with them. I intend to do everything I can to persuade them of our peaceful intent, to remind them that it was the West that refused to use its nuclear monopoly in the 1940s and 1950s for territorial gain, and which now proposes a 50-percent cut in strategic ballistic missiles and the elimination of an entire class of land-based, intermediate-range nuclear missiles.

Defending Freedom

At the same time, however, they must be made to understand we will never compromise our principles and standards. We will never give away our freedom. We will never abandon our belief in God. And we will never stop searching for a genuine peace. But we can assure none of these things America stands for through the so-called nuclear freeze solutions proposed by some.

The truth is that a freeze now would be a very dangerous fraud, for that is merely the illusion of peace. The reality is that we must find peace through strength.

I would agree to a freeze if only we could freeze the Soviets' global desires. A freeze at current levels of weapons would remove any incentive for the Soviets to negotiate seriously in Geneva and virtually end our chances to achieve the major arms reductions which we have proposed. Instead, they would achieve their objectives through the freeze.

A freeze would reward the Soviet Union for its enormous and unparalleled military buildup. It would prevent the essential and long overdue modernization of United States and allied defenses and would leave our aging forces increasingly vulnerable. And an honest freeze would require extensive prior negotiations on the systems and numbers to be limited and on the measures to ensure effective verification and compliance. And the kind of a freeze that has been suggested would be virtually impossible to verify. Such a major effort would divert us completely from our current negotiations on achieving substantial reductions.

Evil Empire

A number of years ago, I heard a young father, a very prominent young man in the entertainment world, addressing a tremendous gathering in California. It was during the time of the Cold War, and communism and our own way of life were very much on people's minds. And he was speaking on that subject. And suddenly I heard him saying, "I love my little girls more than anything"—And I said to myself, "Oh, no, don't. You can't—

don't say that." But I had underestimated him. He went on: "I would rather see my little girls die now, still believing in God, than have them grow up under communism and one day die no longer believing in God."

There were thousands of young people in that audience. They came to their feet with shouts of joy. They had instantly recognized the profound truth in what he had said.

Yes, let us pray for the salvation of all of those who live in that totalitarian darkness—pray they will discover the joy of knowing God. But until they do, let us be aware that while they, the Soviets, preach the supremacy of the state, declare its omnipotence over individual man, and predict its eventual domination of all peoples on the Earth, they are the focus of evil in the modern world.

It was C.S. Lewis who, in his unforgettable *Screwtape Letters*, wrote: "The greatest evil is not done now in those sordid 'dens of crime' that Dickens loved to paint. It is not even done in concentration camps and labor camps. In those we see its final result. But it is conceived and ordered (moved, seconded, carried and minuted) in clear, carpeted, warmed, and well-lighted offices, by quiet men with white collars and cut fingernails and smooth-shaven cheeks who do not need to raise their voices."

Because these "quiet men" do not "raise their voices," because they sometimes speak in soothing tones of brotherhood and peace, because, like other dictators before them, they're always making "their final territorial demand," some would have us accept them at their word and accommodate ourselves to their aggressive impulses. But if history teaches anything, it teaches that simple-minded appeasement or wishful thinking about our adversaries is folly. It means the betrayal of our past, the squandering of our freedom.

So, I urge you to speak out against those who would place the United States in a position of military and moral inferiority. You know, I've always believed that old "Screwtape" reserved his best efforts for those of you in the church. So, in your discussions of the nuclear freeze proposals, I urge you to beware the temptation of pride—the temptation of blithely declaring yourselves above it all and label both sides equally at fault, to ignore the facts of history and the aggressive impulses of an evil empire, to simply call the arms race a giant misunderstanding and thereby remove yourself from the struggle between right and wrong and good and evil. I ask you to resist the attempts of those who would have you withhold your support for this administration's efforts, to keep America strong and free, while we negotiate real and verifiable reductions in the world's nuclear arsenals, and one day, with God's help, their total elimination.

Faith in God

While America's military strength is important, let me add here that I've always maintained that the struggle now going on for the world will never be decided by bombs or rockets, by armies or military might. The real crisis we face today is a spiritual one; at root, it is a test of moral will and faith.

Whittaker Chambers,* the man whose own religious conversion made him a witness to one of the terrible traumas of our time, the Hiss-Chambers case, wrote that the crisis of the Western world exists to the degree in which the West is indifferent to God, the degree to which it collaborates in communism's attempt to make man stand alone without God. And then he said, for Marxism-Leninism is actually the second oldest faith, first proclaimed in the Garden of Eden with the words of temptation, "Ye shall be as gods."

The Western world can answer this challenge, he wrote, "but only provided that its faith in God and the freedom He enjoins is as great as communism's faith in Man."

I believe we shall rise to the challenge. I believe that communism is another sad, bizarre chapter in human history whose last pages even now are being written. I believe this because the source of our strength in the quest for human freedom is not material, but spiritual. And because it knows no limitation, it must terrify and ultimately triumph over those who would enslave their fellow man. For in the words of Isaiah: "He giveth power to the faint: and to them that have no might He increaseth strength....But they that wait upon the Lord shall renew their strength; they shall mount up with wings as eagles; they shall run, and not be weary...."

Yes, change your world. One of our Founding Fathers, Thomas Paine, said, "We have it within our power to begin the world over again." We can do it, doing together what no one church could do by itself.

God bless you, and thank you very much.   □

---

*1901-61 Renounced Communist Party membership to become conservative editor and writer Chief accuser in famous 1949 perjury trial of Alger Hiss

A Nation Conceived in Liberty

MESSAGE TO THE NATION FOR INDEPENDENCE DAY

WASHINGTON, D.C.
JULY 3, 1983

Today we join together to celebrate freedom's birthday. America is 207 years old. That makes us the oldest living democracy on Earth. I think there's a good reason for that.

A Land of Heroes

It's always been my belief that by a Divine plan this nation was placed between the two oceans to be sought out and found by those with a special brand of courage and love of freedom. Can we imagine the courage it took back in 1620 to pick up family, bid goodbye to friends, board those small ships, and set sail across a mighty ocean toward a new future in an unknown world?

Can we appreciate what the patriots endured in that bone-cold snow at Valley Forge when they spent a winter without enough food or medicine or even boots to cover their feet? Maybe we can't. Maybe we look around our more comfortable world of 1983 and say, "That's more than we've known or could endure."

But look closer. Look in our own neighborhoods and families, and you will see America is still a land of heroes with all the courage and love of freedom that ever was before. And that's our best hope for the future.

We've seen our heroes at Normandy, Bastogne, Guadalcanal and Pork Chop Hill. We saw the agony of our POW's inside prison camps in North Vietnam. We held our breath, then rejoiced and cried when they finally came home, kissed the ground, and thanked God they were free.

We're a melting pot. And our body and spirit have never been stronger or richer, thanks to hundreds of thousands of new heroes—the brave men, women and children who risked death to escape their communist prisons in Asia and Cuba. They arrived less than 10 years ago. Most were not able to speak a word of English. But with their courage and faith, they brought unbounded determination to work, produce, succeed and excel. Now, more and more of them are becoming leaders in their communities—small business owners, hard-working taxpayers, even valedictorians in their high school graduating classes. We can be proud and thankful that they're joining us today in parades and ball games and backyard barbecues as young members of an old family.

We can salute the heroes of our technological age, like the four-man, one-woman crew of the [space shuttle] *Challenger*. They dazzled America and the world with another perfect mission into the new frontier of space.

How can we ignore the countless other examples of courage and love of neighbor from everyday Americans—people like that grandmother in New York who collared a robber and gave him the back of her hand until the police arrived; people all across the country who've been battling angry spring floods and rising rivers so they could save the property and maybe the lives of their families and friends.

To Serve Liberty

Don't let anyone tell us that America's best days are behind her, that the American spirit has been lost. I've never felt stronger than I do now that our people are coming together and that America is moving forward again. I've never been more convinced that fundamental problems of the economy, education, and national defense—neglected for too many years—are now being addressed and can be solved.

They will be solved if we believe in each other and in those values that make us a great and loving people. Think about it. We work and educate for freedom, for service of the ideal of liberty, not for subservience to the state.

Our notion of education is the most revolutionary idea conceived by mankind. When our scholars and teachers learn something new, they can't wait to teach it to our children. But in a totalitarian country, you're not allowed to read books or discuss ideas that aren't approved by censors. You're not allowed to have a computer in your home, because you might obtain information or knowledge that would make you a threat to the state.

Let us remember this July 4th that America's Revolution remains unique because it's changed the very concept of government. We are the nation which proudly announced to the world: We are conceived in liberty. Each of us is created equal, with God-given rights, and power ultimately resides in "We the people."

Meaning of the Flag

We, the people, have only begun to write a great story that will be passed down through time—the story of America. I'm reminded of a verse I once read about Old Glory [the American flag]. The "Red, White, and Blue" is a testament to the unity and patriotism of our people and to the deep love and commitment we have for our country, our freedom and our way of life. The verse was written as if the flag was speaking to us, now and for generations to come.

It said:

I am whatever you make me, nothing more.
I am your belief in yourself, your dream of what a people may become.
I am a day's work of the weakest man and the largest dream of the most daring.
I am the clutch of an idea and the reasoned purpose of resolution.
I am no more than you believe me to be and I am all that you believe I can be.
I am whatever you make me, nothing more.

Happy Fourth of July, and may God bless America.   □

A New American Emancipation

INAUGURAL ADDRESS

WASHINGTON, D.C.
JANUARY 21, 1985

Thee are no words adequate to express my thanks for the great honor that you've bestowed on me. I'll do my utmost to be deserving of your trust.

This is the 50th time that we, the people, have celebrated this historic occasion. When the first President, George Washington, placed his hand upon the Bible, he stood less than a single day's journey by horseback from raw, untamed wilderness. There were four million Americans in a union of 13 states. Today, we are 60 times as many in a union of 50 states. We've lighted the world with our inventions, gone to the aid of mankind wherever in the world there was a cry for help, journeyed to the moon and safely returned. So much has changed, and yet we stand together as we did two centuries ago.

New Beginnings

When I took this oath four years ago, I did so in a time of economic stress. Voices were raised saying that we had to look to our past for the greatness and glory. But we, the present-day Americans, are not given to looking backward. In this blessed land, there is always a better tomorrow.

Four years ago, I spoke to you of a new beginning, and we have accomplished that. But in another sense, our new beginning is a continuation of that beginning created two centuries ago when—for the first time in history—government, the people said, was not our master, it is our servant; its only power that which we the people allow it to have.

That system has never failed us, but for a time we failed the system. We asked things of government that government was not

-61-

equipped to give. We yielded authority to the national government that properly belonged to states or to local governments or to the people themselves. We allowed taxes and inflation to rob us of our earnings and savings, and watched the great industrial machine that had made us the most productive people on Earth slow down and the number of unemployed increase.

By 1980 we knew it was time to renew our faith, to strive with all our strength toward the ultimate in individual freedom, consistent with an orderly society.

We believed then and now: There are no limits to growth and human progress when men and women are free to follow their dreams. And we were right to believe that. Tax rates have been reduced, inflation cut dramatically, and more people are employed than ever before in our history.

We are creating a nation once again vibrant, robust and alive. But there are many mountains yet to climb. We will not rest until every American enjoys the fullness of freedom, dignity and opportunity as our birthright. It is our birthright as citizens of this great Republic.

And if we meet this challenge, these will be years when Americans have restored their confidence and tradition of progress; when our values of faith, family, work and neighborhood were restated for a modern age; when our economy was finally freed from government's grip; when we made sincere efforts at meaningful arms reductions and—by rebuilding our defenses, our economy, and developing new technologies—helped preserve peace in a troubled world; when America courageously supported the struggle for individual liberty, self-government and free enterprise throughout the world, and turned the tide of history away from totalitarian darkness and into the warm sunlight of human freedom.

With Heart and Hand

My fellow citizens, our nation is poised for greatness. We must do what we know is right, and do it with all our might. Let history say of us, "These were golden years—when the American Revolution was reborn, when freedom gained new life, and America reached for her best."

Our two-party system has served us well over the years, but never better than in those times of great challenge when we came together not as Democrats or Republicans, but as Americans united in a common cause.

Two of our Founding Fathers, a Boston lawyer named Adams and a Virginia planter named Jefferson, members of that remarkable group who met in Independence Hall and dared to think they could start the world over again, left us an important lesson. They had become, in the years then in government, bitter political rivals in the presidential election of 1800. Then, years later, when both were retired and age had softened their anger, they began to speak to each other again through letters. A bond was reestablished between those two who had helped create this government of ours.

In 1826, the 50th anniversary of the Declaration of Independence, they both died. They died on the same day, within a few hours of each other, and that day was the Fourth of July.

In one of those letters exchanged in the sunset of their lives, Jefferson wrote, "It carries me back to the times when, beset with difficulties and dangers, we were fellow laborers in the same cause, struggling for what is most valuable to man, his right of self-government. Laboring always at the same oar, with some wave ever ahead threatening to overwhelm us, and yet passing harmless...we rode through the storm with heart and hand."

Well, with heart and hand, let us stand as one today—one people under God, determined that our future shall be worthy of our past. As we do, we must not repeat the well-intentioned errors of our past. We must never again abuse the trust of working men and women by sending their earnings on a futile chase after the spiraling demands of a bloated federal establishment. You elected us in 1980 to end this prescription for disaster, and I don't believe you reelected us in 1984 to reverse course.

Freedom Unleashes Human Progress

At the heart of our efforts is one idea vindicated by 25 straight months of economic growth: Freedom and incentives unleash the drive and entrepreneurial genius that are the core of human progress. We have begun to increase the rewards for work, savings and investment; reduce the increase in the cost and size of government and its interference in people's lives.

We must simplify our tax system, make it more fair and bring the rates down for all who work and earn. We must think anew and move with a new boldness, so every American who seeks work can find work, so the least among us shall have an equal chance to achieve the greatest things—to be heroes who heal our sick, feed the hungry, protect peace among nations, and leave this world a better place.

The time has come for a new American emancipation—a great national drive to tear down economic barriers and liberate the spirit of enterprise in the most distressed areas of our country. My friends, together we can do this, and do it we must, so help me God.

From new freedom will spring new opportunities for growth, a more productive, fulfilled and united people, and a stronger America— an America that will lead the technological revolution and also open its mind and heart and soul to the treasures of literature, music and poetry, and the values of faith, courage and love.

Balanced Budget

A dynamic economy, with more citizens working and paying taxes, will be our strongest tool to bring down budget deficits. But an almost unbroken 50 years of deficit spending has finally brought us to a time of reckoning. We've come to a turning point, a moment for hard decisions. I have asked the Cabinet and my staff a question, and now I put the same question to all of you: If not us, who? And if not now, when? It must be done by all of us going forward with a program aimed at reaching a balanced budget. We can then begin reducing the national debt.

I will shortly submit a budget to the Congress aimed at freezing government program spending for the next year. Beyond this, we must take further steps to permanently control government's power to tax and spend. We must act now to protect future generations from government's desire to spend its citizens' money and tax them into servitude when the bills come due. Let us make it unconstitutional for the federal government to spend more than the federal government takes in.

Compassion and Government

We have already started returning to the people and to state and local governments responsibilities better handled by them. Now, there is a place for the federal government in matters of social compassion. But our fundamental goals must be to reduce dependency and upgrade the dignity of those who are infirm or disadvantaged. And here, a growing economy and support from family and community offer our best chance for a society where compassion is a way of life, where the old and infirm are cared for, the young and, yes, the unborn protected, and the unfortunate looked after and made self-sufficient.

Now, there is another area where the federal government can play a part. As an older American, I remember a time when people of different race, creed, or ethnic origin in our land found hatred and prejudice installed in social custom and, yes, in law. There's no story more heartening in our history than the progress that we've made toward the brotherhood of man that God intended for us. Let us resolve there will be no turning back or hesitation on the road to an America rich in dignity and abundant with opportunity for all our citizens.

Let us resolve that we, the people, will build an American Opportunity Society in which all of us—white and black, rich and poor, young and old—will go forward together, arm in arm. Again, let us remember that though our heritage is one of bloodlines from every corner of the Earth, we are all Americans, pledged to carry on this last, best hope of man on Earth.

Freedom and Security

I've spoken of our domestic goals and the limitations we should put on our national government. Now let me turn to a task that is the primary responsibility of national government—the safety and security of our people.

Today, we utter no prayer more fervently than the ancient prayer for peace on Earth. Yet history has shown that peace does not come, nor will our freedom be preserved, by good will alone. There are those in the world who scorn our vision of human dignity and freedom. One nation, the Soviet Union, has conducted the greatest military buildup in the history of man, building arsenals of awesome offensive weapons.

We've made progress in restoring our defense capability. But much remains to be done. There must be no wavering by us, nor any doubts by others, that America will meet her responsibilities to remain free, secure and at peace.

There is only one way safely and legitimately to reduce the cost of national security, and that is to reduce the need for it. And this we're trying to do in negotiations with the Soviet Union. We're not just discussing limits on a further increase of nuclear weapons; we seek, instead, to reduce their number. We seek the total elimination one day of nuclear weapons from the face of the Earth.

Now, for decades, we and the Soviets have lived under the threat of mutual assured destruction—if either resorted to the use of nuclear weapons, the other could retaliate and destroy the one who had started it. Is there either logic or morality in believing that if one side threatens to kill tens of millions of our people our only recourse is to threaten killing tens of millions of theirs?

I have approved a research program to find, if we can, a security shield that will destroy nuclear missiles before they reach their target. It wouldn't kill people; it would destroy weapons. It wouldn't militarize space; it would help demilitarize the arsenals of Earth. It would render nuclear weapons obsolete. We will meet with the Soviets, hoping that we can agree on a way to rid the world of the threat of nuclear destruction.

Freedom our Best Ally

We strive for peace and security, heartened by the changes all around us. Since the turn of the century, the number of democracies in the world has grown fourfold. Human freedom is on the march, and nowhere more so than in our own hemisphere. Freedom is one of the deepest and noblest aspirations of the human spirit. People, worldwide, hunger for the right of self-determination, for those inalienable rights that make for human dignity and progress.

America must remain freedom's staunchest friend, for freedom is our best ally and it is the world's only hope to conquer poverty and preserve peace. Every blow we inflict against poverty will be a blow against its dark allies of oppression and war. Every victory for human freedom will be a victory for world peace.

So, we go forward today, a nation still mighty in its youth and powerful in its purpose. With our alliances strengthened, with our economy leading the world to a new age of economic expansion, we look to a future rich in possibilities. And all of this is because we worked and acted together, not as members of political parties but as Americans.

My friends, we live in a world that's lit by lightning. So much is changing and will change, but so much endures and transcends time.

History is a ribbon, always unfurling. History is a journey. As we continue our journey, we think of those who traveled before us. We stand...inside this symbol of our democracy [the Capitol], and we see and hear again the echoes of our past: a general falls to his knees in the hard snow of Valley Forge; a lonely President paces the darkened halls and ponders his struggle to preserve the Union; the men of the Alamo call out encouragement to each other; a settler pushes west and sings a song, and the song echoes out forever and fills the unknowing air.

It is the American sound. It is hopeful, big-hearted, idealistic, daring, decent and fair. That's our heritage, that's our song. We sing it still. For all our problems, our differences, we are together as of old. We raise our voices to the God who is the Author of this most tender music. And may He continue to hold us close as we fill the world with our sound—in unity, affection and love—one people under God, dedicated to the dream of freedom that He has placed in the human heart, called upon now to pass that dream on to a waiting and hopeful world.

God bless you, and God bless America. □

Explosion of the Space Shuttle *Challenger*

ADDRESS TO THE NATION

WASHINGTON, D.C.
JANUARY 28, 1986

L adies and gentlemen, I'd planned to speak to you tonight to report on the state of the Union, but the events of earlier today have led me to change those plans. Today is a day for mourning and remembering.

Nancy and I are pained to the core by the tragedy of the shuttle *Challenger*. We know we share this pain with all of the people of our country. This is truly a national loss.

Courage and Loss

Nineteen years ago, almost to the day, we lost three astronauts in a terrible accident on the ground. But we've never lost an astronaut in flight; we've never had a tragedy like this. And perhaps we've forgotten the courage it took for the crew of the shuttle; but they, the *Challenger* Seven, were aware of the dangers, but overcame them and did their jobs brilliantly. We mourn seven heroes: Michael Smith, Dick Scobee, Judith Resnik, Ronald McNair, Ellison Onizuka, Gregory Jarvis and Christa McAuliffe. We mourn their loss as a nation together.

For the families of the seven, we cannot bear, as you do, the full impact of this tragedy. But we feel the loss, and we're thinking about you so very much. Your loved ones were daring and brave, and they had that special grace, that special spirit that says, "Give me a challenge and I'll meet it with joy." They had a hunger to explore the universe and discover its truths. They wished to serve, and they did. They served all of us.

Future Belongs to the Brave

We've grown used to wonders in this century. It's hard to dazzle us. But for 25 years the United States space program has been doing just that. We've grown used to the idea of space, and perhaps we forget that we've only just begun. We're still pioneers. They, the members of the *Challenger* crew, were pioneers.

And I want to say something to the schoolchildren of America who were watching the live coverage of the shuttle's takeoff. I know it is hard to understand, but sometimes painful things like this happen. It's all part of the process of exploration and discovery. It's all part of taking a chance and expanding man's horizons. The future doesn't belong to the fainthearted; it belongs to the brave. The *Challenger* crew was pulling us into the future, and we'll continue to follow them.

I've always had great faith in and respect for our space program, and what happened today does nothing to diminish it. We don't hide our space program. We don't keep secrets and cover things up. We do it all up front and in public. That's the way freedom is, and we wouldn't change it for a minute.

Their Dedication Was Complete

We'll continue our quest in space. There will be more shuttle flights and more shuttle crews and, yes, more volunteers, more civilians, more teachers in space. Nothing ends here; our hopes and our journeys continue.

I want to add that I wish I could talk to every man and woman who works for NASA or who worked on this mission and tell them: "Your dedication and professionalism have moved and impressed us for decades. And we know of your anguish. We share it."

There's a coincidence today. On this day 390 years ago, the great explorer Sir Francis Drake died aboard ship off the coast of Panama. In his lifetime the great frontiers were the oceans, and an historian later said, "He lived by the sea, died on it, and was buried in it." Well, today we can say of the *Challenger* crew: Their dedication was, like Drake's, complete.

The crew of the space shuttle *Challenger* honored us by the manner in which they lived their lives. We will never forget them, nor the last time we saw them, this morning, as they prepared for their journey and waved good-bye and "slipped the surly bonds of earth" to "touch the face of God." □

Seven Americans

REMARKS AT THE MEMORIAL SERVICE
FOR THE CREW OF THE SPACE SHUTTLE *CHALLENGER*

JOHNSON SPACE CENTER, HOUSTON, TEXAS
JANUARY 31, 1986

We come together today to mourn the loss of seven brave Americans, to share the grief that we all feel, and perhaps in that sharing, to find the strength to bear our sorrow and the courage to look for the seeds of hope.

Our nation's loss is first a profound personal loss to the family and the friends and the loved ones of our shuttle astronauts. To those they left behind—the mothers, the fathers, the husbands and wives, brothers and sisters, yes, and especially the children—all of America stands beside you in your time of sorrow.

Dedication and Honor

What we say today is only an inadequate expression of what we carry in our hearts. Words pale in the shadow of grief; they seem insufficient even to measure the brave sacrifice of those you loved and we so admired. Their truest testimony will not be in the words we speak, but in the way they led their lives and in the way they lost their lives—with dedication, honor and an unquenchable desire to explore this mysterious and beautiful universe.

The best we can do is remember our seven astronauts, our *Challenger* Seven, remember them as they lived, bringing life and love and joy to those who knew them and pride to a nation.

They came from all parts of this great country—from South Carolina to Washington State; Ohio to Mohawk, New York; Hawaii to North Carolina to Concord, New Hampshire. They were so different; yet in their mission, their quest, they held so much in common.

Soaring Achievements

We remember Dick Scobee, the commander who spoke the last words we heard from the space shuttle *Challenger*. He served as a fighter pilot in Vietnam earning many medals for bravery and later as a test pilot of advanced aircraft before joining the space program. Danger was a familiar companion to Commander Scobee.

We remember Michael Smith, who earned enough medals as a combat pilot to cover his chest, including the Navy Distinguished Flying Cross, three Air Medals, and the Vietnamese Cross of Gallantry with Silver Star in gratitude from a nation he fought to keep free.

We remember Judith Resnik, known as J.R. to her friends, always smiling, always eager to make a contribution, finding beauty in the music she played on her piano in her off-hours.

We remember Ellison Onizuka, who, as a child running barefoot through the coffee fields and macadamia groves of Hawaii, dreamed of someday traveling to the moon. Being an Eagle Scout, he said, had helped him soar to the impressive achievements of his career.

We remember Ronald McNair, who said that he learned perseverance in the cotton fields of South Carolina. His dream was to live aboard the space station, performing experiments and playing his saxophone in the weightlessness of space. Well, Ron, we will miss your saxophone; and we will build your space station.

We remember Gregory Jarvis. On that ill-fated flight he was carrying with him a flag of his university in Buffalo, New York—a small token, he said, to the people who unlocked his future.

We remember Christa McAuliffe, who captured the imagination of the entire nation; inspiring us with her pluck, her restless spirit of discovery; a teacher, not just to her students, but to an entire people, instilling us all with the excitement of this journey we ride into the future.

We will always remember them, these skilled professionals, scientists and adventurers, these artists and teachers and family men and women; and we will cherish each of their stories, stories of triumph and bravery, stories of true American heroes.

The Sacrifice of a Nation

On the day of the disaster, our nation held a vigil by our television sets. In one cruel moment our exhilaration turned to horror; we waited and watched and tried to make sense of what we had seen. That night I listened to a call-in program on the radio; people of every age spoke of their sadness and the pride they felt in our astronauts. Across America we are reaching out, holding hands, and finding comfort in one another.

The sacrifice of your loved ones has stirred the soul of our nation and through the pain our hearts have been opened to a profound truth: The future is not free; the story of all human progress is one of a struggle against all odds. We learned again that this America, which Abraham Lincoln called the last, best hope of man on Earth, was built on heroism and noble sacrifice. It was built by men and women like our seven star voyagers, who answered a call beyond duty, who gave more than was expected or required, and who gave it little thought to worldly reward.

Pioneers

We think back to the pioneers of an earlier century, the sturdy souls who took their families and their belongings and set out into the frontier of the American West. Often they met with terrible hardship. Along the Oregon Trail, you could still see the gravemarkers of those who fell on the way. But grief only steeled them to the journey ahead.

Today the frontier is space and the boundaries of human knowledge. Sometimes when we reach for the stars, we fall short. But we must pick ourselves up again and press on despite the pain. Our nation is indeed fortunate that we can still draw on immense reservoirs of courage, character and fortitude; that we're still blessed with heroes like those of the space shuttle *Challenger.*

The Dream Lives On

Dick Scobee knew that every launching of a space shuttle is a technological miracle. And he said, "If something ever does go wrong, I hope that doesn't mean the end to the space shuttle program." Every family member I talked to asked specifically that we continue the program, that that is what their departed loved one would want above all else. We will not disappoint them.

Today we promise Dick Scobee and his crew that their dream lives on, that the future they worked so hard to build will become reality. The dedicated men and women of NASA have lost seven members of their family. Still, they, too, must forge ahead with a space program that is effective, safe and efficient, but bold and committed.

Man will continue his conquest of space. To reach out for new goals and ever greater achievements—that is the way we shall commemorate our seven *Challenger* heroes.

Dick, Mike, Judy, El, Ron, Greg and Christa—your families and your country mourn your passing. We bid you good-bye; we will never forget you. For those who knew you well and love you, the pain will be deep and enduring. A nation, too, will long feel the loss of her seven sons and daughters, her seven good friends. We can find consolation only in faith, for we know in our hearts that you who flew so high and so proud now make your home beyond the stars, safe in God's promise of eternal life.

May God bless you all and give you comfort in this difficult time. □

Agenda for the Future

ADDRESS TO THE CONGRESS ON THE STATE OF THE UNION

WASHINGTON, D.C.
FEBRUARY 4, 1986

I have come to review with you the progress of our nation, to speak of unfinished work, and to set our sights on the future. I am pleased to report the state of our Union is stronger than a year ago and growing stronger each day. Tonight we look out on a rising America, firm of heart, united in spirit, powerful in pride and patriotism. America is on the move.

But it wasn't long ago that we looked out on a different land: locked factory gates, long gasoline lines, intolerable prices and interest rates turning the greatest country on Earth into a land of broken dreams. Government growing beyond our consent had become a lumbering giant, slamming shut the gates of opportunity, threatening to crush the very roots of our freedom.

What brought America back? The American people brought us back with quiet courage and common sense, with undying faith that in this nation under God the future will be ours; for the future belongs to the free.

Freedom on the March

Tonight the American people deserve our thanks for 37 straight months of economic growth, for sunrise firms and modernized industries creating nine million new jobs in three years, interest rates cut in half, inflation falling from over 12 percent in 1980 to under four today, and a mighty river of good works—a record $74,000 million in voluntary giving just last year alone.

Despite the pressures of our modern world, family and community remain the moral core of our society, guardians of our values and hopes for the future. Family and community are the costars of this American comeback. They are why we say tonight: Private values must be at the heart of public policies.

What is true for families in America is true for America in the family of free nations. History is no captive of some inevitable force. History is made by men and women of vision and courage. Tonight freedom is on the march. The United States is the economic miracle, the model to which the world once again turns. We stand for an idea whose time is now: Only by lifting the weights from the shoulders of all can people truly prosper and can peace among all nations be secure.

Teddy Roosevelt* said that a nation that does great work lives forever. We have done well, but we cannot stop at the foothills when [Mt.] Everest beckons. It's time for America to be all that we can be.

We speak tonight of an "agenda for the future," an agenda for a safer, more secure world. And we speak about the necessity for actions to steel us for the challenges of growth, trade and security in the next decade and the year 2000. And we will do it—not by breaking faith with bedrock principles, but by breaking free from failed policies.

Federal and Family Budgets

Let us begin where storm clouds loom darkest—right here in Washington, D.C. This week I will send you our detailed proposals; tonight let us speak of our responsibility to redefine government's role: not to control, not to demand or command, not to contain us, but to help in times of need and, above all, to create a ladder of opportunity to full employment so that all Americans can climb toward economic power and justice on their own.

But we cannot win the race to the future shackled to a system that can't even pass a federal budget. We cannot win that race held back by horse-and-buggy programs that waste tax dollars and squander human potential. We cannot win that race if we're swamped in a sea of red ink.

Now, Mr. Speaker [of the House of Representatives], you know, I know, and the American people know the federal budget system is broken. It doesn't work. Before we leave this city, let's you and I work together to fix it, and then we can finally give the American people a balanced budget.

Members of Congress, passage of Gramm-Rudman-Hollings** gives us an historic opportunity to achieve what has eluded our national leadership for decades: forcing the federal government to live within its means.

Your schedule now requires that the budget resolution be passed by April 15th, the very day America's families have to foot the bill for the budgets that you produce.*** How often we read of a husband

---

*26th president, 1901-1909
**Legislation requiring a balanced federal budget
***Deadline for filing federal tax returns

and wife both working, struggling from paycheck to paycheck to raise a family, meet a mortgage, pay their taxes and bills. And yet some in Congress say taxes must be raised. Well, I'm sorry; they're asking the wrong people to tighten their belts. It's time we reduce the federal budget and left the family budget alone. We do not face large deficits because American families are undertaxed; we face those deficits because the federal government overspends.

Reducing the Deficit

The detailed budget that we will submit will meet the Gramm-Rudman-Hollings target for deficit reductions, meet our commitment to ensure a strong national defense, meet our commitment to protect Social Security and the truly less fortunate and, yes, meet our commitment to not raise taxes.

How should we accomplish this? Well, not by taking from those in need. As families take care of their own, government must provide shelter and nourishment for those who cannot provide for themselves. But we must revise or replace programs enacted in the name of compassion that degrade the moral worth of work, encourage family breakups, and drive entire communities into a bleak and heartless dependency.

Gramm-Rudman-Hollings can mark a dramatic improvement. But experience shows that simply setting deficit targets does not assure they'll be met. We must proceed with...reforms against waste. And tonight I ask you to give me what 43 governors have: Give me a line-item veto this year.* Give me the authority to veto waste, and I'll take the responsibility. I'll make the cuts, I'll take the heat. This authority would not give me any monopoly power, but simply prevent spending measures from sneaking through that could not pass on their own merit. And you can sustain and override my veto; that's the way the system should work. Once we've made the hard choices, we should lock in our gains with a balanced budget amendment to the Constitution.

I mentioned that we will meet our commitment to national defense. We must meet it. Defense is not just another budget expense. Keeping America strong, free and at peace is solely the responsibility of the federal government; it is government's prime responsibility. We have devoted five years trying to narrow a dangerous gap born of illusion and neglect, and we've made important gains. Yet the threat from Soviet forces, conventional and strategic, from the Soviet drive for domination, from the increase in espionage and state terror remains great. This is reality. Closing our eyes will not make reality disappear.

We pledged together to hold real growth in defense spending to the bare minimum. My budget honors that pledge, and I'm now asking you, the Congress, to keep its end of the bargain. The Soviets must know that if America reduces her defenses, it will be because of a reduced threat, not a reduced resolve.

*Authority to reject individual spending programs within a single legislative act

Freeing the Economy

Keeping America strong is as vital to the national security as controlling federal spending is to our economic security. But, as I have said before, the most powerful force we can enlist against the federal deficit is an ever-expanding American economy, unfettered and free.

The magic of opportunity—unreserved, unfailing, unrestrained—isn't this the calling that unites us? I believe our tax rate cuts for the people have done more to spur a spirit of risktaking and help America's economy break free than any program since John Kennedy's tax cut almost a quarter century ago.

Now history calls us to press on, to complete efforts for an historic tax reform providing new opportunity for all and ensuring that all pay their fair share, but no more. We've come this far. Will you join me now, and we'll walk this last mile together?

You know my views on this. We cannot and we will not accept tax reform that is tax increase in disguise. True reform must be an engine of productivity and growth, and that means a top personal rate no higher than 35 percent. True reform must be truly fair, and that means raising personal exemptions to $2,000. True reform means a tax system that at long last is pro-family, pro-jobs, pro-future and pro-America.

As we knock down the barriers to growth, we must redouble our efforts for freer and fairer trade. We have already taken actions to counter unfair trading practices and to pry open closed foreign markets. We will continue to do so. We will also oppose legislation touted as providing protection that in reality pits one American worker against another, one industry against another, one community against another, and that raises prices for us all. If the United States can trade with other nations on a level playing field, we can outproduce, outcompete and outsell anybody, anywhere in the world.

The constant expansion of our economy and exports requires a sound and stable dollar at home and reliable exchange rates around the world. We must never again permit wild currency swings to cripple our farmers and other exporters. Farmers, in particular, have suffered from past unwise government policies. They must not be abandoned with problems they did not create and cannot control. We've begun coordinating economic and monetary policy among our major trading partners. But there's more to do, and tonight I am directing Treasury Secretary Jim Baker to determine if the nations of the world should convene to discuss the role and relationship of our currencies.

American Values

Confident and secure in our values, Americans are striving forward to embrace the future. We see it not only in our recovery but in three straight years of falling crime rates, as families and communities band together to fight pornography, drugs and lawlessness, and to give back to their children the safe and, yes, innocent childhood they deserve.

We see it in the renaissance in education, the rising SAT (Scholastic Aptitude Test) scores for three years—last year's increase, the greatest since 1963. It wasn't government and Washington lobbies that turned education around; it was the American people who, in reaching for excellence, know to reach back to basics. We must continue the advance by supporting discipline in our schools, vouchers that give parents freedom of choice*; and we must give back to our children the lost right to acknowledge God in their classrooms.

We are a nation of idealists, yet today there is a wound in our national conscience. America will never be whole as long as the right to life granted by our Creator is denied to the unborn.** For the rest of my time, I shall do what I can to see that this wound is one day healed.

As we work to make the American dream real for all, we must also look to the condition of America's families. Struggling parents today worry how they will provide their children the advantages that their parents gave them. In the welfare culture, the breakdown of the family, the most basic support system, has reached crisis proportions—in female and child poverty, child abandonment, horrible crimes, and deteriorating schools. After millions upon millions of dollars in poverty programs, the plight of the poor grows more painful. But the waste in dollars and cents pales before the most tragic loss: the sinful waste of human spirit and potential.

We can ignore this terrible truth no longer. As Franklin Roosevelt warned 51 years ago, standing before this chamber, he said, "Welfare is a narcotic, a subtle destroyer of the human spirit." And we must now escape the spider's web of dependency. Tonight I am charging the White House Domestic Council to present me by December 1, 1986, an evaluation of programs and a strategy for immediate action to meet the financial, educational, social and safety concerns of poor families. I'm talking about real and lasting emancipation, because the success of welfare should be judged by how many of its recipients become independent of welfare.

Further, after seeing how devastating illness can destroy the financial security of the family, I am directing the Secretary of Health and Human Services, Dr. Otis Bowen, to report to me by year end with recommendations on how the private sector and government can work together to address the problems of affordable insurance for those whose life savings would otherwise be threatened when catastrophic illness strikes.

The Future

And tonight I want to speak directly to America's younger generation, because you hold the destiny of our nation in your hands. With all the temptations young people face, it sometimes seems the allure of the permissive society requires superhuman feats of self-control. But the

---

*To choose between sending their children to public or private school
**By abortion

call of the future is too strong, the challenge too great to get lost in the blind alleyways of dissolution, drugs and despair.

Never has there been a more exciting time to be alive, a time of rousing wonder and heroic achievement. As they said in the film, "Back to the Future": "Where we're going, we don't need roads." Well, today physicists peering into the infinitely small realms of subatomic particles find reaffirmations of religious faith. Astronomers build a space telescope that can see the edge of the universe and possibly back to the moment of creation.

So, yes, this nation remains fully committed to America's space program. We're going forward with our shuttle flights. We're going forward to build our space station. And we are going forward with research on a new Orient Express that could, by the end of the next decade, take off from Dulles Airport (Washington, D.C.), accelerate up to 25 times the speed of sound, attaining low Earth orbit or flying to Tokyo within two hours.

Peace Follows Freedom

And the same technology transforming our lives can solve the greatest problem of the 20th century. A security shield can one day render nuclear weapons obsolete and free mankind from the prison of nuclear terror. America met one historic challenge and went to the moon. Now America must meet another: to make our strategic defense real for all the citizens of planet Earth.

Let us speak of our deepest longing for the future: to leave our children a land that is free and just, and a world at peace. It is my hope that our fireside summit in Geneva and Mr. Gorbachev's upcoming visit to America can lead to a more stable relationship. Surely no people on Earth hate war or love peace more than we Americans.

But we cannot stroll into the future with childlike faith. Our differences with a system that openly proclaims and practices an alleged right to command people's lives and to export its ideology by force are deep and abiding. Logic and history compel us to accept that our relationship be guided by realism—rockhard, clear-eyed, steady and sure. Our negotiators in Geneva have proposed a radical cut in offensive forces by each side with no cheating. They have made clear that Soviet compliance with the letter and spirit of agreements is essential. If the Soviet government wants an agreement that truly reduces nuclear arms, there will be such an agreement.

But arms control is no substitute for peace. We know that peace follows in freedom's path, and conflicts erupt when the will of the people is denied. So, we must prepare for peace not only by reducing weapons but by bolstering prosperity, liberty and democracy however and wherever we can.

We advance the promise of opportunity every time we speak out on behalf of lower tax rates, freer markets, sound currencies around the world. We strengthen the family of freedom every time we work with

- 78 -

allies and come to the aid of friends under siege. And we can enlarge the family of free nations if we will defend the inalienable rights of all God's children to follow their dreams.

To those imprisoned in regimes held captive, to those beaten for daring to fight for freedom and democracy—for their right to worship, to speak, to live and to prosper in the family of free nations—we say to you tonight: You are not alone, freedom fighters. America will support you with moral and material assistance, your right not just to fight and die for freedom, but to fight and win freedom—to win freedom in Afghanistan, in Angola, in Cambodia and in Nicaragua.

This is a great moral challenge for the entire free world. Surely no issue is more important for peace in our own hemisphere, for the security of our frontiers, for the protection of our vital interests, than to achieve democracy in Nicaragua and to protect Nicaragua's democratic neighbors.

This year I will be asking Congress for the means to do what must be done for the great and good cause. As [the late Senator, Henry] "Scoop" Jackson, the inspiration for our Bipartisan Commission on Central America, once said, "In matters of national security, the best politics is no politics."

Reaching Our Dreams

What we accomplish this year, in each challenge we face, will set our course for the balance of the decade, indeed, for the remainder of the century. After all we've done so far, let no one say that this nation cannot reach the destiny of our dreams. America believes, America is ready, America can win the race to the future—and we shall.

The American dream is a song of hope that rings through night winter air—vivid, tender music that warms our hearts when the least among us aspire to the greatest things: to venture a daring enterprise; to unearth new beauty in music, literature and art; to discover a new universe inside a tiny silicon chip or a single human cell.

We see the dream coming true in the spirit of discovery of Richard Cavoli. All his life he's been enthralled by the mysteries of medicine. And, Richard, we know that the experiment that you began in high school was launched and lost last week,* yet your dream lives. And as long as it's real, work of noble note will yet be done, work that could reduce the harmful effects of X-rays on patients and enable astronomers to view the golden gateways of the farthest stars.

We see the dream glow in the towering talent of a 12-year-old, Tyrone Ford. A child prodigy of gospel music, he has surmounted personal adversity to become an accomplished pianist and singer. He also directs the choirs of three churches and has performed at the Kennedy Center. With God as your composer, Tyrone, your music will be the music of angels.

We see the dream being saved by the courage of the 13-year-old

---

*In the explosion of the space shuttle *Challenger*

Shelby Butler, honor student and member of her school's safety patrol. Seeing another girl freeze in terror before an out-of-control school bus, she risked her life and pulled her to safety. With bravery like yours, Shelby, America need never fear for our future.

And we see the dream born again in the joyful compassion of a 13-year-old, Trevor Ferrell. Two years ago, age 11, watching men and women bedding down in abandoned doorways—on television, he was watching—Trevor left his suburban Philadelphia home to bring blankets and food to the helpless and homeless. And now 250 people help him fulfill his mighty vigil. Trevor, yours is the living spirit of brotherly love. Would you four stand up for a moment?*

Thank you. Thank you. You are heroes of our hearts. We look at you and know it's true: In this land of dreams fulfilled, where greater dreams may be imagined, no victory is beyond our reach, no glory will ever be too great.

So, now it's up to us, all of us, to prepare America for that day when our work will pale before the greatness of America's champions in the 21st century. The world's hopes rest with America's future; America's hopes rest with us. So, let us go forward to create our world of tomorrow in faith, in unity and in love.

God bless you, and God bless America.

*In the Capitol's visitors gallery

Foundations of Freedom

PROCLAMATION ESTABLISHING LAW DAY U.S.A., 1986

WASHINGTON, D.C.
APRIL 16, 1986

May 1, 1986, is Law Day U.S.A. It is traditionally a time to focus our nation's attention on the importance of the rule of law in our free society. But this year's Law Day has special significance. Its theme, "Foundations of Freedom," is designed to prepare all citizens for an important event in America's history: the Bicentennial of the United States Constitution in 1987.

Constitution

The foundations of freedom upon which our nation was built include the Magna Carta of 1215, English common law, the Mayflower Compact, the Act of Parliament abolishing the Court of Star Chamber, and numerous colonial charters. These and similar precedents, rooted in a firm conviction of the worth and dignity of the human person, articulated fundamental concepts, such as due process of law, trial by jury and freedom of speech. In drafting the Constitution, our forefathers sought to embody these concepts in a single document, creating a rule of law that continues to "secure the blessings of liberty to ourselves and our posterity...."

Our written Constitution has been in existence for 200 years, longer than that of any other nation in the world. Although our nation has grown from 13 isolated agricultural states to an industrialized society of 240 million people, the text of the Constitution provides today, as it did in 1787, a blueprint for a functioning republic with well-considered

-81-

and workable guidelines for democratic self-government. Its endurance is a tribute not only to the wisdom of the authors of that great document, but to all the citizens who, in our courts and legislatures, have fought to uphold its vital guarantees. It is also a testament to a 200-year-old tradition of freedom through voluntary adherence to the rule of law. Because of the vigilance of the American people, we continue to be a country governed by law, rather than by force or the whim of a few self-proclaimed leaders.

Rule of Law

Law Day U.S.A. is an important opportunity for all Americans to examine the historical precedents that led to the establishment of the rule of law in America through the United States Constitution, and consequently to improve our understanding and appreciation of the important contribution these sources made to the creation of our free society. As we observe Law Day, I urge everyone to join me in renewing our dedication to the foundations of our freedom, principles that ensure that, in this nation, all men and women will continue to be free, enjoying the full and equal protection of the law.

Now, Therefore, I, Ronald Reagan, President of the United States of America, in accordance with Public Law 87-20 of April 7, 1961, do hereby proclaim Thursday, May 1, 1986, as Law Day U.S.A. I urge the people of the United States to use this occasion to renew their commitment to the rule of law and to reaffirm our dedication to the principles embodied in the documents that form the foundations of our freedom. I call upon the legal profession, schools, civic, service and fraternal organizations, public bodies, libraries, the courts, the communications media, business, the clergy, and all interested individuals and organizations to join in efforts to focus attention on the need for the rule of law. I also call upon all public officials to display the flag of the United States on all government buildings on Law Day, May 1, 1986.... □

PART II:

International
Issues

The Caribbean Basin Initiative

**ADDRESS TO THE PERMANENT COUNCIL OF THE
ORGANIZATION OF AMERICAN STATES**

WASHINGTON, D.C.
FEBRUARY 24, 1982

I t's a great honor for me to stand before you today. The principles which the Organization of American States (OAS) embodies—democracy, self-determination, economic development and collective security—are at the heart of U.S. foreign policy. The United States of America is a proud member of this organization. What happens anywhere in the Americas affects us in this country. In that very real sense, we share a common destiny.

Americans

We, the peoples of the Americas, have much more in common than geographical proximity. For over 400 years our peoples have shared the dangers and dreams of building a new world. From colonialism to nationhood, our common quest has been for freedom.

Most of our forebears came to this hemisphere seeking a better life for themselves. They came in search of opportunity and, yes, in search of God. Virtually all descendants of the land and immigrants alike have had to fight for independence. Having gained it, they've had to fight to retain it. There were times when we even fought each other.

Gradually, however, the nations of this hemisphere developed a set of common principles and institutions that provided the basis for mutual protection. Some 20 years ago, John F. Kennedy caught the essence of our unique mission when he said it was up to the New World "to demonstrate that man's unsatisfied aspiration for economic progress and social justice can best be achieved by free men working within a framework of democratic institutions."

In the commitment to freedom and independence, the peoples of this hemisphere are one. In this profound sense, we are all Americans. Our principles are rooted in self-government and nonintervention. We believe in the rule of law. We know that a nation cannot be liberated by depriving its people of liberty. We know that a state cannot be free when its independence is subordinated to a foreign power. And we know that a government cannot be democratic if it refuses to take the test of a free election.

We have not always lived up to these ideals. All of us at one time or another in our history have been politically weak, economically backward, socially unjust or unable to solve our problems through peaceful means. My own country, too, has suffered internal strife, including a tragic civil war. We have known economic misery, and once tolerated racial and social injustice. And, yes, at times we have behaved arrogantly and impatiently toward our neighbors. These experiences have left their scars, but they also help us today to identify with the struggle for political and economic development in the other countries of this hemisphere.

Out of the crucible of our common past, the Americas have emerged as more equal and more understanding partners. Our hemisphere has an unlimited potential for economic development and human fulfillment. We have a combined population of more than 600 million people; our continents and our islands boast vast reservoirs of food and raw materials; and the markets of the Americas have already produced the highest standard of living among the advanced as well as the developing countries of the world. The example that we could offer to the world would not only discourage foes; it would project like a beacon of hope to all of the oppressed and impoverished nations of the world. We are the New World, a world of sovereign and independent states that today stand shoulder to shoulder with a common respect for one another and a greater tolerance of one another's shortcomings.

North American Accord

Some two years ago, when I announced as a candidate for the presidency, I spoke of an ambition I had to bring about an accord with our two neighbors here on the North American continent. Now, I was not suggesting a common market or any kind of formal arrangement. "Accord" was the only word that seemed to fit what I had in mind.

I was aware that the United States has long enjoyed friendly relations with Mexico and Canada, that our borders have no fortifications. Yet it seemed to me that there was a potential for a closer relationship than had yet been achieved. Three great nations share the North American continent with all its human and natural resources. Have we done all we can to create a relationship in which each country can realize its potential to the fullest?

Now, I know in the past the United States has proposed policies that we declared would be mutually beneficial not only for North America but also for the nations of the Caribbean and Central and South America. But there was often a problem. No matter how good our intentions were, our very size may have made it seem that we were exercising a kind of paternalism. At the time I suggested a new North American accord, I said I wanted to approach our neighbors not as someone with yet another plan, but as a friend seeking their ideas, their suggestions as to how we could become better neighbors.

I met with President Lopez Portillo in Mexico before my inauguration and with Prime Minister Trudeau in Canada shortly after I had taken office. We have all met several times since—in the United States, in Mexico and Canada—and I believe that we have established a relationship better than any our three countries have ever known before.

Central America and the Caribbean

Today I would like to talk about our neighbors by the sea—some two dozen countries of the Caribbean and Central America. These countries are not unfamiliar names from some isolated corner of the world far from home. They're very close to home. The country of El Salvador, for example, is nearer to Texas than Texas is to Massachusetts. The Caribbean region is a vital strategic and commercial artery for the United States. Nearly half of our trade, two-thirds of our imported oil and over half of our imported strategic minerals pass through the Panama Canal or the Gulf of Mexico. Make no mistake: The well-being and security of our neighbors in this region are in our own vital interest.

Economic health is one of the keys to a secure future for our Caribbean Basin and to the neighbors there. I'm happy to say that Mexico, Canada and Venezuela have joined in this search for ways to help these countries realize their economic potential.

Each of our four nations has its own unique position and approach. Mexico and Venezuela are helping to offset energy costs to Caribbean Basin countries by means of an oil facility that is already in operation. Canada is doubling its already significant economic assistance. We all seek to ensure that the people of this area have the right to preserve their own national identities, to improve their economic lot, and to develop their political institutions to suit their own unique social and historical needs. The Central American and Caribbean countries differ widely in culture, personality and needs. Like America itself, the Caribbean Basin is an extraordinary mosaic of Hispanics, Africans, Asians and Europeans, as well as native Americans.

At the moment, however, these countries are under economic siege. In 1977, one barrel of oil was worth 2.25 kilos of coffee or 69.75 kilos of sugar. Well, to buy that same barrel of oil today, these small countries must provide five times as much coffee— nearly 11.7 kilos— or almost twice as much sugar— 127.35 kilos. This economic disaster is consuming our neighbors' money, reserves and credit, forcing thousands of people to leave for other countries, for the United States, often illegally, and shaking even the most established democracies. And economic disaster has provided a fresh opening to the enemies of freedom, national independence and peaceful development.

We've taken the time to consult closely with other governments in the region, both sponsors and beneficiaries, to ask them what they need and what they think will work. And we've labored long to develop an economic program that integrates trade, aid and investment—a program that represents a long-term commitment to the countries of the Caribbean and Central America—to make use of the magic of the marketplace, the market of the Americas, to earn their own way toward self-sustaining growth.

At the Cancun Summit last October, I presented a fresh view of development which stressed more than aid and government intervention. As I pointed out then, nearly all of the countries that have succeeded in their development over the past 30 years have done so on the strength of market-oriented policies and vigorous participation in the international economy. Aid must be complemented by trade and investment.

Free Trade Centerpiece

The program I'm proposing today puts these principles into practice. It is an integrated program that helps our neighbors help themselves, a program that will create conditions under which creativity and private entrepreneurship and self-help can flourish. Aid is an important part of this program because many of our neighbors need it to put themselves in a starting position from which they can begin to earn their own way. But this aid will encourage private-sector activities, not displace them.

The centerpiece of the program that I am sending to the Congress is free trade for Caribbean Basin products exported to the United States. Currently some 87 percent of Caribbean exports already enter U.S. markets duty free under the Generalized System of Preferences. These exports, however, cover only the limited range of existing products—not the wide variety of potential products these talented and industrious peoples are capable of producing under the free trade arrangement that I am proposing.

Exports from the area will receive duty-free treatment for 12 years. Thus, new investors will be able to enter the market knowing that their products will receive duty-free treatment for at least the pay-off lifetime of their investments. Before granting duty-free treatment, we will discuss with each country its own self-help measures.

The only exception to the free trade concept will be textile and apparel products because these products are covered now by other international agreements. However, we will make sure that our immediate neighbors have more liberal quota arrangements.

This economic proposal is as unprecedented as today's crisis in the Caribbean. Never before has the United States offered a preferential trading arrangement to any region. This commitment makes unmistakably clear our determination to help our neighbors grow strong.

The impact of this free-trade approach will develop slowly. The economies that we seek to help are small. Even as they grow, all the protections now available to U.S. industry, agriculture and labor against disruptive imports will remain. And growth in the Caribbean will benefit everyone with American exports finding new markets.

CBI Provisions

Secondly, to further attract investment, I will ask the Congress to provide significant tax incentives for investment in the Caribbean Basin. We also stand ready to negotiate bilateral investment treaties with interested Basin countries.

Third, I'm asking for a supplemental fiscal year 1982 appropriation of $350 million to assist those countries which are particularly hard hit economically. Much of this aid will be concentrated on the private sector. These steps will help foster the spirit of enterprise necessary to take advantage of the trade and investment portions of the program.

Fourth, we will offer technical assistance and training to assist the private sector in the Basin countries to benefit from the opportunities of this program. This will include investment promotion, export marketing and technology transfer efforts, as well as programs to facilitate adjustments to greater competition and production in agriculture and industry. I intend to seek the active participation of the business community in this joint undertaking. The Peace Corps already has 861 volunteers in Caribbean Basin countries and will give special emphasis to recruiting volunteers with skills in developing local enterprise.

Fifth, we will work closely with Mexico, Canada and Venezuela, all of whom have already begun substantial and innovative programs of their own, to encourage stronger international efforts to coordinate our own development measures with their vital contributions, and with those of other potential donors like Colombia. We will also encourage our European, Japanese and other Asian allies, as well as multilateral development institutions, to increase their assistance in the region.

Sixth, given our special valued relationship with Puerto Rico and the United States Virgin Islands, we will propose special measures to ensure that they also will benefit and prosper from this program. With their strong traditions of democracy and free enterprise, they can play leading roles in the development of the area.

This program has been carefully prepared. It represents a far-sighted act by our own people at a time of considerable economic difficulty at home. I wouldn't propose it if I were not convinced that it is vital to the security interests of this nation and of this hemisphere. The energy, the time and the treasure we dedicate to assisting the development of our neighbors now can help to prevent the much larger expenditures of treasure as well as human lives which would flow from their collapse.

One early sign is positive. After a decade of falling income and exceptionally high unemployment, Jamaica's new leadership is reducing bureaucracy, dismantling unworkable controls and attracting new investment. Continued outside assistance will be needed to tide Jamaica over until market forces generate large increases in output and employment—but Jamaica is making freedom work.

Totalitarian Threat

I've spoken up to now mainly of the economic and social challenges to development. But there are also other dangers. A new kind of colonialism stalks the world today and threatens our independence. It is brutal and totalitarian. It is not of our hemisphere, but it threatens our hemisphere and has established footholds on American soil for the expansion of its colonialist ambitions.

The events of the last several years dramatize two different futures which are possible for the Caribbean area: either the establishment or restoration of moderate constitutional governments with economic growth and improved living standards, or further expansion of political violence from the extreme left and the extreme right, resulting in the imposition of dictatorships and, inevitably, more economic decline and human suffering.

The positive opportunity is illustrated by the two-thirds of the nations in the area which have democratic governments. The dark future is foreshadowed by the poverty and repression of Castro's Cuba, the tightening grip of the totalitarian left in Grenada and Nicaragua, and the expansion of Soviet-backed, Cuban-managed support for violent revolution in Central America.

The record is clear. Nowhere in its whole sordid history have the promises of communism been redeemed. Everywhere it has exploited and aggravated temporary economic suffering to seize power and then to institutionalize economic deprivation and suppress human rights. Right now, six million people worldwide are refugees from communist systems. Already, more than a million Cubans alone have fled communist tyranny.

Our economic and social program cannot work if our neighbors cannot pursue their own economic and political future in peace, but must divert their resources, instead, to fight imported terrorism and armed attack. Economic progress cannot be made while guerrillas systematically burn, bomb and destroy bridges, farms, and power and transportation systems—all with the deliberate intention of worsening economic and social problems in hopes of radicalizing already suffering people.

Cuba

Our Caribbean neighbors' peaceful attempts to develop are feared by the foes of freedom because their success will make the radical message a hollow one. Cuba and its Soviet backers know this. Since 1978 Havana has trained, armed and directed extremists in guerrilla warfare and economic sabotage as part of a campaign to exploit troubles in Central

America and the Caribbean. Their goal is to establish Cuban-style, Marxist-Leninist dictatorships.

Last year, Cuba received 66,000 tons of war supplies from the Soviet Union—more than in any year since the 1962 missile crisis. Last month, the arrival of additional high performance MIG-23 Floggers gave Cuba an arsenal of more than 200 Soviet warplanes—far more than the military aircraft inventories of all other Caribbean Basin countries combined.

Nicaragua

For almost two years, Nicaragua has served as a platform for covert military action. Through Nicaragua, arms are being smuggled to guerrillas in El Salvador and Guatemala. The Nicaraguan government even admits the forced relocation of about 8,500 Miskito Indians. And we have clear evidence that since late 1981, many Indian communities have been burned to the ground and men, women and children killed.

The Nicaraguan junta cabled written assurances to the OAS in 1979 that it intended to respect human rights and hold free elections. Two years later, these commitments can be measured by the postponement of elections until 1985, by repression against free trade unions, against the media, minorities and, in defiance of all international civility, by the continued export of arms and subversion to neighboring countries.

El Salvador

Two years ago, in contrast, the government of El Salvador began an unprecedented land reform. It has repeatedly urged the guerrillas to renounce violence, to join in the democratic process [in] an election in which the people of El Salvador could determine the government they prefer. Our own country and other American nations through the OAS have urged such a course. The guerrillas have refused. More than that, they now threaten violence and death to those who participate in such an election.

Can anything make more clear the nature of those who pretend to be supporters of so-called wars of liberation?

A determined propaganda campaign has sought to mislead many in Europe and certainly many in the United States as to the true nature of the conflict in El Salvador. Very simply, guerrillas, armed and supported by and through Cuba, are attempting to impose a Marxist-Leninist dictatorship on the people of El Salvador as part of a larger imperialistic plan. If we do not act promptly and decisively in defense of freedom, new Cubas will arise from the ruins of today's conflicts. We will face more totalitarian regimes tied militarily to the Soviet Union—more regimes exporting subversion, more regimes so incompetent yet so totalitarian that their citizens' only hope becomes that of one day migrating to other American nations, as in recent years they have come to the United States.

Ensuring Hemispheric Peace

I believe free and peaceful development of our hemisphere requires us to help governments confronted with aggression from outside their borders to defend themselves. For this reason, I will ask the Congress to provide increased security assistance to help friendly countries hold off those who would destroy their chances for economic and social progress and political democracy. Since 1947 the Rio Treaty has established reciprocal defense responsibilities linked to our common democratic ideals. Meeting these responsibilities is all the more important when an outside power supports terrorism and insurgency to destroy any possibility of freedom and democracy. Let our friends and our adversaries understand that we will do whatever is prudent and necessary to ensure the peace and security of the Caribbean area.

In the face of outside threats, security for the countries of the Caribbean and Central American area is not an end in itself, but a means to an end. It is a means toward building representative and responsive institutions, toward strengthening pluralism and free private institutions—churches, free trade unions and an independent press. It is a means to nurturing the basic human rights freedom's foes would stamp out. In the Caribbean, we—above all—seek to protect those values and principles that shape the proud heritage of this hemisphere.

I have already expressed our support for the coming election in El Salvador. We also strongly support the Central American Democratic Community formed this January by Costa Rica, Honduras and El Salvador. The United States will work closely with other concerned democracies inside and outside the area to preserve and enhance our common democratic values.

We will not, however, follow Cuba's lead in attempting to resolve human problems by brute force. Our economic assistance, including the additions that are part of the program I've just outlined, is more than five times the amount of our security assistance. The thrust of our aid is to help our neighbors realize freedom, justice and economic progress.

We seek to exclude no one. Some, however, have turned from their American neighbors and their heritage. Let them return to the traditions and common values of this hemisphere, and we all will welcome them. The choice is theirs.

Freedom: Our Common Destiny

As I have talked these problems over with friends and fellow citizens here in the United States, I'm often asked, "Well, why bother? Why should the problems of Central America or the Caribbean concern us? Why should we try to help?" Well, I tell them we must help because the people of the Caribbean and Central America are, in a fundamental sense, fellow Americans. Freedom is our common destiny. And freedom cannot survive if our neighbors live in misery and oppression. In short, we must do it because we're doing it for each other.

Our neighbors' call for help is addressed to us all here in this country—to the administration, to the Congress, to millions of Americans from Miami to Chicago, from New York to Los Angeles. This is not Washington's problem; it is the problem of all the people of this great land and of all the other Americas—the great and sovereign republics of North America, the Caribbean Basin and South America. The Western Hemisphere does not belong to any one of us; we belong to the Western Hemisphere. We are brothers historically as well as geographically.

Now, I'm aware that the United States has pursued good neighbor policies in the past. These policies did some good, but they're inadequate for today. I believe that my country is now ready to go beyond being a good neighbor to being a true friend and brother in a community that belongs as much to others as to us. That, not guns, is the ultimate key to peace and security for us all.

We have to ask ourselves, why has it taken so long for us to realize the God-given opportunity that is ours? These two great land masses, north and south, so rich in virtually everything we need. Together our more than 600 million people can develop what is undeveloped, can eliminate want and poverty, can show the world that our many nations can live in peace—each with its own customs and language and culture, but sharing a love for freedom and a determination to resist outside ideologies that would take us back to colonialism.

We return to a common vision. Nearly a century ago a great citizen of the Caribbean and the Americas, José Martí, warned that "mankind is composed of two sorts of men, those who love and create and those who hate and destroy." Today more than ever the compassionate, creative peoples of the Americas have an opportunity to stand together, to overcome injustice, hatred and oppression, and to build a better life for all the Americas.

I have always believed that this hemisphere was a special place with a special destiny. I believe we are destined to be the beacon of hope for all mankind. With God's help, we can make it so. We can create a peaceful, free and prospering hemisphere based on our shared ideals and reaching from pole to pole of what we proudly call the New World. □

Democracy's Foundation

ADDRESS TO THE CONFERENCE ON FREE ELECTIONS

WASHINGTON, D.C.
NOVEMBER 4, 1982

I would like to welcome all of you to the White House. It's a privilege and an inspiration to be host to this distinguished gathering.

In this room today are representatives of thriving democracies on many continents. President Monge [of Costa Rica] leads one of Latin America's strongest democracies. Mr. Shehu Musa is the personal representative of President Shagari of Nigeria, Africa's most populous nation and a democracy. Europe's advanced industrial democracies with traditions of representative governments stretching over generations are represented here. So, too, are Asia's new democracies. And we also welcome representatives of international parliaments: President [José Maria de] Areilza of the Council of Europe Parliamentary Assembly, Vice President Elles of the European Parliament, Vice President Townsend of the Latin American Parliament.

And I would also like to greet the democratic leaders who are with us in spirit only: Prime Minister Spadolini of Italy, who could not attend this luncheon but who has sent a great keynote address to this gathering, which you heard. King Juan Carlos of Spain has sent a message of greetings in which he expressed, on behalf of the Spanish people and himself, support for the principles and objectives of this Conference.

A Common Vision

And we are here today to celebrate a common vision, a vision of a world where right to self-government is openly acknowledged—where the state is seen as not the master, but the servant of man. In particular, this Conference is concerned with free elections, the very foundation of democracy. There's no more striking symbol of democracy than the picture of a citizen casting a ballot, electing a leader, choosing his or her own destiny.

Earlier this week, elections were held here in the United States. I spent the last two weeks on the road working for votes and trying to understand my country's problems better. And so did thousands of candidates for local, state and federal offices with a wide variety of views. On Tuesday of this week, the people gave their verdict in free elections. And the process is the same in your countries.

The free flow and the open competition of ideas is the heart of our free societies. What a striking contrast this is with those nations of the world where the people have no role, but must sit weakly by and wait for a small group of men to conclude their struggle for power behind closed doors and then rule without being accountable to anyone.

Spreading Democracy

But there's something else that brings us together today. It's an excitement that we share about the opportunities for the spread of democracy, the sense of hope about the prospects for the future. One of my predecessors in this office shared this excitement. General Eisenhower wrote in his personal diary less than a year after the end of the Second World War, "Our most effective security step is to develop in every country where there is any chance or opportunity a democratic form of government. To lead others to democracy we must help actively, but more than this we must be an example of the worth of democracy." I can think of no better way to express the challenge to those of us participating in this Conference and free men everywhere than those words of Dwight Eisenhower's.

That this Conference is taking place is testimony to the growing power of democratic ideals. And their appeal has led me to suggest to the British Parliament last June that you and I live at a turning point, a moment in time, and when time and circumstance and the sound instincts of good and decent people can unite to redirect history, to bring about a new and more hopeful life for future generations.

Some may see this prognosis as too optimistic. I do not underestimate the capabilities for repression of dictatorships of either the left or the right or the devastating effect of terrorism. But the imperishable democratic ideal and the democratic movement—these are stronger. As shown in country after country on the continents which all of you in this room represent, mankind has an unquenchable aspiration to control its own destiny.

It's our duty to speak out against the evil and the cruelty of misused state power. Unless we speak out, unless we give voice to the decent impulses of mankind and our own deepest held convictions, a kind of moral atrophy sets in, and we too may ultimately lose faith in the appeal and the power of our convictions.

Democracy and Progress

This Conference is a further step in our support for the democratic movement. It's an opportunity to point out to the world that democracy gives to the people of each nation a chance to chart their own course. It's an opportunity to point out how free elections place the hand of the people firmly on the tiller of state, how the free competition of ideas at the ballot box is an invitation to stability and flexibility that is so necessary for economic and social progress, how universal suffrage is the certain route to popular support for institutions and policies, how the accountability of elected officials is the surest guarantee that the people's will is respected and that the fruits of growth will not be channeled to only a few.

All of these realizations provide a powerful antidote to those who argue that state power and armed might are the only means to social or economic progress. In case after case, we have seen the democratic states, which rely on the initiative of their own people, develop their economies and societies far further than centralized states. We must not underestimate the task that we face in supporting the growth of democracy.

Democracy cannot be imposed from outside and it frequently evolves only after patient, incremental steps. It must be the product of free institutions—churches, labor unions, independent judiciary and the press—and its life-giving, rejuvenating process is a citizen placing his vote in a ballot box: the subject of this Conference.

Your presence today already provides inspiration to those who believe in and work for democracy. I'm confident that your deliberation will be a source of new insight and wisdom. Yet, we must do more than note the lessons of the past and the challenges of the future. It is my hope that this Conference will produce not only a new commitment to freedom but a positive program for international action.   □

The Cause of Peace

RADIO ADDRESS TO THE NATION AND PEOPLES OF OTHER COUNTRIES

WASHINGTON, D.C
SEPTEMBER 24, 1983

My fellow Americans and fellow citizens of the world:

This is Ronald Reagan, President of the United States, speaking to you live from the broadcast studios of the Voice of America in Washington, D.C.

In two days I will be going to the United Nations General Assembly to speak for a cause that people everywhere carry close to their hearts—the cause of peace. This subject is so important I wanted to share our message with a larger audience than I usually address each Saturday afternoon in the United States. So today I'm speaking directly to people everywhere, from Los Angeles to New Delhi, Cairo, Bangkok, and I'm attempting to speak directly to the people of the Soviet Union. I'd like to talk about ideas and feelings all of us share which I intend to communicate to the United Nations.

Message of Peace

Let me begin by bringing you greetings from the American people and our heartfelt wishes for peace. In these times of stress, I believe that the people of the world must know and understand how each other feel, their fears as well as their dreams. We Americans are a peace-loving people. We seek friendship not only with our traditional allies but with our adversaries, too. We've had serious differences with the Soviet government, but we should remember that our sons and daughters have never fought each other in war and, if we Americans have our way, we never will.

People don't make wars; governments do. And too many Soviet and American citizens have already shed too much blood because of violence by governments. The American people want less confrontation and more communication and cooperation, more opportunity to correspond, to speak freely with all people over our respective radio and television programs and, most important, to visit each other in our homes so we could better understand your countries and you could know the truth about America.

Freedom

The treasure we Americans cherish most is our freedom—freedom to lead our lives the way we choose, freedom to worship God, to think for ourselves, and freedom to speak our minds even to the point of criticizing our own government. We do not believe in censorship. When another government criticizes us, we know about it. And if they ever say something good, you can bet we'll know that, too. The trouble is, we don't always have that same freedom to speak to others, especially those who live in the Soviet Union. And one-way communication prevents us from better understanding each other.

KAL 007

For example, the Soviet government has taken extraordinary steps to justify its firing on a Korean civilian airliner (KAL 007), killing 269 helpless people from 14 countries. But I ask those who have been told the United States is responsible: If you're hearing the truth, why has the outcry been so intense from members of the United Nations, the International Civil Aviation Organization, and why are pilots all over the world boycotting flights to Moscow? We have no quarrel with you, the Soviet people. But please understand, the world believes no government has a right to shoot civilian airliners out of the sky. Your airline, Aeroflot, has violated sensitive U.S. airspace scores of times, yet we would never fire on your planes and risk killing one of your friends or your loved ones.

Now, I guess the picture painted of me by the officials in some countries is pretty grim. May I just say—and I speak not only as the President of the United States but also as a husband, a father, a grandfather, and as a person who loves God and whose heart yearns deeply for a better future—my dream is for our peoples to come together in a spirit of faith and friendship, to help build and leave behind a far safer world. But dreams for the future cannot be realized by words alone. Words must be matched by deeds, by an honest, tireless effort to reduce the risks of war and the loss of life. In this era of nuclear weapons, no achievement could be more meaningful than a verifiable agreement that would dramatically reduce the level of nuclear armaments.

American negotiators in Geneva are offering fair-minded, equitable proposals in the interests of both our countries. In the Strategic Arms Reduction Talks, we propose deep cuts in both the number of warheads carried by intercontinental ballistic missiles and in the number of missiles themselves. This proposal offered cuts to far below current United States levels. The Soviet government declined to consider them. We tried again. Last June we proposed a more flexible approach. Then, during the last round of talks in Geneva, we presented a draft treaty responding to concerns expressed by the Soviet government.

Intermediate-Range Nuclear Forces

Also, from the outset of the Intermediate-Range Nuclear Force talks two years ago, I made clear that the United States was ready to join with the Soviet Union in the total elimination of an entire class of intermediate-range, land-based nuclear missiles. That offer still stands. I regret that the Soviet government continues to reject this proposal. What could possibly be better than to rid the world of an entire class of nuclear weapons?

But in the effort to move the negotiations forward, we proposed an interim solution—some number on both sides below current levels. Again, the Soviet government refused. I'm deeply aware of people's feelings and frustrations. I share them. And I intend to keep trying. On Monday, I will go to the United Nations to propose another package of steps designed to advance the negotiations. All we seek are agreements to reduce substantially the number and destructive power of nuclear forces.

Yes, we insist on balanced agreements that protect our security, that provide greater stability, and that are truly verifiable, but these requirements are the essence of fairness. They would provide greater security for all nations.

Peace

We, the American people, deeply yearn for peace. If our dreams and hopes are to mean anything, we must sit down together and in good faith let honest negotiations bring us a safer world. But I must speak plainly. Just as government censorship is a barrier to understanding, the inflexibility of the Soviet government on arms control is holding back successful negotiations.

I have said to my own people, you have the right to expect a better world and to demand that your government work for it. In two days I will have the honor to carry that message to the 38th General Session of the United Nations. It will be a commitment from the heart and one that I know all people share. For the sake of our children and our children's children, I pray that the Soviet government will not censor my words but will let their people listen to them and then negotiate with us in good faith.

Thank you for listening, and God bless you all. □

Central America Democracy, Peace and Development Initiative

ADDRESS TO CONGRESS ANNOUNCING PROPOSED LEGISLATION

WASHINGTON, D C
FEBRUARY 3, 1984

I n the coming days we'll send legislation to the Congress based on a remarkable consensus of the National Bipartisan Commission on Central America. And I urge prompt congressional action and support.

Bipartisan Commission

Last April, in an address to a joint session of the Congress, I spoke to the American people about what is at stake in Central America and asked for bipartisan cooperation in our efforts to help make a better life for the people of that region. Shortly after that speech, the late Senator Henry Jackson called for the appointment of a bipartisan commission to chart a long-term course for democracy, economic improvement and peace in Central America. And as "Scoop" Jackson so rightly observed, "Whatever policy options might be available to us, ignoring threats to the stability of Central America and refusing to engage ourselves in the problems of the region are not among them."

It was against this background that I did establish the National Bipartisan Commission on Central America. Its mission was to recommend a long-term policy appropriate to the economic, social, political and military challenges to the region.

The distinguished Americans who served on that Commission have performed a great service to all Americans, all of us—from Point Barrow to Tierra del Fuego. Henry Kissinger and the Commission members and senior counselors: My appreciation for a tough job well done.

Comprehensive Program

Our proposed legislation, the Central America Democracy, Peace and Development Initiative Act, is based on the Commission's analysis and embodies its recommendations, and it's in the spirit of Senator Jackson who first proposed the idea of a bipartisan commission and served until his death as one of its senior counselors. He represented something very special in American politics. "Scoop" Jackson stood for national security and human rights because he knew that one without the other is meaningless. He said what he believed and stuck to it with vision, integrity and grace.

The legislation does not offer a quick fix to the crisis in Central America; there is none. Our plan offers a comprehensive program to support democratic development, improve human rights and bring peace to this troubled region that's so close to home.

The approach is right. It includes a mix of developmental, political, diplomatic and security initiatives, equitably and humanely pursued. We either do them all, or we jeopardize the chance for real progress in the region. The plan responds to decades of inequity and indifference through its support of democracy, reform and human freedom. It responds to the economic challenges of the region.

The legislation calls for $400 million in supplementary economic assistance for fiscal year 1984. And during the next five years, economic assistance will amount to $5,900 million in appropriated funds and $2,000 million in insurance and guarantees.

To support the security of the region's threatened nations, the legislation will provide $515 million over the next two years. At the same time, it will require semiannual reports to the Congress assessing Salvadoran policies for achieving political and economic development and conditions of security.

To support dialogue and negotiations both among the countries of the region and within each country, the legislation provides guidance for cooperation with the Central American countries in establishing, then working with, the Central American Development Organization.

Call to Congress

Our plan is for the long haul. It won't be easy, and it won't be cheap. But it can be done. And for strategic and moral reasons, it must be done. I ask the Congress to study the Commission report and to give our legislative proposal its urgent attention and bipartisan support. It is not an impossible dream. We have the resources to do it. This initiative serves the interest of the United States and of the Western Hemisphere. The beleaguered people in Central America want our help. Our enemies, extremists of the left and the right, would be delighted if we refused to give it. And if we don't help now, we'll surely pay dearly in the future.

With the support of the Congress, we will not let down all those in Central America who yearn for democracy and peace. And in so doing, we'll not let ourselves down. □

Achieving a Safer, More Humane World

**ADDRESS TO THE NATIONAL LEADERSHIP FORUM,
CENTER FOR STRATEGIC AND INTERNATIONAL STUDIES, GEORGETOWN UNIVERSITY**

WASHINGTON, D.C
APRIL 6, 1984

I'd like to address the theme of bipartisanship with a view toward America's foreign policy—the challenges for the '80s.

All Americans share two great goals for foreign policy: a safer world, and a world in which individual rights can be respected and precious values may flourish. These goals are at the heart of America's traditional idealism and our aspirations for world peace. Yet, while cherished by us, they do not belong exclusively to us. They're not made in America. They're shared by people everywhere.

Tragically, the world in which these fundamental goals are so widely shared is a very troubled world. While we and our allies may enjoy peace and prosperity, many citizens of the industrial world continue to live in fear of conflict and the threat of nuclear war. And all around the globe, terrorists threaten innocent people and civilized values. And in developing countries, the dreams of human progress have too often been lost to violent revolution and dictatorship.

Quite obviously, the widespread desire for a safer and more human world is, by itself, not enough to create such a world. In pursuing our worthy goals, we must go beyond honorable intentions and good will to practical means.

Foreign Policy Principles

We must be guided by these key principles:

— Realism. The world is not as we wish it would be. Reality is often harsh. We will not make it less so, if we do not first see it for what it is.

— Strength. We know that strength alone is not enough, but without it there can be no effective diplomacy and negotiations, no secure democracy and peace. Conversely, weakness or hopeful passivity are only self-defeating. They invite the very aggression and instability that they would seek to avoid.

— Economic growth. This is the underlying base that ensures our strength and permits human potential to flourish. Neither strength nor creativity can be achieved or sustained without economic growth, both at home and abroad.

— Intelligence. Our policies cannot be effective unless the information on which they're based is accurate, timely and complete.

— Shared responsibility with allies. Our friends and allies share the heavy responsibility for the protection of freedom. We seek and need their partnership, sharing burdens in pursuit of our common goals.

— Nonaggression. We have no territorial ambitions. We occupy no foreign lands. We build our strength only to assure deterrence and to secure our interests if deterrence fails.

— Dialogue with adversaries. Though we must be honest in recognizing fundamental differences with our adversaries, we must always be willing to resolve these differences by peaceful means.

— Bipartisanship at home. In our two-party democracy, an effective foreign policy must begin with bipartisanship, and the sharing of responsibility for a safer and more humane world must begin at home.

During the past three years, we've been steadily rebuilding America's capacity to advance our foreign policy goals through renewed attention to these vital principles. Many threats remain, and peace may still seem precarious. But America is safer and more secure today because the people of this great nation have restored the foundation of its strength.

We began with renewed realism, a clear-eyed understanding of the world we live in and of our inescapable global responsibilities. Our industries depend on the importation of energy and minerals from distant lands. Our prosperity requires a sound international financial system and free and open trading markets. And our security is inseparable from the security of our friends and neighbors.

I believe Americans today see the world with realism and maturity. The great majority of our people do not believe the stark differences between democracy and totalitarianism can be wished away. They understand that keeping America secure begins with keeping America strong and free.

Defense Modernization

When we took office in 1981, the Soviet Union had been engaged for 20 years in the most massive military buildup in history. Clearly, their goal was not to catch us, but to surpass us. Yet the United States remained a virtual spectator in the 1970s, a decade of neglect that took a severe toll on our defense capabilities.

With bipartisan support, we embarked immediately on a major defense rebuilding program. We've made good progress in restoring the morale of our men and women in uniform, restocking spare parts and ammunition, replacing obsolescent equipment and facilities, improving basic training and readiness, and pushing forward with long overdue weapons programs.

The simple fact is that, in the last half of the 1970s, we were not deterring, as events from Angola to Afghanistan made clear. Today we are. And that fact has fundamentally altered the future for millions of human beings. Gone are the days when the United States was perceived as a rudderless superpower, a helpless hostage to world events. American leadership is back. Peace through strength is not a slogan. It's a fact of life. And we will not return to the days of handwringing, defeatism, decline and despair.

We have also upgraded significantly our intelligence capabilities, restoring morale in the intelligence agencies and increasing our capability to detect, analyze and counter hostile intelligence threats.

Economic strength, the underlying base of support for our defense buildup, has received a dramatic new boost. We've transformed a no-growth economy, crippled by disincentives, double-digit inflation, 21.5 percent interest rates, plunging productivity and a weak dollar, into a dynamic growth economy bolstered by new incentives, stable prices, lower interest rates, a rebirth of productivity and restored confidence in our currency.

Alliances

Renewed strength at home has been accompanied by closer partnerships with America's friends and allies. Far from buckling under Soviet intimidation, the unity of the NATO alliance has held firm, and we're moving forward to modernize our strategic deterrent. The leader of America's oldest ally, French President Francois Mitterand, recently reminded us that peace, like liberty, is never given. The pursuit of both is a continual one. In the turbulent times we live in, solidarity among friends is essential.

Our principles don't involve just rebuilding our strength; they also tell us how to use it. We remain true to the principle of nonaggression. On an occasion when the United States, at the request of its neighbors, did use force in Grenada, we acted decisively, but only after it was clear a bloodthirsty regime had put American and Grenadian lives in danger, and the security of neighboring islands in danger. As soon as stability and freedom were restored in the island, we left. The Soviet Union had no such legitimate justification for its massive invasion of Afghanistan four years ago. And today, over a hundred thousand occupation troops remain there. The United States, by stark contrast, occupies no foreign nation, nor do we seek to.

Though we and the Soviet Union differ markedly, living in this nuclear age makes it imperative that we talk with each other. If the new Soviet leadership truly is devoted to building a safer and more humane world, rather than expanding armed conquests, it will find a sympathetic partner in the West.

In pursuing these practical principles, we have throughout sought to revive the spirit that was once the hallmark of our postwar foreign policy: bipartisan cooperation between the executive and legislative branches of our government.

Much has been accomplished, but much remains to be done. If Republicans and Democrats will join together to confront four great challenges to American foreign policy in the '80s, then we can and will make great strides toward a safer and more humane world.

Preventing Nuclear War

Challenge number one is to reduce the risk of nuclear war and to reduce the levels of nuclear armaments in a way that also reduces the risk they will ever be used. We have no higher challenge, for a nuclear war cannot be won and must never be fought. But merely to be against nuclear war is not enough to prevent it.

For 35 years the defense policy of the United States and her NATO allies has been based on one simple premise: We do not start wars; we maintain our conventional and strategic strength to deter aggression by convincing any potential aggressor that war could bring no benefit, only disaster. Deterrence has been and will remain the cornerstone of our national security policy to defend freedom and preserve peace.

But as I mentioned, the 1970s were marked by neglect of our defenses, and nuclear safety was no exception. Too many forgot John Kennedy's warning that only when our arms are certain beyond doubt can we be certain beyond doubt they will never be used. By the beginning of this decade, we faced three growing problems: the Soviet SS-20 [intermediate-range nuclear missile] monopoly in Europe and Asia; the vulnerability of our land-based ICBMs (intercontinental ballistic missiles), the entire force; and the failure of arms control agreements to slow the overall growth in strategic weapons. The Carter Administration acknowledged these problems. In fact, almost everyone did.

Arms Reductions

There is a widespread, but mistaken, impression that arms agreements automatically produce arms control. In 1969, when (Strategic Arms Limitation Talks) SALT I negotiations began, the Soviet Union had about 1,500 strategic nuclear weapons. Today, the Soviet nuclear arsenal can grow to over 15,000 nuclear weapons and still stay within all past arms control agreements, including the SALT I and SALT II guidelines.

The practical means for reducing the risks of nuclear war must, therefore, follow two parallel paths: credible deterrence and real arms reductions with effective verification. It is on this basis that we've responded to the problems I just described. This is why we've moved forward to implement NATO's dual-track decision of 1979. While actually reducing the number of nuclear weapons in Europe, it is also why we have sought bipartisan support for the recommendations of the Scowcroft Commission* and the builddown concept, and why we've proposed deep reductions in strategic forces at the Strategic Arms Reduction Talks (START).

Without exception, every arms control proposal that we have offered would reverse the arms buildup and help bring a more stable balance at lower force levels. At the START talks, we seek to reduce substantially the number of ballistic missile warheads, reduce the destructive capacity of nuclear missiles, and establish limits on bombers and cruise missiles below the levels of SALT II. At the talks on Intermediate-Range Nuclear Forces (INF), our negotiators have tabled four initiatives to address Soviet concerns and improve prospects for a fair and equitable agreement that would reduce or eliminate an entire class of such nuclear weapons. Our flexibility in the START and INF negotiations has been demonstrated by numerous modifications to our positions. But they have been met only by the silence of Soviet walkouts.

At the Mutual and Balanced Force Reduction (MBFR) talks in Vienna, we and our NATO partners presented a treaty that would reduce conventional forces to parity at lower levels. To reduce the risk of war in times of crisis, we have proposed to the Soviet Union important measures to improve direct communications and increase mutual confidence. And just recently, I directed Vice President Bush to go to the Conference on Disarmament in Geneva to present a new American initiative, a worldwide ban on the production, possession and use of chemical weapons.

Our strategic policy represents a careful response to a nuclear agenda upon which even our critics agreed. Many who would break the bonds of partisanship, claiming they know how to bring greater security, seem to ignore the likely consequences of their own proposals.

Those who wanted a last-minute moratorium on INF deployment would have betrayed our allies and reduced the chances for a safer Europe. Those who would try to implement a unilateral freeze would find it unverifiable and destabilizing, because it would prevent restoration of a stable balance that keeps the peace. And those who would advocate unilateral cancellation of the Peacekeeper (MX) missile would ignore a central recommendation of the bipartisan Scowcroft report and leave the Soviets with little incentive to negotiate meaningful reductions. Indeed, the Soviets would be rewarded for leaving the bargaining table.

These simple solutions and others put forward by our critics would take meaningful agreements and increased security much further

---

* Study of U S strategic nuclear forces

from our grasp. Our critics can best help us move closer to the goals that we share by accepting practical means to achieve them. Granted, it's easy to support a strong defense. It's much harder to support a strong defense budget. And granted, it's easy to call for arms agreements. It's more difficult to support patient, firm, fair negotiations with those who want to see how much we will compromise with ourselves first. Bipartisanship can only work if both forces, both sides, face up to real-world problems and meet them with real-world solutions.

Securing Regional Stability

Our safety and security depend on more than credible deterrence and nuclear arms reductions. Constructive regional development is also essential. Therefore, our second great challenge is strengthening the basis for stability in troubled and strategically sensitive regions.

Regional tensions often begin in long-standing social, political and economic inequities, and in ethnic and religious disputes. But throughout the 1970s, increased Soviet support for terrorism, insurgency and aggression, coupled with the perception of weakening U.S. power and resolve, greatly exacerbated these tensions.

The results were not surprising: the massacres of Cambodia followed by the Vietnamese invasion, the Soviet invasion of Afghanistan, the rise of Iranian extremism and the holding of Americans hostage, Libyan coercion in Africa, Soviet and Cuban military involvement in Angola and Ethiopia, their subversion in Central America, and the rise of state-supported terrorism.

Taken together, these events defined a pattern of mounting instability and violence that the U.S. could not ignore. And we have not. As with defense, by the beginning of the '80s, there was an emerging consensus in this country that we had to go do better in dealing with problems that affect our vital interests.

Obviously, no single abstract policy could deal successfully with all problems or all regions. But as a general matter, effective regional stabilization requires a balanced approach—a mix of economic aid, security assistance and diplomatic mediation—tailored to the needs of each region.

It's also obvious that we alone cannot save embattled governments or control terrorism. But doing nothing only ensures far greater problems down the road. So, we strive to expand cooperation with states who support our common interests, to help friendly nations in danger, and to seize major opportunities for peacekeeping.

Central America and Southern Africa

Perhaps the best example of this comprehensive approach is the report and recommendations of the National Bipartisan Commission on Central America. It is from this report that we drew our proposals for bringing peaceful development to Central America. They are now before the Congress and will be debated at length.

I welcome a debate, but if it's to be productive we must put aside mythology and uninformed rhetoric. Some, for example, insist that the root of regional violence is poverty, but not communism. Well, three-fourths of our requests and of our current program is economic and humanitarian assistance. America is a good and generous nation, but economic aid alone cannot stop Cuban- and Soviet-inspired guerrillas determined to terrorize, burn, bomb and destroy everything from bridges and industries to electric power and transportation. And neither individual rights nor economic health can be advanced if stability is not secured.

Other critics say that we shouldn't see the problems of this or any other region as an East-West struggle. Our policies in Central America and elsewhere are in fact designed precisely to keep East-West tensions from spreading, from intruding into the lives of nations that are struggling with great problems of their own.

Events in southern Africa are showing what persistent mediation and ability to talk to all sides can accomplish. The states of this region have been poised for war for decades, but there is new hope for peace. South Africa, Angola and Mozambique are implementing agreements to break the cycle of violence. Our administration has been active in this process, and we'll stay involved, trying to bring an independent Namibia into being, end foreign military interference, and keep the region free from East-West conflict. I have hope that peace and democratic reform can be enjoyed by all the peoples of southern Africa.

In Central America we've also seen progress. El Salvador's presidential election expresses that nation's desire to govern itself in peace. Yet the future of the region remains open. We have a choice. Either we help America's friends defend themselves and give democracy a chance, or we abandon our responsibilities and let the Soviet Union and Cuba shape the destiny of our hemisphere. If this happens, the East-West conflict will only become broader and much more dangerous.

Seeking Stability

In dealing with regional instability, we have to understand how it is related to other problems. Insecurity and regional violence are among the driving forces of nuclear proliferation. Peacekeeping in troubled regions and strengthening barriers to nuclear proliferation are two sides of the same coin. Stability and safeguards go together.

Now no one says this approach is cheap, quick or easy. But the cost of this commitment is bargain-basement compared to the tremendous sacrifices that we will have to make if we do nothing or do too little. The Kissinger Commission warned that an outbreak of Cuban-type regimes in Central America will bring subversion closer to our own borders, and the specter of millions of uprooted refugees fleeing in desperation to the north.

In the Middle East, which has so rarely known peace, we seek a similar mix of economic aid, diplomatic mediation, and military assistance and cooperation. These will, we believe, make the use of U.S. forces unnecessary and make the risk of East-West conflict less. But, given the importance of the region, we must also be ready to act when the presence of American power and that of our friends can help stop the spread of violence. I have said, for example, that we'll keep open the Straits of Hormuz, the vital lifeline through which so much oil flows to the United States and other industrial democracies. Making this clear beforehand and making it credible makes a crisis much less likely.

We must work with quiet persistence and without illusions. We may suffer setbacks, but we mustn't jump to the conclusion that we can defend our interests without ever committing ourselves. Nor should other nations believe that mere setbacks will turn America inward again. We know our responsibilities, and we must live up to them.

Because effective regional problem solving requires a balanced and sustained approach, it is essential that the Congress give full, not piecemeal, support. Indeed, where we have foundered in regional stabilization, it has been because the Congress has failed to provide such support. Halfway measures, refusing to take responsibility for means, produce the worst possible results.

Economic Growth

Expanding opportunities for economic development and personal freedom is our third great challenge. The American concept of peace is more than absence of war. We favor the flowering of economic growth and individual liberty in a world of peace. And this, too, is a goal to which most Americans subscribe. Our political leaders must be judged by whether the means they offer will help us to reach it.

Our belief in individual freedom and opportunity is rooted in practical experience. Free people build free markets that ignite dynamic development for everyone. And in America, incentives, risktaking and entrepreneurship are reawakening the spirit of capitalism and strengthening economic expansion and human progress throughout the world. Our goal has always been to restore and sustain noninflationary, worldwide growth, thereby ending for good the stagflation of the 1970s, which saw a drastic weakening of the fabric of the world economy.

We take our leadership responsibilities seriously, but we alone cannot put the world's economic house in order. At [the] Williamsburg [Economic Summit], the industrial countries consolidated their views on economic policy. The proof is not in the communique; it's in the results. France is reducing inflation and seeking greater flexibility in its economy. Japan is slowly, to be sure, but steadily—we will insist—liberalizing its trade and capital markets. Germany and the United Kingdom are moving forward on a steady course of low inflation and moderate, sustained growth.

Just as we believe that incentives are key to greater growth in America and throughout the world, so, too, must we resist the sugar-coated poison of protectionism everywhere it exists. Here at home we're opposing inflationary, self-defeating bills like domestic content. At the London Economic Summit in June, I hope that we can lay the groundwork for a new round of negotiations that will open markets for our exports of goods and services and stimulate greater growth, efficiency and jobs for all.

Trade and Debt

We're advancing other key initiatives to promote more powerful worldwide growth by expanding trade and investment relationships. The dynamic growth of Pacific Basin nations has made them the fastest growing markets for our goods, services and capital. Last year I visited Japan and Korea—two of America's most important allies—to forge closer partnerships. This month I will visit the People's Republic of China, another of the increasingly significant relationships that we hold in the Pacific. I see America and our Pacific neighbors as nations of the future, going forward together in a mighty enterprise to build dynamic growth economies and a safer world.

We're helping developing countries grow by presenting a fresh view of development—the magic of the marketplace—to spark greater growth and participation in the international economy. Developing nations earn twice as much from exports to the United States as they received in aid from all the other nations combined.

And practical proposals like the Caribbean Basin Initiative will strengthen the private sectors of some 20 Caribbean neighbors, while guaranteeing fairer treatment for U.S. companies and nationals and increasing demand for American exports.

We've recently sent to the Congress a new economic policy initiative for Africa. And it, too, is designed to support the growth of private enterprise in African countries by encouraging structural economic change in international trade. We've also asked the Congress to increase humanitarian assistance to Africa to combat the devastating effects of extreme drought.

In building a strong global recovery, of course, nothing is more important than to keep the wheels of world commerce turning and to create jobs without renewing the spiral of inflation. The International Monetary Fund (IMF) is a linchpin in our efforts to restore a sound world economy [and] resolve the debt problems of many developing countries. With bipartisan support, we implemented a major increase in IMF resources. In cooperation with the IMF, we're working to prevent the problems of individual debtor nations from disrupting the stability and strength of the entire international financial system. It was this goal that brought nations of north and south together to help resolve the debt difficulties of the new democratic government of Argentina.

Trust the People

Because we know that democratic governments are the best guarantors of human rights, and that economic growth will always flourish when men and women are free, we seek to promote not just material products but the values of faith and human dignity for which America and all democratic nations stand—values which embody the culmination of 5,000 years of Western civilization.

When I addressed the British Parliament in June of 1982, I called for a bold and lasting effort to assist people struggling for human rights. We've established the National Endowment for Democracy, a partnership of people from all walks of life dedicated to spreading the positive message of democracy. To succeed we must oppose the doublespeak of totalitarian propaganda. And so, we're modernizing the Voice of America and our other broadcasting facilities, and we're working to start up Radio Marti, a voice of truth to the imprisoned people of Cuba.

Americans have always wanted to see the spread of democratic institutions, and that goal is coming closer. In our own hemisphere, 26 countries of Latin America and the Caribbean are either democracies or formally embarked on a democratic transition. This represents 90 percent of the region's population, up from under 50 percent a decade ago.

Trust the people—this is the crucial lesson of history and America's message to the world. We must be staunch in our conviction that freedom is not the sole possession of a chosen few, but the universal right of men and women everywhere.

President Truman said, "If we should pay merely lip service to inspiring ideals, and later do violence to simple justice, we would draw down upon us the bitter wrath of generations yet unborn." Well, let us go forward together, faithful friends of democracy and democratic values, confident in our conviction that the tide of the future is a freedom tide. But let us go forward with practical means.

Speaking with One Voice

This brings me to our fourth great challenge. We must restore bipartisan consensus in support of U.S. foreign policy. We must restore America's honorable tradition of partisan politics stopping at the water's edge, Republicans and Democrats standing united in patriotism and speaking with one voice as responsible trustees for peace, democracy, individual liberty and the rule of law.

In the 1970s we saw a rash of congressional initiatives to limit the President's authority in the areas of trade, human rights, arms sales, foreign assistance, intelligence operations and the dispatch of troops in time of crisis. Over a hundred separate prohibitions and restrictions on executive branch authority to formulate and implement foreign policy were enacted.

The most far-reaching consequence of the past decade's congressional activism is this: Bipartisan consensus-building has become a central responsibility of congressional leadership as well as of executive leadership. If we're to have a sustainable foreign policy, the Congress must support the practical details of policy, not just the general goals.

We have demonstrated the capacity for such jointly responsible leadership in certain areas, but we've seen setbacks for bipartisanship, too. I believe that once we established bipartisan agreement on our course in Lebanon, the subsequent second-guessing about whether we ought to keep our men there severely undermined our policy. It hindered the ability of our diplomats to negotiate, encouraged more intransigence from the Syrians, and prolonged the violence. Similarly, congressional wavering on support for the Jackson Plan, which reflects the recommendations of the National Bipartisan Commission on Central America, can only encourage the enemies of democracy who are determined to wear us down.

Presidential-Congressional Partnership

To understand and solve this problem—this problem of joint responsibility—we have to go beyond the familiar questions as to who should be stronger, the President or the Congress. The more basic problem is, in this post-Vietnam era, Congress has not yet developed capacities for coherent, responsible action needed to carry out the new foreign policy powers it has taken for itself. To meet the challenges of this decade, we need a strong President and a strong Congress.

Unfortunately, many in the Congress seem to believe they're still in the troubled Vietnam era, with their only task to be vocal critics and not responsible partners in developing positive, practical programs to solve real problems.

Much was learned from Vietnam—lessons ranging from increased appreciation of the need for careful discrimination in the use of U.S. force or military assistance, to increased appreciation of the need for domestic support for any such military element or policy. Military force, either direct or indirect, must remain an available part of America's foreign policy. But clearly the Congress is less than wholly comfortable with both the need for a military element in foreign policy and its own responsibility to deal with that element.

Presidents must recognize Congress as a more significant partner in foreign policymaking and, as we've tried to do, seek new means to reach bipartisan executive-legislative consensus. But legislators must realize that they, too, are partners. They have a responsibility to go beyond mere criticism to consensus-building that will produce positive, practical and effective action.

Bipartisan consensus is not an end in itself. Sound and experienced U.S. foreign policy leadership must always reflect a deep understanding of fundamental American interests, values and principles. Consensus on the broad goals of a safer and more humane world is easy to achieve. The harder part is making progress in developing concrete, realistic means to reach these goals. We've made some progress, but there is still a congressional reluctance to assume responsibility for positive bipartisan action to go with their newly claimed powers.

We've set excellent examples with the bipartisan Scowcroft Commission, bipartisan support for IMF funding, and the bipartisan work of the Kissinger Commission. But it's time to lift our efforts to a higher level of cooperation, time to meet—together with realism and idealism—America's great challenges for the '80s.

We have the right to dream great dreams, the opportunity to strive for a world at peace enriched by human dignity, and the responsibility to work as partners so that we might leave these blessed gifts to our children and to our children's children.

We might remember the example of a legislator who lived in a particularly turbulent era, Henry Clay. Abraham Lincoln called him "my beau ideal of a statesman." He knew Clay's loftiness of spirit and vision never lost sight of his country's interest and, election year or not, Clay would set love of country above all political considerations.

The stakes for America, for peace and for freedom demand every bit as much from us in 1984 and beyond. This is our challenge.... □

Catalysts for an Era of World Peace

ADDRESS BEFORE THE 39TH SESSION OF THE UNITED NATIONS GENERAL ASSEMBLY

NEW YORK CITY
SEPTEMBER 24, 1984

The responsibility of this Assembly, the peaceful resolution of disputes between peoples and nations, can be discharged successfully only if we recognize the great common ground upon which we all stand—our fellowship as members of the human race, our oneness as inhabitants of this planet, our place as representatives of thousands of millions of our countrymen whose fondest hope remains the end to war and to the repression of the human spirit. These are the important central realities that bind us, that permit us to dream of a future without the antagonisms of the past. Just as shadows can be seen only where there is light, so too can we overcome what is wrong only if we remember how much is right. And we will resolve what divides us only if we remember how much more unites us.

Political and Economic Freedom

This chamber has heard enough about the problems and dangers ahead. Today, let us dare to speak of a future that is bright and hopeful and can be ours only if we seek it. I believe that future is far nearer than most of us would dare to hope.

At the start of this decade, one scholar at the Hudson Institute noted that mankind also had undergone enormous changes for the better in the past two centuries—changes which aren't always readily noticed or written about.

"Up until 200 years ago, there were relatively few people in the world," he wrote. "All human societies were poor. Disease and early death dominated most people's lives. People were ignorant and largely at the mercy of the forces of nature.

"Now," he said, "we are somewhere near the middle of a process of economic development. At the end of that process, almost no one will live in a country as poor as the richest country of the past. There will be many more people...living long, healthy lives with immense knowledge and more to learn than anybody has time for." They will be "able to cope with the forces of nature and almost indifferent to distance."

We do live today, as the scholar suggested, in the middle of one of the most important and dramatic periods in human history—one in which all of us can serve as catalysts for an era of world peace and unimagined human freedom and dignity.

And today I would like to report to you, as distinguished and influential members of the world community, on what the United States has been attempting to do to help move the world closer to this era. On many fronts enormous progress has been made, and I think our efforts are complemented by the trend of history.

If we look closely enough, I believe we can see all the world moving toward a deeper appreciation of the value of human freedom in both its political and economic manifestations. This is partially motivated by a worldwide desire for economic growth and higher standards of living. And there's an increasing realization that economic freedom is a prelude to economic progress and growth and is intricately and inseparably linked to political freedom.

Everywhere, people in governments are beginning to recognize that the secret of a progressive new world is to take advantage of the creativity of the human spirit, to encourage innovation and individual enterprise, to reward hard work, and to reduce barriers to the free flow of trade and information.

Our opposition to economic restrictions and trade barriers is consistent with our view of economic freedom and human progress. We believe such barriers pose a particularly dangerous threat to the developing nations and their chance to share in world prosperity through expanded export markets. Tomorrow at the International Monetary Fund, I will address this question more fully, including America's desire for more open trading markets throughout the world.

This desire to cut down trade barriers and our open advocacy of freedom as the engine of human progress are two of the most important ways the United States and the American people hope to assist in bringing about a world where prosperity is commonplace, conflict an aberration, and human dignity and freedom a way of life.

Let me place these steps more in context by briefly outlining the major goals of American foreign policy, and then exploring with you the practical ways we're attempting to further freedom and prevent war. By that I mean, first, how we have moved to strengthen ties with old allies and new friends; second, what we're doing to help avoid the regional conflicts that could contain the seeds of world conflagration; and third, the status of our efforts with the Soviet Union to reduce the level of arms.

Let me begin with a word about the objectives of American foreign policy, which have been consistent since the postwar era, and which fueled the formation of the United Nations and were incorporated into the U.N. Charter itself.

Reaffirming Fundamental Human Rights

The U.N. Charter states two overriding goals: "to save succeeding generations from the scourge of war, which twice in our lifetime has brought untold sorrow to mankind," and "to reaffirm faith in fundamental human rights, in the dignity and worth of the human person, in the equal rights of men and women and of nations large and small."

The founders of the United Nations understood full well the relationship between these two goals. And I want you to know that the government of the United States will continue to view this concern for human rights as the moral center of our foreign policy. We can never look at anyone's freedom as a bargaining chip in world politics. Our hope is for a time when all the people of the world can enjoy the blessings of personal liberty. But I would like also to emphasize that our concern for protecting human rights is part of our concern for protecting the peace.

The answer is for all nations to fulfill the obligations they freely assumed under the Universal Declaration of Human Rights. It states, "The will of the people shall be the basis of the authority of government; this will shall be expressed in periodic and genuine elections." The Declaration also includes these rights: "to form and to join trade unions," "to own property alone as well as in association with others," "to leave any country including his own and return to his country," and to enjoy "freedom of opinion and expression." Perhaps the most graphic example of the relationship between human rights and peace is the right of peace groups to exist and to promote their views. In fact, the treatment of peace groups may be a litmus test of government's true desire for peace.

Alliances and Friends

In addition to emphasizing this tie between the advocacy of human rights and the prevention of war, the United States has taken important steps, as I mentioned earlier, to prevent world conflict. The starting point and cornerstone of our foreign policy is our alliance and partnership with our fellow democracies. For 35 years, the North Atlantic Alliance has guaranteed the peace in Europe. In both Europe and Asia, our alliances have been the vehicle for a great reconciliation among nations that had fought bitter wars in decades and centuries past. And here in the Western Hemisphere, north and south are being lifted on the tide of freedom and are joined in a common effort to foster peaceful economic development.

We're proud of our association with all those countries that share our commitment to freedom, human rights, the rule of law and international peace. Indeed, the bulwark of security that the democratic alliance provides is essential and remains essential to the maintenance of world peace. Every alliance involves burdens and obligations, but these are far less than the risks and sacrifices that would result if the peace-loving nations were divided and neglectful of their common security. The people of the United States will remain faithful to their commitments.

But the United States is also faithful to its alliances and friendships with scores of nations in the developed and developing worlds with differing political systems, cultures and traditions. The development of ties between the United States and China, a significant global event of the last dozen years, shows our willingness to improve relations with countries ideologically very different from ours.

We're ready to be the friend of any country that is a friend to us and a friend of peace. And we respect genuine nonalignment. Our own nation was born in revolution. We helped promote the process of decolonization that brought about the independence of so many members of this body. And we're proud of that history.

We're proud, too, of our role in the formation of the United Nations and our support of this body over the years. And let me again emphasize our unwavering commitment to a central principle of the United Nations system—the principle of universality, both here and in the United Nations' technical agencies around the world. If universality is ignored, if nations are expelled illegally, then the U.N. itself cannot be expected to succeed.

Constructive Negotiations

The United States welcomes diversity and peaceful competition. We do not fear the trends of history. We are not ideologically rigid. We do have principles, and we will stand by them, but we will also seek the friendship and good will of all, both old friends and new.

We've always sought to lend a hand to help others—from our

relief efforts in Europe after World War I, to the Marshall Plan and massive foreign assistance programs after World War II. Since 1946 the United States has provided over $115,000 million in economic aid to developing countries and, today, provides about one-third of the nearly $90,000 million in financial resources, public and private, that flows to the developing world. And the U.S. imports about one-third of the manufactured exports of the developing world.

But any economic progress as well as any movement in the direction of greater understanding between the nations of the world are, of course, endangered by the prospect of conflict at both the global and regional level. In a few minutes, I will turn to the menace of conflict on a worldwide scale and discuss the status of negotiations between the United States and the Soviet Union. But permit me first to address the critical problem of regional conflicts, for history displays tragic evidence that it is these conflicts which can set off the sparks leading to worldwide conflagration.

In a glass display case across the hall from the Oval Office at the White House, there is a gold medal—the Nobel Peace Prize won by Theodore Roosevelt for his contribution in mediating the Russo-Japanese War in 1905. It was the first such prize won by an American, and it's part of a tradition of which the American people are very proud—a tradition that is being continued today in many regions of the globe.

Southern Africa, Central America

We're engaged, for example, in diplomacy to resolve conflicts in Southern Africa, working with the Front Line States and our partners in the Contact Group. Mozambique and South Africa have reached an historic accord on non-aggression and cooperation. South Africa and Angola have agreed on a disengagement of forces from Angola, and the groundwork has been laid for the independence of Namibia, with virtually all aspects of Security Council Resolution 435 agreed upon. Let me add that the United States considers it a moral imperative that South Africa's racial policies evolve peacefully but decisively toward a system compatible with basic norms of justice, liberty and human dignity.

I'm pleased that American companies in South Africa, by providing equal employment opportunities, are contributing to the economic advancement of the black population. But, clearly, much more must be done.

In Central America, the United States has lent support to a diplomatic process to restore regional peace and security. We have committed substantial resources to promote economic development and social progress.

The growing success of democracy in El Salvador is the best proof that the key to peace lies in a political solution. Free elections brought into office a government dedicated to democracy, reform, economic progress and regional peace. Regrettably, there are forces in the region eager to thwart democratic change—but these forces are now on the defensive. The tide is turning in the direction of freedom. We call upon Nicaragua, in particular, to abandon its policies of subversion and militarism, and to carry out the promises it made to the Organization of American States to establish democracy at home.

The Middle East

The Middle East has known more than its share of tragedy and conflict for decades, and the United States has been actively involved in peace diplomacy for just as long. We consider ourselves a full partner in the quest for peace. The record of the 11 years since the October War shows that much can be achieved through negotiations; it also shows that the road is long and hard:

— Two years ago, I proposed a fresh start toward a negotiated solution to the Arab-Israeli conflict. My initiative of September 1, 1982 contains a set of positions that can serve as a basis for a just and lasting peace. That initiative remains a realistic and workable approach, and I am committed to it as firmly as on the day I announced it. And the foundation stone of this effort remains Security Council Resolution 242, which in turn was incorporated in all its parts in the Camp David Accords.

— The tragedy of Lebanon has not ended. Only last week, a despicable act of barbarism* by some who are unfit to associate with humankind reminded us once again that Lebanon continues to suffer. In 1983 we helped Israel and Lebanon reach an agreement that, if implemented, could have led to the full withdrawal of Israeli forces in the context of the withdrawal of all foreign forces. This agreement was blocked, and the long agony of the Lebanese continues. Thousands of people are still kept from their homes by continuous violence and are refugees in their own country. The once flourishing economy of Lebanon is near collapse. All of Lebanon's friends should work together to help end this nightmare.

— In the Gulf, the United States has supported a series of Security Council resolutions that call for an end to the war between Iran and Iraq that has meant so much death and destruction and put the world's economic well-being at risk. Our hope is that hostilities will soon end, leaving each side with its political and territorial integrity intact, so that both may devote their energies to addressing the needs of their people and a return to relationships with other states.

— The lesson of experience is that negotiations work. The peace treaty between Israel and Egypt brought about the peaceful return of the Sinai, clearly showing that the negotiating process brings results when the parties commit themselves to it. The time is bound to come when the same wisdom and courage will be applied with success to reach peace between Israel and all of its Arab neighbors in a manner that assures security for all in the region, the recognition of Israel and a solution to the Palestinian problem.

---

* On September 20, 1984, a car bomb exploded in front of the U S Embassy annex in Aukar, Lebanon, killing an estimated 23 people, including two Americans

In every part of the world, the United States is similarly engaged in peace diplomacy as an active player or a strong supporter.

— In Southeast Asia, we have backed the efforts of ASEAN (Association of Southeast Asian Nations) to mobilize international support for a peaceful resolution of the Cambodian problem, which must include the withdrawal of Vietnamese forces and the election of a representative government. ASEAN's success in promoting economic and political development has made a major contribution to the peace and stability of the region.

— In Afghanistan, the dedicated efforts of the Secretary General and his representatives to find a diplomatic settlement have our strong support. I assure you that the United States will continue to do everything possible to find a negotiated outcome which provides the Afghan people with the right to determine their own destiny, allows the Afghan refugees to return to their own country in dignity and protects the legitimate security interests of all neighboring countries.

— On the divided and tense Korean peninsula, we have strongly backed the confidence-building measures proposed by the Republic of Korea and by the U.N. Command at Panmunjon. These are an important first step toward peaceful reunification in the long term.

— We take heart from progress by others in lessening the tensions, notably the efforts by the Federal Republic of Germany to reduce barriers between the two German states.

— And the United States strongly supports the Secretary General's efforts to assist the Cypriot parties in achieving a peaceful and reunited Cyprus.

The United States has been and will always be a friend to peaceful solutions. This is no less true with respect to my country's relations with the Soviet Union.

When I appeared before you last year, I noted that we cannot count on the instinct for survival alone to protect us against war. Deterrence is necessary but not sufficient. America has repaired its strength; we have invigorated our alliances and friendships. We are ready for constructive negotiations with the Soviet Union.

We recognize that there is no sane alternative to negotiations on arms control and other issues between our two nations, which have the capacity to destroy civilization as we know it. I believe this is a view shared by virtually every country in the world and by the Soviet Union itself. And I want to speak to you today on what the United States and the Soviet Union can accomplish together in the coming years, and the concrete steps that we need to take.

You know, as I stand here and look out from this podium, there in front of me, I can see the seat of the representative from the Soviet Union. And not far from that seat, just over to the side, is the seat of the representative from the United States. In this historic assembly hall, it is clear there is not a great distance between us. Outside this room, while there still will be clear differences, there is every reason why we should do all that is possible to shorten that distance. And that is why we are here. Isn't that what this organization is all about?

Establishing a Working Relationship

On January 16, 1984, I set out three objectives for U.S.-Soviet relations that can provide an agenda for our work over the months ahead. First, I said, we need to find ways to reduce and, eventually, to eliminate the threat and use of force in solving international disputes. Our concern over the potential for nuclear war cannot deflect us from the terrible human tragedies occurring every day in the regional conflicts I just discussed. Together, we have a particular responsibility to contribute to political solutions to these problems, rather than to exacerbate them through the provision of even more weapons.

I propose that our two countries agree to embark on periodic consultations at policy level about regional problems. We will be prepared, if the Soviets agree, to make senior experts available at regular intervals for in-depth exchanges of views....Spheres of influence are a thing of the past. Differences between American and Soviet interests are not. The objectives of this political dialogue will be to help avoid miscalculation, reduce the potential risk of U.S.-Soviet confrontation, and help the people in areas of conflict to find peaceful solutions.

The United States and the Soviet Union have achieved agreements of historic importance on some regional issues. The Austrian State Treaty and the Berlin Accords are notable and lasting examples. Let us resolve to achieve similar agreements in the future.

Reducing Arms

Our second task must be to find ways to reduce the vast stockpiles of armaments in the world. I am committed to redoubling our negotiating efforts to achieve real results: in Geneva, a complete ban on chemical weapons; in Vienna, real reductions to lower and equal levels in Soviet and American, Warsaw Pact and NATO conventional forces; in Stockholm, concrete practical measures to enhance mutual confidence, to reduce the risk of war, and to reaffirm commitments concerning non-use of force. In the field of nuclear testing, improvements in verification essential to ensure compliance with the Threshhold Test Ban and Peaceful Nuclear Explosions agreements; and in the field of nonproliferation, close cooperation to strengthen the international institutions and practices aimed at halting the spread of nuclear weapons, together with redoubled efforts to meet the legitimate expectations of all nations that the Soviet Union and the United States will substantially reduce their own nuclear arsenals.

We and the Soviets have agreed to upgrade our Hotline communications facility, and our discussions of nuclear nonproliferation in recent years have been useful to both sides. We think there are other possibilities for improving communications in this area that deserve serious exploration.

I believe the proposal of the Soviet Union for opening U.S.-Soviet talks in Vienna provided an important opportunity to advance these objectives. We've been prepared to discuss a wide range of issues of concern to both sides, such as the relationship between defensive and offensive forces and what has been called the militarization of space. During the talks we would consider what measures of restraint both sides might take while negotiations proceed. However, any agreement must logically depend on our ability to get the competition in offensive arms under control and to achieve genuine stability at substantially lower levels of nuclear arms.

Our approach in all these areas will be designed to take into account concerns the Soviet Union has voiced. It will attempt to provide a basis for an historic breakthrough in arms control....

Bilateral Relations

The third task I set in January was to establish a better working relationship between the Soviet Union and the United States, one marked by greater cooperation and understanding. We have made some modest progress. We have reached agreements to improve our Hotline extend our 10-year economic agreement, enhance consular cooperation and explore coordination of search and rescue efforts at sea.

We have also offered to increase significantly the amount of U.S. grain for purchase by the Soviet Union, and to provide the Soviets a direct fishing allocation off U.S. coasts. But there is much more we could do together. I feel particularly strongly about breaking down the barriers between the peoples of the United States and the Soviet Union, and between our political, military and other leaders.

Now, all of these steps that I have mentioned, and especially the arms control negotiations, are extremely important to a step-by-step process toward peace. But let me also say that we need to extend the arms control process to build a bigger umbrella under which it can operate—a road map, if you will, showing where, during the next 20 years or so, these individual efforts can lead. This can greatly assist step-by-step negotiations and enable us to avoid having all our hopes or expectations ride on any single set or series of negotiations. If progress is temporarily halted at one set of talks, this newly established framework for arms control could help us take up the slack at other negotiations.

A Fresh Approach

Today, to the great end of lifting the dread of nuclear war from the peoples of the earth, I invite the leaders of the world to join in a new beginning. We need a fresh approach to reducing international tensions. History demonstrates that just as the arms competition has its root in political suspicions and anxieties, so it can be channeled in more stabilizing directions and eventually be eliminated, if those political suspicions and anxieties are addressed as well.

Toward this end, I will suggest to the Soviet Union that we institutionalize regular ministerial- or cabinet-level meetings between our two countries on the whole agenda of issues before us, including the problem of needless obstacles to understanding. To take but one idea for discussion: In such talks, we could consider the exchange of outlines of five-year military plans for weapons development and our schedules of intended procurement. We would also welcome the exchange of observers at military exercises and locations. And I propose that we find a way for Soviet experts to come to the United States nuclear test site and for ours to go to theirs to measure directly the yields of tests of nuclear weapons. I hope that the Soviet Union will cooperate in this undertaking and reciprocate in a manner that will enable the two countries to establish the basis for verification for effective limits on underground nuclear testing.

I believe such talks could work rapidly toward developing a new climate of policy understanding, one that is essential if crises are to be avoided and real arms control is to be negotiated. Of course, summit meetings have a useful role to play. But they need to be carefully prepared, and the benefit here is that meetings at the ministerial level would provide the kind of progress that is the best preparation for higher-level talks between ourselves and the Soviet leaders.

How much progress we will make and at what pace, I cannot say. But we have a moral obligation to try and try again.

"Beginning the World Over"

Some may dismiss such proposals and my own optimism as simplistic American idealism, and they will point to the burdens of the modern world and to history. Well, yes, if we sit down and catalog year by year, generation by generation, the famines, the plagues, the wars, the invasions mankind has endured, the list will grow so long and the assault on humanity so terrific that it seems too much for the human spirit to bear.

But isn't this narrow and shortsighted and not at all how we think of history? Yes, the deeds of infamy or injustice are all recorded, but what shines out from the pages of history is the daring of the dreamers and the deeds of the builders and the doers. These things make up the stories we tell and pass on to our children. They comprise the most enduring and striking fact about human history—that through the heartbreak and tragedy man has always dared to perceive the outline of human progress, the steady growth in not just the material well-being, but the spiritual insight of mankind.

"There have been tyrants and murderers, and for a time they can seem invincible. But in the end, they always fall. Think on it...always. All through history, the way of truth and love has always won." That was the belief and the vision of Mahatma Gandhi. He described that, and it remains today a vision that is good and true.

"All is gift," is said to have been the favorite expression of another great spiritualist, a Spanish soldier who gave up the ways of war for that of love and peace. And if we're to make realities of the two great goals of the United Nations Charter—the dreams of peace and human dignity—we must take to heart these words of Ignatius Loyola*; we must pause long enough to contemplate the gifts received from Him who made us: the gift of life, the gift of this world and the gift of each other.

And the gift of the present. It is this present, this time that now we must seize. I leave you with a reflection from Mahatma Gandhi, spoken with those in mind who said that the disputes and conflicts of the modern world are too great to overcome; it was spoken shortly after Gandhi's quest for independence had taken him to Britain.

"I am not conscious of a single experience throughout my three months' stay in England and Europe," he said, "that made me feel that after all East is East and West is West. On the contrary, I have been convinced more than ever that human nature is much the same, no matter under what clime it flourishes, and that if you approached people with trust and affection, you would have ten-fold trust and thousand-fold affection returned to you."

For the sake of a peaceful world, a world where human dignity and freedom is respected and enshrined, let us approach each other with ten-fold trust and thousand-fold affection. A new future awaits us. The time is here, the moment is now.

One of the Founding Fathers of our nation, Thomas Paine, spoke words that apply to all of us gathered here today. He said, "We have it in our power to begin the world over again."

Thank you and God bless you. ◻

---

* 1491-1556 Founder of the Jesuits

The Cause of Human Freedom

ADDRESS AT A CEREMONY ESTABLISHING INTERNATIONAL HUMAN RIGHTS DAY

WASHINGTON, D.C
DECEMBER 10, 1984

T his ceremony marks more than another event on the White House calendar or another worthy cause for the national agenda, for in observing Human Rights Day we rededicate ourselves to the cause of human dignity and freedom, a cause that goes to the heart of our national character and defines our national purpose.

Today, we dare to affirm again the commitment of the American people to the inalienable rights of all human beings. In reaffirming the moral beliefs that began our nation, we strive to make the United States what we pray to God it will always be—a beacon of hope to all the persecuted and oppressed of the world. And we resolve that, as a people, we'll never rest until the blessings of liberty and self-government are extended to all the nation's of the Earth.

Hemisphere of Democracy

Two years ago in London, when I called for a crusade for freedom and human rights, I noted that these ideals—embodied in the rule of law, under God, and in the institutions of democratic self-government—were on the march. Because these ideals represent the oldest and noblest aspirations of the human spirit, I said then that this power is irresistible when compared to totalitarian ideologies that seek to roll back mankind's march to freedom.

Today I want to take special note of evidence that this desire for self-determination, this recognition by the state of the inalienable rights of men and women everywhere, is nowhere stronger than close to our own borders in the lands of Latin America. In contrast to only a few years ago, today more than 90 percent of the people in Latin America and the Caribbean live in nations either democratically governed or moving in that direction.

While we're still doing all that we can to promote democratic change in nations such as Paraguay and Chile, we must not forget that over the last five years in Argentina, Bolivia, Ecuador, El Salvador, Honduras, Panama, Peru and, most recently, in Uruguay, military juntas have been replaced by elected civilian governments. And just last Monday, democratic values triumphed again as the people of Grenada freely elected a new civilian prime minister.

Today, all who cherish human rights and individual freedom salute the people of the Americas for their great achievements. And we pledge to our neighbors the continued support and assistance of the United States as they transform our entire hemisphere into a haven for democracy, peace and human rights.

In other nations farther from our shores, we've also seen progress toward reducing the repression of human rights and some strengthening of democratic institutions. In some of these nations, which have authoritarian governments but friendly ties to the United States and the community of democratic nations, quiet diplomacy has brought about humane and democratic change.

But we know there are occasions when quiet diplomacy is not enough, when we must remind the leaders of nations who are friendly to the United States that such friendship also carries responsibilities for them and for us. And that's why the United States calls for all governments to advance the democratic process and work toward a system of government based on the consent of the governed.

South Africa

From our beginning, regard for human rights and the steady expansion of human freedom have defined the American experience. And they remain today the real, moral core of our foreign policy.

The United States has said on many occasions that we view racism with repugnance. We feel moral responsibility to speak out on this matter, to emphasize our concerns and our grief over the human and spiritual costs of apartheid in South Africa, to call upon the government of South Africa to reach out to its black majority by ending the forced removal of blacks from their communities and the detention, without trial, and lengthy imprisonment of black leaders. Such action can comfort only those whose vision of South Africa's future is one of polarization, violence and the final extinction of any hope for peaceful, democratic government. At the same time, we note with satisfaction that the South African government has released 11 black leaders, including the top leaders of two of that country's most important labor unions.

Because we care deeply about the people of South Africa and the future of that nation, we ask that the constructive changes of recent years be broadened to address the aspirations of all South Africans. Peaceful change in South Africa, and throughout southern Africa, can come only when blacks and whites find a durable basis to live together, when they establish an effective dialogue, a dialogue sustained by adherence to democratic values and a belief in governments based on the consent of the governed.

We urge both the government and the people of South Africa to move toward a more just society. We pledge here today that if South Africans address the imperatives of constructive change, they will have the unswerving support of our government and people in this effort.

A Moral Distinction

A few years ago, when I spoke of totalitarian ideologies as the greatest threat to personal freedom in the world today and the most persistent source of human suffering in our century, I also pointed out that the United States, too, has faced evils like racism, anti-Semitism and other forms of intolerance and disregard for human freedom. So, while we work to see human rights extended throughout the world, this observance of Human Rights Day reminds us of our responsibility to assure against injustice and intolerance in our own land as well. And today, I call on the American people to reaffirm, in our daily lives and in the workings of our private and governmental institutions, a commitment to brotherhood and equal justice under the law.

But we do a serious disservice to the cause of human rights if we forget that, however mistaken and wrong, however stumbling the actions of democracies in seeking to achieve the ideals of freedom and brotherhood, our philosophy of government permits us to acknowledge, debate and then correct mistakes, injustices and violations of human rights.

Let us always remember the critical moral distinction of our time—the clear difference between a philosophy of government that acknowledges wrongdoing and injustice and one that refuses to admit to such injustices and even justifies its own assaults on individual liberty in the name of a chimeric utopian vision. Such brutal affronts to the human conscience as the systematic suppression of individual liberty in the Soviet Union and the denial of religious expression by Christians, Jews and Muslims in that country are tragic examples. Today, for example, the largest remaining Jewish community in Europe, Soviet Jewry, is again being exposed to a systematic anti-Semitic campaign. Ominously, teachers of the Hebrew language have been arrested and their efforts to preserve their culture and religion treated as a crime.

Soviet authorities are continuing to threaten many "refuseniks" with confinement in psychiatric hospitals, expulsion from their jobs and internal exile. Yet thousands of Soviet Jews have applied for permission to emigrate. We have and shall continue to insist that those who wish to leave must be allowed to do so.

-129-

Sakharov

Our heart also goes out today to an individual who has worked so hard for human rights progress in the Soviet Union and suffered so much for his efforts—the Nobel Prize Laureate, Dr. Andrei Sakharov. Nothing more clearly illustrates the absence of what our Founding Fathers called a "decent respect to the opinions of mankind" than the cruel treatment of this great humanitarian. The Soviet Union, itself, would do much to regain respect within the international community if it would allow academician Sakharov and his wife, Yelena Bonner, to live the rest of their lives in dignity in a place of their own choosing. We're pleased to have the Sakharovs' son-in-law here with us today.

The Sakharovs are the best-known victims of human rights violations in the Soviet Union, but thousands of other Soviet citizens, such as Yuriy Orlov, and Anatoly Shcharanskiy—whose wife, Avital, is here with us today—suffer in Soviet prisons and labor camps for the sole crimes of expressing a personal opinion, seeking to emigrate or openly expressing their love of God.

We Americans recognize a special responsibility to speak for the oppressed, wherever they may be. We think here of special cases like the persecution of the Baha'i religious minority in Iran. But we also acknowledge a special obligation to speak for those who suffer the repression of totalitarian regimes, regimes that refuse to acknowledge and correct injustice and that justify absolute state power even as they seek to extend their cruel rule to other lands.

The Cause of Human Freedom

So, we call today for all free peoples of the world to unite in resisting and bringing to an end such intolerable practices as the suppression of free trade unionism, the campaign against the church and against political freedom in Nicaragua, the continuing Vietnamese occupation of Cambodia, and the barbaric war waged by Soviet troops in Afghanistan—a war which began five years ago this month with the Soviet invasion of that once nonaligned country.

As but one of the tragic consequences of Soviet actions in Afghanistan, more than one-third of the people of that country have fled from their homes and sought refuge in internal or external exile.

Finally, we welcome the recent steps taken by the Polish Government, but we urge that they are followed by lasting efforts for genuine, national reconciliation through effective dialogue with the Polish people.

So, today, we the people of the United States, in conjunction with other freedom-loving people everywhere in the world, rededicate ourselves to the cause of human rights, to the cause of democratic self-rule and human freedom. We reassert our belief that some day the repression of the human spirit and the special tragedy of totalitarian rule will be only a distant chapter in the human past. In doing so, we're deeply aware of our nation's long struggle toward achieving these goals and our own heritage of seeking to promote these ideals throughout the world.

Thomas Jefferson told us, "The mass of mankind has not been born with saddles on their backs." And the poet Archibald MacLeish once said: Some say the hope for "the liberation of humanity, the freedom of man and mind, is nothing but a dream. They are right. It is. It is the American dream."

Another great American literary figure, F. Scott Fitzgerald, suggested that America is "a willingness of the heart." We've recently read a great deal about the young people of this nation about whom, some say, this willingness of the heart no longer exists. Well, my own experiences with this generation suggest that the traditional idealism of the young, their hope to accomplish great things, their willingness to serve the cause of humanity, is not only intact but stronger than ever. And like every generation before it, this generation hungers for a cause, for a mission that will take it outside itself and let it help lift humanity beyond the material and the immediate to new heights of human and spiritual progress.

A Challenge to Youth

So today, let us challenge these young Americans to make our nation an even better example of what she was always meant to be—champion of the oppressed, defender of all who reach for freedom and for the right of self-determination. Let us challenge young Americans, excited by technological and material progress, to ensure that this progress enriches political freedom and human dignity as well. Here's a challenge that's worthy of our youth, of their vision, their energy, and their vigor. Let our younger generation lead young people throughout the world to join the democratic nations in promoting human rights and self-government and the cause of human freedom.

The other night at the Kennedy Center, they had a United Nations choir of 90 young people, children, in the costumes of their native countries from all over the world. And looking at them down there, singing together, I couldn't help but think, "Good Lord, if we turn it all over to them, they'd get along just fine together." And maybe the world should follow their lead.

There is in the Book of Genesis a story of great loss. It's a story of man alienated from his fellow man and turning to persecution and hatred for others. Well, I believe that history is slowly working itself back to the restoration of brotherhood and mutual respect among all the peoples of the Earth. So today, we rededicate ourselves to this vision and mission. We do so mindful that human might and will alone cannot achieve this goal, aware that our ultimate success will be determined by our faith in the power of prayer, in the promises of Him who made us and even now guides us in our quest for human dignity and freedom. □

Democracy is the Road to Peace

ADDRESS ANNOUNCING A PEACE PROPOSAL FOR CENTRAL AMERICA

WASHINGTON, D.C.
APRIL 4, 1985

I want to announce today a proposal for peace in Central America that can enable liberty and democracy to prevail in this troubled region and that can protect the security of our own borders, economy and people.

On March 1st in San Jose, Costa Rica, the leaders of the Nicaraguan democratic resistance met with a broad coalition of other exiled Nicaraguan democrats. They agreed upon and signed an historic proposal to restore peace and democracy in their country. The members of the democratic resistance offered a cease-fire in return for an agreement by the Nicaraguan regime to begin a dialogue, mediated by the Bishops' Conference of the Roman Catholic Church, with the goal of restoring democracy through honest elections. To date the Nicaraguan regime has refused this offer.

National Reconciliation

The Central American countries, including Nicaragua, have agreed that internal reconciliation is indispensable to regional peace. But we know that, unlike President Duarte of El Salvador, who seeks a dialogue with his opponents, the communists in Nicaragua have turned—at least up until now—a cold shoulder to appeals for national reconciliation from the Pope and the Nicaraguan bishops. And we know that without incentives, none of this will change.

For these reasons, great numbers of Nicaraguans are demanding change and taking up arms to fight for the stolen promise of freedom and democracy. Over 15,000 farmers, small merchants, whites, blacks and Miskito Indians have united to struggle for a true democracy.

We supported democracy in Nicaragua before, and we support democracy today. We supported national reconciliation before, and we support it today. We believe that democracy deserves as much support in Nicaragua as it has received in El Salvador. And we're proud of the help that we've given to El Salvador.

You may recall that in 1981 we were told that the communist guerrillas were mounting a final offensive, the government had no chance and our approach would lead to greater American involvement. Well, our critics were wrong: democracy and freedom are winning in El Salvador. President Duarte is pulling his country together and enjoys wide support from the people. And all of this with America's help kept strictly limited.

The formula that worked in El Salvador—support for democracy, self-defense, economic development and dialogue—will work for the entire region. And we couldn't have accomplished this without bipartisan support in Congress, backed up by the National Bipartisan Commission on Central America, headed by Henry Kissinger. And that's why, after months of consulting with congressional leaders and listening carefully to their concerns, I am making the following proposal: I'm calling upon both sides to lay down their arms and accept the offer of church-mediated talks on internationally supervised elections and an end to the repression now in place against the church, the press and individual rights.

Proposal for Peace

To the members of the democratic resistance, I ask them to extend their offer of a cease-fire until June 1st.

To the Congress, I ask for immediate release of the $14 million already appropriated. While the cease-fire offer is on the table, I pledge these funds will not be used for arms or munitions. These funds will be used for food, clothing and medicine, and other support for survival. The democratic opposition cannot be a partner in negotiations without these basic necessities.

If the Sandinistas accept this peace offer, I will keep my funding restrictions in effect. But peace negotiations must not become a cover for deception and delay. If there is no agreement after 60 days of negotiations, I will lift these restrictions, unless both sides ask me not to.

U.S. Objectives

I want to emphasize that, consistent with the 21 goals of the Contadoran process, the United States continues to seek:

— One, Nicaragua's implementation of its commitment to democracy made to the Organization of American States;

— Two, an end to Nicaragua's aggression against its neighbors;

— Three, a removal of the thousands of Soviet bloc, Cuban, PLO (Palestinian Liberation Organization), Libyan, and other military and security personnel; and

— Four, a return of the Nicaraguan military to a level of parity with their neighbors.

Now, later today I will be meeting with [the leaders of the United Nicaraguan Opposition] Arturo Cruz, Adolpho Calero, and Alfonso Robelo to discuss my proposal.

Incentives to Democracy

Democracy is the road to peace. But, if we abandon the brave members of the democratic resistance, we will also remove all constraints on the communists.

Democracy can succeed in Central America. But Congress must release the funds that can create incentives for dialogue and peace. If we provide too little help, our choice will be a communist Central America with communist subversion spreading southward and northward. We face the risk that a hundred million people, from Panama to our open southern border, could come under the control of pro-Soviet regimes and threaten the United States with violence, economic chaos and a human tidal wave of refugees.

Central America is not condemned to that dark future of endless violence. If the United States meets its obligations to help those now striving for democracy, they can create a bright future in which peace for all Americans will be secure.

Let us make this so. I look forward to working with the Congress on this important matter in the coming weeks.   □

America's Vision — a World of Democracy

ADDRESS BEFORE THE 42nd SESSION OF THE UNITED NATIONS GENERAL ASSEMBLY

NEW YORK CITY
SEPTEMBER 21, 1987

Hundreds of thousands have already fallen in the bloody conflict between Iran and Iraq. All men and women of good will pray that the carnage can soon be stopped. We pray that the Secretary-General [Perez de Cuellar] proves to be not only a pilgrim but also the architect of a lasting peace between those two nations. Mr. Secretary-General, the United States supports you. May God guide you in your labors ahead.

Diplomacy of Peace

Like the Secretary-General, all of us here today are on a kind of pilgrimage. We come from every continent, every race and most religions to this great hall of hope, where in the name of peace, we practice diplomacy. Now, diplomacy, of course, is a subtle and nuanced craft—so much so that it is said that when one of the most wily diplomats of the 19th century passed away, other diplomats asked, on reports of his death, "What do you suppose the old fox meant by that?"

But true statesmanship requires not merely skill but something greater. Something we call vision—a grasp of the present and of the possibilities of the future. I have come here today to map out for you my own vision of the world's future—one I believe that, in its essential elements, is shared by all Americans. And I hope those who see things differently will not mind if I say that we in the United States believe that the place to look first for the shape of the future is not in continental masses and sea lanes, although geography is, obviously, of great importance. Neither is it in national reserves of blood and iron or, on the other hand, of money and industrial capacity—although military and economic strength are also, of course, crucial. We begin with something that is far simpler and yet far more profound—the human heart.

A Move Toward Democracy

All over the world today, the yearnings of the human heart are redirecting the course of international affairs, putting the lie to the myth of materialism and historical determinism. We have only to open our eyes to see the simple aspirations of ordinary people writ large on the record of our times.

Last year in the Philippines, ordinary people rekindled the spirit of democracy and restored the electoral process. Some said they had performed a miracle, and, if so, a similar miracle—a transition to democracy—is taking place in the Republic of Korea. Haiti, too, is making a transition. Some despair when these new, young democracies face conflicts or challenges, but growing pains are normal in democracies. The United States had them—as has every other democracy on Earth.

In Latin America, too, one can hear the voices of freedom echo from the peaks and across the plains. It is the song of ordinary people marching, not in uniforms and not in military file, but, rather, one by one in simple, everyday working clothes—marching to the polls. Ten years ago, only a third of the people of Latin America and the Caribbean lived in democracies or in countries that were turning to democracy. Today over 90 percent do.

But this worldwide movement to democracy is not the only way in which simple, ordinary people are leading us—we who are said to be the makers of history—into the future. Around the world, new businesses, new economic growth, new technologies are emerging from the workshops of ordinary people with extraordinary dreams.

Economic Freedom

Here in the United States, entrepreneurial energy—reinvigorated when we cut taxes and regulations—has fueled the current economic expansion. According to scholars at the Massachusetts Institute of Technology (MIT), three-quarters of the more than 13.5 million new jobs that we have created since the beginning of our expansion came from businesses with fewer than 100 employees—businesses started by ordinary people who dared to take a chance. And many of our new high technologies were first developed in the garages of fledgling entrepreneurs. Yet America is not the only or perhaps even the best example of the dynamism and dreams of free markets.

In India and China, freer markets for farmers have led to an explosion in production. In Africa, governments are rethinking their policies and, where they are allowing greater economic freedom to farmers, crop production has improved. Meanwhile, in the newly industrialized countries of the Pacific Rim, free markets in services and manufacturing as well as agriculture have led to a soaring of growth and standards of living. The ASEAN nations (Association of Southeast Asian Nations), Japan, Korea and Taiwan have created the true economic miracle of the last two decades and, in each of them, much of the magic came from ordinary people who succeeded as entrepreneurs.

In Latin America, this same lesson of free markets, greater opportunity and growth is being studied and acted on. President Sarney of Brazil spoke for many others when he said that "private initiative is the engine of economic development. In Brazil we have learned that every time the state's penetration in the economy increases, our liberty decreases." Yes, policies that release to flight ordinary people's dreams are spreading around the world. From Colombia to Turkey to Indonesia, governments are cutting taxes, reviewing their regulations, and opening opportunities for initiative.

There has been much talk in the halls of this building about the "right to development." But more and more the evidence is clear that development is not itself a right. It is the product of rights—the right to own property; the right to buy and sell freely; the right to contract; the right to be free of excessive taxation and regulation, of burdensome government. There have been studies that have determined that countries with low tax rates have greater growth than those with high rates.

We are all familiar with the phenomenon of the "underground economy." The scholar, Hernando de Soto, and his colleagues have examined the situation of one country—Peru—and described an economy of the poor that bypasses crushing taxation and stifling regulation. This "informal economy," as the researchers call it, is the principal supplier of many goods and services, and often the only ladder for upper mobility. In the capital city, it accounts for almost all public transportation and most street markets. And the researchers concluded that, thanks to the informal economy, "the poor can work, travel and have a roof over their heads." They might have added that, by becoming underground entrepreneurs themselves or by working for them, the poor have become less poor and the nation itself richer.

Democracy and Peace

Those who advocate statist solutions to development should take note—the free market is the other path to development and the one true path. It is the people's path. And, unlike many other paths, it leads somewhere. It works. So this is where I believe we can find the map to the world's future—in the hearts of ordinary people; in their hopes for themselves and their children; in their prayers as they lay themselves and their families to rest each night. These simple people are the giants of the Earth, the true builders of the world and shapers of the centuries to come. And if indeed they triumph, as I believe they will, we will at last know a world of democracy—a world in which the spirit of mankind at last conquers the old, familiar enemies of famine, disease, tyranny and war.

This is my vision—America's vision. I recognize that some governments represented in this hall have other ideas. Some do not believe in democracy or in political, economic or religious freedom. Some believe in dictatorship—whether by one man, one party, one class, one race or one vanguard. To those governments I would only say that the price of oppression is clear. Your economies will fall farther and farther behind. Your people will become more restless. Isn't it better to listen to the people's hopes now, rather than their curses later?

And yet, despite our differences, there is one common hope that brought us all to make this common pilgrimage—the hope that mankind will one day beat its swords into plowshares; the hope of peace.

Iran-Iraq War

In no place on Earth today is peace more in need of friends than the Middle East. Its peoples' yearning for peace is growing. The United States will continue to be an active partner in the efforts of the parties to come together to settle their differences and build a just and lasting peace.

And this month marks the beginning of the eighth year of the Iran-Iraq War. Two months ago, the U.N. Security Council adopted a mandatory resolution demanding a cease-fire, withdrawal and negotiations to end the war. The United States fully supports implementation of Resolution 598, as we support the Secretary-General's recent mission. We welcomed Iraq's acceptance of that resolution, and remain disappointed at Iran's unwillingness to accept it.

In that regard, I know that the president of Iran will be addressing you tomorrow. I take this opportunity to call upon him clearly and unequivocally to state whether Iran accepts 598 or not. If the answer is positive, it would be a welcome step and major breakthrough. If it is negative, the Council has no choice but to rapidly adopt enforcement measures.

For 40 years the United States has made clear its vital interest in the security of the Persian Gulf and the countries that border it. The oil reserves there are of strategic importance to the economies of the free world. We are committed to maintaining the free flow of this oil and to preventing the domination of the region by any hostile power.

We do not seek confrontation or trouble with Iran or anyone else. Our objective is now, and has been at every stage, finding a means to end the war with no victor and no vanquished. The increase in our naval presence in the Gulf does not favor one side or the other. It is a response to heightened tensions and followed consultations with our friends in the region. When the tension diminishes, so will our presence.

The United States is gratified by many recent diplomatic developments—the unanimous adoption of Resolution 598, the Arab League's statement at its recent meeting in Tunis, and the Secretary-General's visit. Yet problems remain.

The Soviet Union helped in drafting and reaching an agreement on Resolution 598. But outside the Security Council, the Soviets have acted differently. They called for removal of our Navy from the Gulf, where it has been for 40 years. They made the false accusation that somehow the United States—rather than the war itself—is the source of tension in the Gulf. Such statements are not helpful. They divert attention from the challenge facing us all—a just end to the war.

The United States hopes the Soviets will join the other members of the Security Council in vigorously seeking an end to a conflict that should never have begun, should have ended long ago, and has become one of the great tragedies of the postwar era.

Afghanistan

Elsewhere in the region, we see the continuing Soviet occupation of Afghanistan. After nearly eight years, a million casualties, nearly four million others driven into exile, and more intense fighting than ever— it's time for the Soviet Union to leave.

The Afghan people must have the right to determine their own future free of foreign coercion. There is no excuse for prolonging a brutal war or propping up a regime whose days are clearly numbered. That regime offers political proposals that pretend compromise, but really would ensure the perpetuation of the regime's power. Those proposals have failed the only significant test: they have been rejected by the Afghan people. Every day the resistance grows in strength. It is an indispensable party in the quest for a negotiated solution.

The world community must continue to insist on genuine self-determination; prompt and full Soviet withdrawal; and the return of the refugees to their homes in safety and honor. The attempt may be made to pressure a few countries to change their vote this year, but this body, I know, will vote overwhelmingly, as every year before, for Afghan independence and freedom.

We have noted General Secretary Gorbachev's statement of readiness to withdraw. In April I asked the Soviet Union to set a date this year when this withdrawal would begin. I repeat that request now, in this forum for peace. I pledge that, once the Soviet Union shows convincingly that it's ready for a genuine political settlement, the United States is ready to be helpful.

Let me add one final note on this matter. Pakistan, in the face of enormous pressure and intimidation, has given sanctuary to Afghan refugees. We salute the courage of Pakistan and the Pakistani people. They deserve strong support from all of us.

Nicaragua and Human Rights

Another regional conflict, we all know, is taking place in Central America—in Nicaragua. To the Sandinista delegation here today I say: Your people know the true nature of your regime. They have seen their liberties suppressed. They have seen the promises of 1979 go unfulfilled. They have seen their real wages and personal income fall by half—yes, half—since 1979, while your party elite live lives of privilege and luxury.

This is why, despite $1,000 million in Soviet-bloc aid last year alone, despite the largest and best equipped army in Central America, you face a popular revolution at home. It is why the democratic resistance is able to operate freely deep in your heartland. But this revolution should come as no surprise to you. It is only the revolution you promised the people that you then betrayed.

The goal of U.S. policy towards Nicaragua is simple. It is the goal of the Nicaraguan people and the freedom fighters as well: It is democracy—real, free, pluralistic, constitutional democracy. Understand this: We will not, and the world community will not, accept phony "democratization" designed to mask the perpetuation of dictatorship.

In this 200th year of our own Constitution, we know that real democracy depends on the safeguards of an institutional structure that prevents a concentration of power. It is that which makes rights secure. The temporary relaxation of controls—which can later be tightened—is not democratization.

Again, to the Sandinistas, I say: We continue to hope that Nicaragua will become part of the genuine democratic transformation we have seen throughout Central America in this decade. We applaud the principles embodied in the Guatemala agreement, which links the security of the Central American democracies to democratic reform in Nicaragua. Now is the time for you to shut down the military machine that threatens your neighbors and assaults your own people. You must end your stranglehold on internal political activity. You must hold free and fair national elections. The media must be truly free—not censored or intimidated or crippled by indirect measures like the denial of news or threats against journalists or their families. Exiles must be allowed to return to minister, to live, to work and to organize politically. Then, when persecution of religion has ended, and the jails no longer contain political prisoners, national reconciliation and democracy will be possible. Unless this happens, democratization will be a fraud. And until it happens, we will press for true democracy by supporting those fighting for it.

Freedom in Nicaragua or Angola or Afghanistan or Cambodia or Eastern Europe or South Africa or anyplace else on the globe is not just an internal matter. Some time ago, the Czech dissident writer Vaclav Havel warned the world that "respect for human rights is the fundamental condition and the sole genuine guarantee of true peace." And Andrei Sakharov in his Nobel Lecture said: "I am convinced that international confidence, mutual understanding, disarmament and international security are inconceivable without an open society with freedom of information, freedom of conscience, the right to publish, and the right to travel and choose the country in which one wishes to live."

Progress in U.S.-Soviet Relations

Freedom serves peace. The quest for peace must serve the cause of freedom. Patient diplomacy can contribute to a world in which both can flourish. We are heartened by new prospects for improvement in East-West and particularly U.S.-Soviet relations.

Last week Soviet Foreign Minister Shevardnadze visited Washington for talks with me and with Secretary of State Shultz. We discussed the full range of issues, including my longstanding efforts to achieve, for the first time, deep reductions in U.S. and Soviet nuclear arms. It was six years ago, for example, that I proposed the "zero option" for U.S. and Soviet longer-range, intermediate-range nuclear missiles. I am pleased that we have now agreed in principle to a truly historic treaty that will eliminate an entire class of U.S. and Soviet nuclear weapons. We also agreed to intensify our diplomatic efforts in all areas of mutual interest.

Toward that end, Secretary Shultz and the Foreign Minister will meet again, a month from now, in Moscow, and I will meet again with General Secretary Gorbachev later this fall.

We continue to have our differences and probably always will. But that puts a special responsibility on us to find ways—realistic ways—to bring greater stability to our competition and to show the world a constructive example of the value of communication and of the possibility of peaceful solutions to political problems.

And here let me add that we seek, through our Strategic Defense Initiative (SDI), to find a way to keep the peace through relying on defense—not offense—for deterrence and for eventually rendering ballistic missiles obsolete. SDI has greatly enhanced the prospects for real arms reduction. It is a crucial part of our efforts to ensure a safer world and a more stable strategic balance.

We will continue to pursue the goal of arms reduction, particularly the goal that the General Secretary and I agreed upon—a 50-percent reduction in our respective strategic nuclear arms. We will continue to press the Soviets for more constructive conduct in the settling of regional conflicts. We look to the Soviets to honor the Helsinki Accords. We look for greater freedom for the Soviet peoples within their country, more people-to-people exchanges with our country, and Soviet recognition in practice of the right of freedom of movement.

We look forward to a time when things we now regard as sources of friction and even danger can become examples of cooperation between ourselves and the Soviet Union. For instance, I have proposed a collaboration to reduce the barriers between East and West in Berlin, and more broadly in Europe as a whole. Let us work together for a

Europe in which force or the threat of force, whether in the form of walls or of guns, is no longer an obstacle to free choice by individuals and whole nations. I have also called for more openness in the flow of information from the Soviet Union about its military forces, policies and programs so that our negotiations about arms reduction can proceed with greater confidence.

We hear much about changes in the Soviet Union. We are intensely interested in these changes. We hear the word, *glasnost,* which is translated as "openness" in English. "Openness" is a broad term. It means the free, unfettered flow of information, ideas and people. It means political and intellectual liberty in all its dimensions. We hope, for the sake of the peoples of the U.S.S.R., that such changes will come. And we hope, for the sake of peace, that it will include a foreign policy that respects the freedom and independence of other peoples.

A Universal Ideal

No place should be better suited for discussions of peace than this hall. The first Secretary-General, Trygve Lie, said of the United Nations: "With the danger of fire, and in the absence of an organized fire department, it is only common sense for the neighbors to join in setting up their own fire brigades."

Joining together to drown the flames of war—this, together with a Universal Declaration of Human Rights, was the founding ideal of the United Nations. It is our continuing challenge to ensure that the United Nations lives up to these hopes.

As the Secretary-General noted some time ago, the risk of anarchy in the world has increased because the fundamental rules of the U.N. Charter have been violated. The General Assembly has repeatedly acknowledged this with regard to the occupation of Afghanistan. The Charter has a concrete practical meaning today because it touches on all the dimensions of human aspiration that I mentioned earlier—the yearning for democracy and freedom, for global peace and for prosperity.

This is why we must protect the Universal Declaration of Human Rights from being debased as it was through the infamous "Zionism is Racism" resolution. We cannot permit attempts to control the media and promote censorship under the ruse of a so-called "New World Information Order." We must work against efforts to introduce contentious and nonrelevant issues into the work of the specialized and technical agencies where we seek progress on urgent problems from terrorism to drug trafficking to nuclear proliferation, which threaten us all. Such efforts corrupt the Charter and weaken this organization.

There have been important administrative and budget reforms. They have helped. The United States is committed to restoring its contribution as reforms progress. But there is still much to do. The United Nations was built on great dreams and great ideals. Sometimes it has strayed. It is time for it to come home.

It was Dag Hammarskjold who said, "The end of all political effort must be the well-being of the individual in a life of safety and freedom." Should this not be our credo in the years ahead?

Swords into Plowshares

I have spoken today of a vision and of the obstacles to its realization. More than a century ago a young Frenchman, Alexis de Tocqueville, visited America. After that visit he predicted that the great powers of the future would be, on one hand, the United States, which would be built, as he said, "by the plowshare," and, on the other, Russia, which would go forward, again, as he said, "by the sword." Yet need it be so? Cannot swords be turned to plowshares? Can we and all nations not live in peace?

In our obsession with antagonisms of the moment, we often forget how much unites all the members of humanity. Perhaps we need some outside, universal threat to make us recognize this common bond. I occasionally think how quickly our differences worldwide would vanish if we were facing an alien threat from outside this world. And yet, I ask you, is not an alien force already among us? What could be more alien to the universal aspirations of our peoples than war and the threat of war?

Two centuries ago in Philadelphia, in a hall much smaller than this one, Americans met to draft a Constitution. In the course of their debates, one of them said that the new government, if it was to rise high, must be built on the broadest base, the will and consent of the people. And so it was. And so it has been.

My message today is that dreams of ordinary people reach to astonishing heights. If we diplomatic pilgrims are to achieve equal altitudes, we must build all we do on the full breadth of humanity's will and consent and the full expanse of the human heart.   □

PART III

Defense Policy and Arms Reduction

Forging Real and Lasting Peace

ADDRESS TO THE SECOND SPECIAL SESSION ON DISARMAMENT, UNITED NATIONS GENERAL ASSEMBLY

NEW YORK CITY
JUNE 17, 1982

I speak today as both a citizen of the United States and of the world. I come with the heartfelt wishes of my people for peace, bearing honest proposals, and looking for genuine progress.

Dag Hammarskjold said 24 years ago this month, "We meet in a time of peace which is no peace." His words are as true today as they were then. More than 100 disputes have disturbed the peace among nations since World War II, and today the threat of nuclear disaster hangs over the lives of all our peoples. The Bible tells us there will be a time for peace, but so far this century mankind has failed to find it.

The United Nations is dedicated to world peace, and its Charter clearly prohibits the international use of force. Yet the tide of belligerence continues to rise. The Charter's influence has weakened even in the four years since the first Special Session on Disarmament. We must not only condemn aggression, we must enforce the dictates of our Charter and resume the struggle for peace.

The record of history is clear: Citizens of the United States resort to force reluctantly and only when they must. Our foreign policy, as President Eisenhower once said, "...is not difficult to state. We are for peace, first, last and always, for very simple reasons. We know that it is only in a peaceful atmosphere, a peace with justice, one in which we can be confident, that America can prosper as we have known prosperity in the past."

To those who challenge the truth of those words let me point out that, at the end of World War II, we were the only undamaged industrial power in the world. Our military supremacy was unquestioned. We had harnessed the atom and had the ability to unleash its destructive force anywhere in the world. In short, we could have achieved world domination but that was contrary to the character of our people.

Instead, we wrote a new chapter in the history of mankind. We used our power and wealth to rebuild the war-ravaged economies of the world, both East and West, including those nations who had been our enemies. We took the initiative in creating such international institutions as this United Nations, where leaders of goodwill could come together to build bridges for peace and prosperity.

America has no territorial ambitions, we occupy no countries, and we have built no walls to lock our people in. Our commitment to self-determination, freedom and peace is the very soul of America. That commitment is as strong today as it ever was.

The United States has fought four wars in my lifetime. In each we struggled to defend freedom and democracy. We were never the aggressors. America's strength and, yes, her military power have been a force for peace, not conquest; for democracy, not despotism; for freedom, not tyranny.

Watching, as I have, succeeding generations of American youth bleed their lives onto far-flung battlefields to protect our ideals and secure the rule of law, I have known how important it is to deter conflict. But since coming to the presidency, the enormity of the responsibility of this office has made my commitment even deeper. I believe that responsibility is shared by all of us here today.

On our recent trip to Europe, my wife Nancy told me of a bronze statue, six and a half meters high, that she saw on a cliff on the coast of France. The beach at the base of that cliff is called Saint Laurent, but countless American families have it written in the flyleaf of their Bibles and know it as Omaha Beach. The pastoral quiet of that French countryside is in marked contrast to the bloody violence that took place there on a June day 38 years ago, when the Allies stormed the continent. At the end of just one day of battle, 10,500 Americans were wounded, missing or killed in what became known as the Normandy landing.

The statue atop that cliff is called "The Spirit of American Youth Rising From the Waves." Its image of sacrifice is almost too powerful to describe. The pain of war is still vivid in our national memory. It sends me to this special session of the United Nations eager to comply with the plea of Pope Paul VI when he spoke in this chamber nearly 17 years ago. "If you want to be brothers," His Holiness said, "let the arms fall from your hands."

We Americans yearn to let them go. But we need more than mere words, more than empty promises, before we can proceed. We look around the world and see rampant conflict and aggression. There are many sources of this conflict—expansionist ambitions, local rivalries, the striving to obtain justice and security. We must all work to resolve such discords by peaceful means and to prevent them from escalation.

The Soviet Record

In the nuclear era, the major powers bear a special responsibility to ease these sources of conflict and to refrain from aggression. And that's why we're so deeply concerned by Soviet conduct. Since World War II, the record of tyranny has included Soviet violation of the Yalta agreements leading to domination of Eastern Europe, symbolized by the Berlin Wall—a grim, gray monument to repression that I visited just a week ago. It includes the takeovers of Czechoslovakia, Hungary and Afghanistan, and the ruthless repression of the proud people of Poland. Soviet-sponsored guerrillas and terrorists are at work in Central and South America, in Africa, the Middle East, in the Caribbean, and in Europe, violating human rights and unnerving the world with violence. Communist atrocities in Southeast Asia, Afghanistan and elsewhere continue to shock the free world as refugees escape to tell of their horror.

The decade of so-called detente witnessed the most massive Soviet buildup of military power in history. They increased their defense spending by 40 percent while American defense spending actually declined in the same real terms. Soviet aggression and support for violence around the world have eroded the confidence needed for arms negotiations. While we exercised unilateral restraint, they forged ahead and today possess nuclear and conventional forces far in excess of an adequate deterrent capability.

Soviet oppression is not limited to the countries they invade. At the very time the Soviet Union is trying to manipulate the peace movement in the West, it is stifling a budding peace movement at home. In Moscow, banners are scuttled, buttons are snatched, and demonstrators are arrested when even a few people dare to speak about their fears.

Deeds, Not Words

Eleanor Roosevelt, one of our first ambassadors to this body, reminded us that the high-sounding words of tyrants stand in bleak contradiction to their deeds. "Their promises," she said, "are in deep contrast to their performances."

My countrymen learned a bitter lesson in this century: The scourge of tyranny cannot be stopped with words alone. So we have embarked on an effort to renew our strength that had fallen dangerously low. We refuse to become weaker while potential adversaries remain committed to their imperialist adventures.

My people have sent me here today to speak for them as citizens of the world, which they truly are, for we Americans are drawn from every nationality represented in this chamber today. We understand that men and women of every race and creed can and must work together for peace. We stand ready to take the next steps down the road of cooperation through verifiable arms reduction. Agreements on arms control and disarmament can be useful in reinforcing peace, but they're not magic. We should not confuse the signing of agreements with the solving of problems. Simply collecting agreements will not bring peace. Agreements genuinely reinforce peace only when they are kept. Otherwise we are building a paper castle that will be blown away by the winds of war. Let me repeat, we need deeds, not words, to convince us of Soviet sincerity should they choose to join us on this path.

Since the end of World War II, the United States has been the leader in serious disarmament and arms control proposals.

— In 1946, in what became known as the Baruch Plan, the United States submitted a proposal for control of nuclear weapons and nuclear energy by an international authority. The Soviets rejected this plan.

— In 1955, President Eisenhower made his "Open Skies" proposal, under which the United States and the Soviet Union would have exchanged blueprints of military establishments and provided for aerial reconnaissance. The Soviets rejected this plan.

— In 1963, the Limited Test Ban Treaty came into force. This treaty ended nuclear weapons testing in the atmosphere, outer space or under water by participating nations.

— In 1970, the Treaty on the Nonproliferation of Nuclear Weapons took effect. The United States played a major role in this key effort to prevent the spread of nuclear explosives and to provide for international safeguards on civil nuclear activities. My country remains deeply committed to those objectives today and to strengthening the nonproliferation framework. This is essential to international security.

— In the early 1970s, again at U.S. urging, agreements were reached between the United States and the U.S.S.R. providing for ceilings on some categories of weapons. They could have been more meaningful if Soviet actions had shown restraint and commitment to stability at lower levels of force.

Agenda for Peace

The United Nations designated the 1970s as the First Disarmament Decade, but good intentions were not enough. In reality, that 10-year period included an unprecedented buildup in military weapons and the flaring of aggression and use of force in almost every region of the world. We are now in the Second Disarmament Decade. The task at hand is to assure civilized behavior among nations, to unite behind an agenda for peace.

Over the past seven months, the United States has put forward a broad-based comprehensive series of proposals to reduce the risk of war. We have proposed four major points as an agenda for peace:

1. Elimination of land-based intermediate-range missiles;

2. A one-third reduction in strategic ballistic missile warheads;

3. A substantial reduction in NATO and Warsaw Pact ground and air forces; and

4. New safeguards to reduce the risk of accidental war.

We urge the Soviet Union today to join with us in this quest. We must act not for ourselves alone but for all mankind.

On November 18th of last year, I announced U.S. objectives in arms control agreements: They must be equitable and militarily significant, they must stabilize forces at lower levels, and they must be verifiable.

The United States and its allies have made specific, reasonable and equitable proposals. In February our negotiating team in Geneva offered the Soviet Union a draft treaty on intermediate-range nuclear forces. We offered to cancel deployment of our Pershing II ballistic missiles and ground-launched cruise missiles in exchange for Soviet elimination of their SS-20, SS-4 and SS-5 missiles. This proposal would eliminate with one stroke those systems about which both sides have expressed the greatest concern.

The United States is also looking forward to beginning negotiations on strategic arms reductions with the Soviet Union. We will work hard to make these talks an opportunity for real progress in our quest for peace.

On May 9th, I announced a phased approach to the reduction of strategic arms. In a first phase, the number of ballistic missile warheads on each side would be reduced to about 5,000. No more than half the remaining warheads would be on land-based missiles. All ballistic missiles would be reduced to an equal level at about one-half the current U.S. number.

In the second phase, we would reduce each side's overall destructive power to equal levels, including a mutual ceiling on ballistic missile throw-weight below the current U.S. level. We are also prepared to discuss other elements of the strategic balance.

Before I returned from Europe last week, I met in Bonn with the leaders of the North Atlantic Treaty Organization. We agreed to introduce a major new Western initiative for the Vienna negotiations on mutual and balanced force reductions. Our approach calls for common collective ceilings for both NATO and the Warsaw Treaty Organization. After seven years, there would be a total of 700,000 ground forces and 900,000 ground and air force personnel combined. It also includes a package of associated measures to encourage cooperation and verify compliance.

We urge the Soviet Union and members of the Warsaw Pact to view our Western proposal as a means to reach agreement in Vienna after nine long years of inconclusive talks. We also urge them to implement the 1975 Helsinki Agreement on security and cooperation in Europe.

Let me stress that for agreements to work, both sides must be able to verify compliance. The building of mutual confidence in compliance can only be achieved through greater openness. I encourage the Special Session on Disarmament to endorse the importance of these principles in arms control agreements.

I have instructed our representatives at the 40-nation Committee on Disarmament to renew emphasis on verification and compliance. Based on a U.S. proposal, a committee has been formed to examine these issues as they relate to restrictions on nuclear testing. We are also pressing the need for effective verification provisions in agreements banning chemical weapons.

Chemical and Toxin Weapons

The use of chemical and biological weapons has long been viewed with revulsion by civilized nations. No peace-making institution can ignore the use of these dread weapons and still live up to its mission. The need for a truly effective and verifiable chemical weapons agreement has been highlighted by recent events. The Soviet Union and their allies are violating the Geneva Protocol of 1925, related rules of international law, and the 1972 Biological Weapons Convention. There is conclusive evidence that the Soviet government has provided toxins for use in Laos and Cambodia and are themselves using chemical weapons against freedom fighters in Afghanistan.

We have repeatedly protested to the Soviet government, as well as to the governments of Laos and Vietnam, their use of chemical and toxin weapons. We call upon them now to grant full and free access to their countries or to territories they control so that U.N. experts can conduct an effective, independent investigation to verify cessation of these horrors.

Conference on Military Expenditures

Evidence of noncompliance with existing arms control agreements underscores the need to approach negotiation of any new agreements with care. The democracies of the West are open societies. Information on our defenses is available to our citizens, our elected officials and the world. We do not hesitate to inform potential adversaries of our military forces and ask in return for the same information concerning theirs. The amount and type of military spending by a country are important for the world to know, as a measure of its intensions, and the threat that country may pose to its neighbors. The Soviet Union and other closed societies go to extraordinary lengths to hide their true military spending not only from other nations, but from their own people. This practice contributes to distrust and fear about their intentions.

Today, the United States proposes an international conference on military expenditures to build on the work of this body in developing a common system for accounting and reporting. We urge the Soviet Union, in particular, to join this effort in good faith, to revise the universally discredited official figures it publishes, and to join with us in giving the world a true account of the resources we allocate to our armed forces.

Improved Communications

Last Friday in Berlin, I said that I would leave no stone unturned in the effort to reinforce peace and lessen the risk of war. It's been clear to me that steps should be taken to improve mutual communication and confidence and lessen the likelihood of misinterpretation.

I have, therefore, directed the exploration of ways to increase understanding and communication between the United States and the Soviet Union in times of peace and of crisis. We will approach the Soviet Union with proposals for reciprocal exchanges in such areas as advance notification of major strategic exercises that otherwise might be misinterpreted; advance notification of ICBM (intercontinental ballistic missile) launches within, as well as beyond, national boundaries; and an expanded exchange of strategic forces data.

While substantial information on U.S. activities and forces in these areas already is provided, I believe that jointly and regularly sharing information would represent a qualitative improvement in the strategic nuclear environment and would help reduce the chance of misunderstandings. I call upon the Soviet Union to join the United States in exploring these possibilities to build confidence, and I ask for your support of our efforts.

International Recommitment

One of the major items before this conference is the development of a comprehensive program of disarmament. We support the effort to chart a course of realistic and effective measures in the quest for peace. I have come to this hall to call for international recommitment to the basic tenet of the U.N. Charter—that all members practice tolerance and live together in peace as good neighbors under the rule of law, forsaking armed force as a means of settling disputes between nations. America urges you to support the agenda for peace that I have outlined today. We ask you to reinforce the bilateral and multilateral arms control negotiations between members of NATO and the Warsaw Pact and to rededicate yourselves to maintaining international peace and security and removing threats to peace.

We, who have signed the U.N. Charter, have pledged to refrain from the threat or use of force against the territory or independence of any state. In these times when more and more lawless acts are going unpunished—as some members of this very body show a growing disregard for the U.N. Charter—the peace-loving nations of the world must condemn aggression and pledge again to act in a way that is worthy of the ideals that we have endorsed. Let us finally make the Charter live.

In late spring, 37 years ago, representatives of 50 nations gathered on the other side of this continent, in the San Francisco Opera House. The League of Nations had crumbled and World War II still raged, but those men and nations were determined to find peace. The result was this Charter for peace that is the framework of the United Nations.

President Harry Truman spoke of the revival of an old faith. He said the everlasting moral force of justice prompting that U.N. conference—such a force remains strong in America and in other countries where speech is free and citizens have the right to gather and make their opinions known.

President Truman said, "If we should pay merely lip service to inspiring ideals, and later do violence to simple justice, we would draw down upon us the bitter wrath of generations yet unborn." Those words of Harry Truman have special meaning for us today as we live with the potential to destroy civilization.

"We must learn to live together in peace," he said. "We must build a new world—a far better world."

Peace with Freedom

What a better world it would be if the guns were silent, if neighbor no longer encroached on neighbor, and all peoples were free to reap the rewards of their toil and determine their own destiny and system of government—whatever their choice.

During my recent audience with His Holiness Pope John Paul II, I gave him the pledge of the American people to do everything possible for peace and arms reduction. The American people believe forging real and lasting peace to be their sacred trust.

Let us never forget that such a peace would be a terrible hoax if the world were no longer blessed with freedom and respect for human rights. The United Nations, Hammarskjold said, was born out of the cataclysms of war. It should justify the sacrifices of all those who have died for freedom and justice. "It is our duty to the past," Hammarskjold said, "and it is our duty to the future, so to serve both our nations and the world."

As both patriots of our nations and the hope of all the world, let those of us assembled here in the name of peace deepen our understandings, renew our commitment to the rule of law, and take new and bolder steps to calm an uneasy world. Can any delegate here deny that in so doing he would be doing what the people—the rank and file of his own country or her own country—want him or her to do?

Isn't it time for us to really represent the deepest, most heartfelt yearnings of all of our people? Let no nation abuse this common longing to be free of fear. We must not manipulate our people by playing upon their nightmares; we must serve mankind through genuine disarmament. With God's help we can secure life and freedom for generations to come.   □

Peace is a Goal, not a Policy

**TELEVISED ADDRESS TO THE NATION ON
STRATEGIC ARMS REDUCTION AND NUCLEAR DETERRENCE**

WASHINGTON, D.C.
NOVEMBER 22, 1982

T he week before last was an especially moving one here in Washington. The Vietnam veterans finally came home once and for all to America's heart. They were welcomed with tears, with pride, and with a monument to their great sacrifice.* Many of their names, like those of our Republic's greatest citizens, are now engraved in stone in this city that belongs to all of us. On behalf of the nation, let me again thank the Vietnam veterans from the bottom of my heart for their courageous service to America.

Seeking Peace

Seeing those moving scenes, I know mothers of a new generation must have worried about their children and about peace. And that's what I'd like to talk to you about tonight—the future of our children in a world where peace is made uneasy by the presence of nuclear weapons.

A year ago, I said the time was right to move forward on arms control. I outlined several proposals and said nothing would have a higher priority in this administration. Now, a year later, I want to report on those proposals and on other efforts we're making to ensure the safety of our children's future.

The prevention of conflict and the reduction of weapons are the most important public issues of our time. Yet, on no other issue are there more misconceptions and misunderstandings. You, the American

*Vietnam Veteran's Memorial in Washington, D C

-154-

people, deserve an explanation from your government on what our policy is on these issues. Too often, the experts have been content to discuss grandiose strategies among themselves and cloud the public debate in technicalities no one can understand. The result is that many Americans have become frightened. And let me say, fear of the unknown is entirely understandable. Unfortunately, much of the information emerging in this debate bears little semblance to the facts.

A Look Back

To begin, let's go back to what the world was like at the end of World War II. The United States was the only undamaged industrial power in the world. Our military power was at it peak, and we alone had the atomic weapon. But we didn't use this wealth and this power to bully; we used it to rebuild. We raised up the war-ravaged economies, including the economies of those who had fought against us. At first, the peace of the world was unthreatened because we alone were left with any real power, and we were using it for the good of our fellow man. Any potential enemy was deferred from aggression because the cost would have far outweighed the gain.

As the Soviet's power grew, we still managed to maintain the peace. The United States had established a system of alliances, with NATO as the centerpiece. In addition, we grew even more respected as a world leader with a strong economy and deeply held moral values.

With our commitment to help shape a better world, the United States also pursued—and always pursued—every diplomatic channel for peace. For at least 30 years after World War II, the United States still continued to possess a large military advantage over the Soviet Union. Our strength deterred—that is, prevented—aggression against us.

This nation's military objective has always been to maintain peace by preventing war. This is neither a Democratic nor a Republican policy. It's supported by our allies. And most important of all, it's worked for nearly 40 years.

Deterrence and Reductions

What do we mean when we speak of "nuclear deterrence"? Certainly we don't want such weapons for their own sake. We don't desire excessive forces or what some people have called "overkill." Basically, it's a matter of others knowing that starting a conflict would be more costly to them than anything they might hope to gain. Yes, it is sadly ironic that in these modern times, it still takes weapons to prevent war. I wish it did not.

We desire peace. But peace is a goal, not a policy. Lasting peace is what we hope for at the end of our journey; it doesn't describe the steps we must take nor the paths we should follow to reach the goal.

I intend to search for peace along two parallel paths: deterrence and arms reductions. I believe these are the only paths that offer any real hope for an enduring peace.

I believe that if we follow prudent policies, the risk of nuclear conflict will be reduced. Certainly, the United States will never use its forces except in response to attack. Through the years, Soviet leaders have also expressed a sober view of nuclear war. If we maintain a strong deterrent, they are exceedingly unlikely to launch an attack.

Soviet Military Buildup

Now, while the policy of deterrence has stood the test of time, the things we must do in order to maintain deterrence have changed. You often hear that the United States and the Soviet Union are in an arms race. Well, the truth is that while the Soviet Union has raced, we have not....In constant dollars, our defense spending in the 1960s went up because of Vietnam. And then it went downward through much of the 1970s....Soviet spending (has) gone up and up and up. In spite of a stagnating Soviet economy, Soviet leaders invest 12 to 14 percent of their country's gross national product in military spending—two to three times the level we invest.

I might add that the defense share of our United States federal budget has gone way down, too....In 1962, when John Kennedy was President, 46 percent, almost half of the federal budget, went to our national defense. In recent years, about one quarter of our budget has gone to defense, while the share for social programs has nearly doubled. And most of our defense budget is spent on people, not weapons.

The combination of the Soviets spending more and the United States spending proportionately less changed the military balance and weakened our deterrent. Today, in virtually every measure of military power, the Soviet Union enjoys a decided advantage.

[With regard to] the total number of intercontinental missiles and bombers, in 1962 and in 1972, the United States forces remained about the same—even dropping some by 1982. But consider the Soviet side. In 1962, at the time of the Cuban missile crisis, the Soviets could not compare with us in terms of strength. In 1972, when we signed the SALT I treaty, we were nearly equal. But in 1982 [we are not].

I could show you chart after chart where there's a great deal of Soviet [growth] compared to the U.S. For example, the Soviet Union has deployed a third more land-based intercontinental ballistic missiles than we have. Believe it or not, we froze our number in 1965 and have deployed no additional missiles since then.

The Soviet Union put to sea 60 new ballistic missile submarines in the last 15 years. Until last year, we hadn't commissioned one in that same period.

The Soviet Union has built over 200 modern Backfire bombers and is building 30 more a year. For 20 years, the United States has deployed no new strategic bombers. Many of our B-52 bombers are now older than the pilots who fly them.

The Soviet Union now has 600 of the missiles considered most threatening by both sides—the intermediate-range missiles based on land. We have none. The United States withdrew its intermediate-range, land-based missiles from Europe almost 20 years ago.

The world has also witnessed unprecedented growth in the area of Soviet conventional forces. The Soviets far exceed us in the number of tanks, artillery pieces, aircraft and ships they produce every year. What is more, when I arrived in this office, I learned that in our own forces we had planes that couldn't fly and ships that couldn't leave port mainly for lack of spare parts and crew members.

Modernization

The Soviet military buildup must not be ignored. We've recognized the problem and, together with our allies, we've begun to correct the imbalance. [Let's look at]...projected real defense spending for the next several years.... Let us assume the Soviets' rate of spending remains at the level they've followed since the 1960s.... If my defense proposals are passed, it will still take five years before we come close to the Soviet level. Yet, the modernization of our strategic and conventional forces will assure that deterrence works and peace prevails.

Our deployed nuclear forces were built before the age of micro-circuits. It's not right to ask our young men and women in uniform to maintain and operate such antiques. Many have already given their lives to missile explosions and aircraft accidents caused by the old age of their equipment. We must replace and modernize our forces, and that's why I decided to proceed with the production and deployment of the new ICBM (intercontinental ballistic missile) known as the MX.

Three earlier Presidents worked to develop this missile. Based on the best advice that I could get, I concluded that the MX is the right missile at the right time. On the other hand, when I arrived in office I felt the proposal on where and how to base the missile simply cost too much in terms of money and the impact on our citizens' lives. I've concluded, however, it's absolutely essential that we proceed to produce this missile and that we base it in a series of closely based silos at Warren Air Force Base, near Cheyenne, Wyoming.

This plan requires only half as many missiles as the earlier plan and will fit in an area of only 5,180 hectares. It is the product of around-the-clock research that has been underway since I directed a search for a better, cheaper way. I urge the members of Congress who must pass this plan to listen and examine the facts before they come to their own conclusion.

Some may question what modernizing our military has to do with peace. Well, as I explained earlier, a secure force keeps others from threatening us, and that keeps the peace. Just as important, it also increases the prospects of reaching significant arms reductions with the Soviets, and that's what we really want.

Incentives to Negotiate

The United States wants deep cuts in the world's arsenal of weapons, but unless we demonstrate the will to rebuild our strength and restore the military balance, the Soviets—since they're so far ahead—have little incentive to negotiate with us. Let me repeat that point because it goes to the heart of our policies. Unless we demonstrate the will to rebuild our strength, the Soviets have little incentive to negotiate. If we hadn't begun to modernize, the Soviet negotiators would know we had nothing to bargain with except talk. They would know we were bluffing without a good hand because they know what cards we hold just as we know what's in their hand.

You may recall that in 1969 the Soviets didn't want to negotiate a treaty banning antiballistic missiles. It was only after our Senate narrowly voted to fund an antiballistic missile program that the Soviets agreed to negotiate. We then reached an agreement. We also know that one-sided arms control doesn't work. We've tried time and time again to set an example by cutting our own forces in the hope that the Soviets would do likewise. The result has always been that they keep building.

I believe our strategy for peace will succeed. Never before has the United States proposed such a comprehensive program of nuclear arms control. Never in our history have we engaged in so many negotiations with the Soviets to reduce nuclear arms and to find a stable peace. What we are saying to them is this: We will modernize our military in order to keep the balance for peace, but wouldn't it be better if we both simply reduced our arsenals to a much lower level?

Intermediate-Range Nuclear Forces

Let me begin with the negotiations on the intermediate-range nuclear forces (INF) that are currently underway in Geneva. As I said earlier, the most threatening of these forces are the land-based missiles which the Soviet Union now has aimed at Europe, the Middle East and Asia.

In 1972 there were 600 warheads on these Soviet missiles. The United States was at zero. In 1977 there [still] were 600. The United States was still at zero. Then the Soviets began deploying powerful new missiles with three warheads and a reach of thousands of miles—the SS-20. Since then, the number has gone through the roof—the Soviets have added a missile with three warheads every week. Still, no United States warheads. Although the Soviet leaders earlier this year declared they'd frozen deployment of this dangerous missile, they have in fact continued deployment.

Last year, on November 18th, I proposed the total, global elimination of all these missiles. I proposed that the United States would deploy no comparable missiles, which are scheduled for late 1983, if the Soviet Union would dismantle theirs. We would follow agreement on the land-based missiles with limits on other intermediate-range systems.

The European governments strongly support our initiative. The Soviet Union has thus far shown little inclination to take this major step to zero levels. Yet I believe and I'm hoping that as the talks proceed and as we approach the scheduled placement of our new systems in Europe, the Soviet leaders will see the benefits of such a far-reaching agreement.

Strategic Arms Reductions

This summer we also began negotiations on strategic arms reductions, the proposal we call START. Here we're talking about intercontinental missiles, the weapons with a longer range than the intermediate-range ones I was just discussing. We're negotiating on the basis of deep reductions. I proposed in May that we cut the number of warheads on these missiles to an equal number, roughly one-third below current levels. I also proposed that we cut the number of missiles themselves to an equal number, about half the current U.S. level. Our proposals would eliminate some 4,700 warheads and some 2,250 missiles. I think that would be quite a service to mankind....

We intend to convince the Soviets it would be in their own best interest to reduce these missiles. Consider the reduced numbers both sides would have under our proposal—quite a dramatic change. We also seek to reduce the total destructive power of these missiles and other elements of United States and Soviet strategic forces.

In 1977, when the last administration proposed more limited reductions, the Soviet Union refused even to discuss them. This time their reaction has been quite different. Their opening position is a serious one and, even though it doesn't meet our objective of deep reductions, there's no question we're heading in the right direction. One reason for this change is clear: The Soviet Union knows that we are now serious about our own strategic programs and that they must be prepared to negotiate in earnest.

Conventional Arms

We also have other important arms control efforts underway. In the talks in Vienna on mutual and balanced force reductions, we've proposed cuts in military personnel to a far lower and equal level. And in the 40-nation Committee on Disarmament in Geneva, we're working to develop effective limitations on nuclear testing and chemical weapons. The whole world remains outraged by the Soviets and their allies use of biological and chemical weapons against defenseless people in Afghanistan, Cambodia and Laos. This experience makes ironclad verification all the more essential for arms control.

There is, of course, much more that needs to be done. In an age when intercontinental missiles can span half the globe in less than half an hour, it's crucial that Soviet and American leaders have a clear understanding of each other's capabilities and intentions.

Last June in Berlin, and again at the United Nations Special Session on Disarmament, I vowed that the United States would make every effort to reduce the risks of accident and misunderstanding and, thus, to strengthen mutual confidence between the United States and the Soviet Union. Since then, we've been actively studying detailed measures to implement this Berlin initiative.

Today I would like to announce some of the measures which I've proposed in a special letter just sent to the Soviet leadership and which I've instructed our ambassadors in Geneva to discuss with their Soviet counterparts. They include, but also go beyond, some of the suggestions I made in Berlin.

The first of these measures involves advance notification of all United States and Soviet test launches of intercontinental ballistic missiles. We will also seek Soviet agreement on notification of all sea-launched ballistic missiles as well as intermediate-range, land-based ballistic missiles of the type we're currently negotiating. This would remove surprise and uncertainty at the sudden appearance of such missiles on the warning screens of the two countries.

In another area of potential misunderstanding, we propose to the Soviets that we provide each other with advance notification of our major military exercises. Here again, our objective is to reduce the surprise and uncertainty surrounding otherwise sudden moves by either side.

These sorts of measures are designed to deal with the immediate issues of miscalculation in time of crisis. But there are deeper, longer-term problems as well. In order to clear away some of the mutual ignorance and suspicion between our two countries, I will propose that we both engage in a broad-ranging exchange of basic data about our nuclear forces. I am instructing our ambassadors at the negotiations on both strategic and intermediate forces to seek Soviet agreement on an expanded exchange of information. The more one side knows about what the other side is doing, the less room there is for surprise and miscalculation.

Probably everyone has heard of the so-called Hotline, which enables me to communicate directly with the Soviet leadership in the event of a crisis. The existing Hotline is dependable and rapid, with both ground and satellite links. But because it's so important, I've also directed that we carefully examine any possible improvements to the existing Hotline system.

Now, although we've begun negotiations on these many proposals, this doesn't mean we've exhausted all the initiatives that could help to reduce the risk of accidental conflict. We'll leave no opportunity unexplored, and we'll consult closely with... members of the Congress who've made important suggestions in this field.

We're also making strenuous efforts to prevent the spread of nuclear weapons to additional countries. It would be tragic if we succeeded in reducing existing arsenals only to have new threats emerge in other areas of the world.

Earlier, I spoke of America's contributions to peace following World War II, of all we did to promote peace and prosperity for our fellow man. Well, we're still those same people. We still seek peace above all else.

I want to remind our own citizens and those around the world of this tradition of American good will because I am concerned about the effects the nuclear fear is having on our people. The most upsetting letters I receive are from schoolchildren who write to me as a class assignment. It's evident they've discussed the most nightmarish aspects of a nuclear holocaust in their classrooms. Their letters are often full of terror. Well, this should not be so.

The philosopher Spinoza said, "Peace is a virtue, a state of mind, a disposition for benevolence, confidence, justice." Well, those are the qualities we want our children to inherit, not fear. They must grow up confident if they're to meet the challenges of tomorrow as we will meet the challenges of today.

I began these remarks speaking of our children. I want to close on the same theme. Our children should not grow up frightened. They should not fear the future. We're working to make it peaceful and free. I believe their future can be the brightest, most exciting of any generation. We must reassure them and let them know that their parents and the leaders of this world are seeking, above all else, to keep them safe and at peace. I consider this to be a sacred trust.

My fellow Americans, on this Thanksgiving holiday, when we have so much to be grateful for, let us give special thanks for our peace, our freedom and our good people.

I've always believed that this land was set aside in an uncommon way, that a Divine plan placed this great continent between the oceans to be found by a people from every corner of the Earth who had a special love of faith, freedom and peace.

Let us reaffirm America's destiny of goodness and good will. Let us work for peace and, as we do, let us remember the lines of the famous old hymn: "O God of Love, O King of Peace, make wars throughout the world to cease." □

The Only Guarantee of Peace and Freedom is Strength

TELEVISED ADDRESS TO THE NATION ON NATIONAL SECURITY

WASHINGTON, D.C.
FEBRUARY 26, 1986

I want to speak to you this evening about my highest duty as President: to preserve peace and defend these United States.

But before I do, let me take a moment to speak about the situation in the Philippines. We've just seen a stirring demonstration of what men and women committed to democratic ideas can achieve. The remarkable people of those 7,000 islands joined together with faith in the same principles on which America was founded: that men and women have the right to freely choose their own destiny. Despite a flawed election, the Filipino people were understood. They carried their message peacefully, and they were heard across their country and across the world.

We salute the remarkable restraint shown by both sides to prevent bloodshed during these last tense days. Our hearts and hands are with President Aquino and her new government as they set out to meet the challenges ahead. Today the Filipino people celebrate the triumph of democracy and the world celebrates with them.

Concern for Security

One cannot sit in this office reviewing intelligence on the military threat we face, making decisions from arms control to Libya to the Philippines, without having that concern for America's security weigh constantly on your mind.

We know that peace is the condition under which mankind was meant to flourish. Yet peace does not exist of its own will. It depends on us, on our courage to build it and guard it and pass it on to future generations. George Washington's words may seem hard and cold today, but history has proven him right again and again. "To be prepared for war," he said, "is one of the most effective means of preserving peace." Well, to those who think strength provokes conflict, Will Rogers* had his own answer. He said of the world heavyweight champion of his day: "I've never seen anyone insult Jack Dempsey."

The past five years have shown that American strength is once again a sheltering arm for freedom in a dangerous world. Strength is the most persuasive argument we have to convince our adversaries to negotiate seriously and to cease bullying other nations.

But tonight the security program that you and I launched to restore America's strength is in jeopardy, threatened by those who would quit before the job is done. Any slackening now would invite the very dangers America must avoid and could fatally compromise our negotiating position. Our adversaries, the Soviets—we know from painful experience—respect only nations that negotiate from a position of strength. American power is the indispensable element of a peaceful world; it is America's last, best hope of negotiating real reductions in nuclear arms. Just as we are sitting down at the bargaining table with the Soviet Union, let's not throw America's trump card away.

America in the '70s

We need to remember where America was five years ago. We need to recall the atmosphere of that time: the anxiety that events were out of control, that the West was in decline, that our enemies were on the march.

It was not just the Iranian hostage crisis or the Soviet invasion of Afghanistan, but the fear felt by many of our friends that America could not, or would not, keep her commitments. Pakistan, the country most threatened by the Afghan invasion, ridiculed the first offer of American aid as "peanuts." Other nations were saying that it was dangerous—deadly dangerous—to be a friend of the United States.

It was not just years of declining defense spending, but a crisis in recruitment and retention—and the outright cancellation of programs vital to our security. The Pentagon horror stories at the time were about ships that couldn't sail, planes that couldn't fly for lack of spare parts and army divisions unprepared to fight.

It was not just a one-sided arms agreement that made it easy for one side to cheat, but a treaty that actually permitted increases in nucle-

*1879-1935 American humorist

-163-

ar arsenals. Even supporters of SALT II were demoralized, saying, "Well, the Soviets just won't agree to anything better." And when President Carter had to abandon the treaty because Senate leaders of his own party wouldn't support it, the United States was left without a national strategy for control of nuclear weapons.

We knew immediate changes had to be made. So, here's what we did: We set out to show that the long string of governments falling under communist domination was going to end, and we're doing it.

In the 1970s one strategic country after another fell under the domination of the Soviet Union. The fall of Laos, Cambodia and South Vietnam gave the Soviet Union a strategic position on the South China Sea. The invasion of Afghanistan cut nearly in half Soviet flying time to the Persian Gulf. Communist takeovers in South Yemen and Ethiopia put the Soviets astride the Red Sea, entryway to the Suez Canal. Pro-Soviet regimes in Mozambique and Angola strengthened the Soviet position in southern Africa. And finally, Grenada and Nicaragua gave Moscow two new beachheads right on the doorstep of the United States.

Halting the Communist Advance

In these last five years, not one square inch of territory has been lost, and Grenada has been set free. When we arrived in 1981, guerrillas in El Salvador had launched what they called their final offensive to make that nation the second communist state on the mainland of North America. Many people said the situation was hopeless; they refused to help. We didn't agree; we did help. And today those guerrillas are in retreat. El Salvador is a democracy, and freedom fighters are challenging communist regimes in Nicaragua, Afghanistan, Angola, Cambodia and Ethiopia.

We set out to show that the Western Alliance could meet its security needs, despite Soviet intimidation, and we're doing it. Many said that to try to counter the Soviet SS-20 missiles would split NATO because Europe no longer believed in defending itself. Well, that was nonsense. Today Pershing and cruise missile deployments are on schedule, and our allies support the decision.

We set out to reverse the decline in morale in our armed forces, and we're doing it. Pride in our armed forces has been restored. More qualified men and women want to join and remain in the military. In 1980 about half of our Army's recruits were high school graduates; last year 91 percent had high school diplomas.

Our armed forces may be smaller in size than in the 1950s, but they're some of the finest young people this country has ever produced. And as long as I'm President, they'll get the quality equipment they need to carry out their mission.

We set out to narrow the growing gaps in our strategic deterrent, and we're beginning to do that. Our modernization program—the MX [missile], the Trident submarine, the B-1 and Stealth bombers—represents the first significant improvement in America's strategic deterrent in 20 years.

Those who speak so often about the so-called arms race ignore a central fact: In the decade before 1981, the Soviets were the only ones racing.

Controlling Defense Costs

During my 1980 campaign, I called federal waste and fraud a national scandal. We knew we could never rebuild America's strength without first controlling the exploding cost of defense programs, and we're doing it. When we took office in 1981, costs had been escalating at an annual rate of 14 percent. Then we began our reforms. And in the last two years, cost increases have fallen to less than one percent. We've made huge savings. Each F-18 fighter costs nearly four million dollars less today than in 1981. One of our air-to-air missiles costs barely half as much.

Getting control of the defense bureaucracy is no small task. Each year the Defense Department signs hundreds of thousands of contracts. So, yes a horror story will sometimes turn up despite our best efforts. That's why we appointed the first Inspector General in the history of the Defense Department. And virtually every case of fraud or abuse has been uncovered by our Defense Department, our Inspector General. Secretary Weinberger should be praised, not pilloried, for cleaning the skeletons out of the closet. As for those few who have cheated taxpayers or have swindled our armed forces with faulty equipment, they are thieves stealing from the arsenal of democracy, and they will be prosecuted to the fullest extent of the law.

Nuclear Arms Reduction

Finally, we set out to reduce the danger of nuclear war. Here, too, we're achieving what some said couldn't be done. We've put forth a plan for deep reductions in nuclear systems. We're pushing forward our highly promising Strategic Defense Initiative, a security shield that may one day protect us and our allies from nuclear attack, whether launched by deliberate calculation, freak accident or the isolated impulse of a madman. Isn't it better to use our talents and technology to build systems that destroy missiles, not people?

Our message has gotten through. The Soviets used to contend that real reductions in nuclear missiles were out of the question. Now they say they accept the idea. Well, we shall see. Just this week, our negotiators presented a new plan for the elimination of intermediate-range nuclear missiles, and we're pressing the Soviets for cuts in other offensive forces as well. One thing is certain: If the Soviets truly want fair and verifiable agreements that reduce nuclear forces, we will have those agreements.

Our defense programs five years ago were immense, and drastic action was required. Even my predecessor in this office recognized that and projected sizable increases in defense spending. And I'm proud of what we've done.

The Price of Strength

Now the biggest increases in defense spending are behind us. And that's why last summer I agreed with Congress to freeze defense funding for one year and after that to resume a modest three-percent annual growth. Frankly, I hesitated to reach this agreement on a freeze because we still have far too much to do. But I thought that congressional support for steady increases over several years was a step forward.

But this didn't happen. Instead of a freeze, there was sharp cut, a cut of over five percent. And some are now saying that we need to chop another 20, 30, or even $50,000 million out of national defense.

This is reckless, dangerous and wrong. It's backsliding of the most irresponsible kind, and you need to know about it. You, after all, paid the bill for all we've accomplished these past five years. But we still have a way to go. Millions of Americans actually believe that we are now superior to the Soviet Union in military power. Well, I'm sorry, but if our country's going to have a useful debate on national security, we have to get beyond the drumbeat of propaganda and get the facts on the table.

Over the next few months, you'll be hearing this debate. I'd like you to keep in mind the two simple reasons not to cut defense now. One, it's not cheap. Two, it's not safe. If we listen to those who would abandon our defense program, we will not only jeopardize negotiations with the Soviet Union; we may put peace itself at risk.

I said it wouldn't be cheap to cut. How can cutting not be cheap? Well, simple. We tried that in the '70s, and the result was waste, enormous waste—hundreds of millions of dollars lost because the cost of each plane and tank and ship went up, often, way up. The old shoppers' adage proved true: They are cheaper by the dozen.

Arbitrary cuts only bring phony savings, but there's a more important reason not to abandon our defense program. It's not safe.

The Soviet Threat

Almost 25 years ago, when John Kennedy occupied this office during the Cuban missile crisis, he commanded the greatest military power on Earth. Today we Americans must live with a dangerous new reality. Year in and year out, at the expense of its own people, the Soviet leadership has been making a relentless effort to gain military superiority over the United States.

Between 1970 and 1985 alone, the Soviets invested $500,000 million more than the United States in defense and built nearly three times as many strategic missiles. As a consequence of their enormous weapons investment, major military imbalances still exist between our two countries.

Today the Soviet Union has deployed over one-and-a-half times as many combat aircraft as the United States, over two-and-a-half times as many submarines, over five times as many tanks, and over 11 times as many artillery pieces.

We have begun to close some of these gaps, but if we're to regain our margins of safety, more must be done. Where the Soviets once relied on numbers alone, they now strive for both quantity and quality. We anticipate that over the next five years they will deploy on the order of 40 nuclear submarines, 500 new ballistic missiles and 18,000 modern tanks. My five-year defense budget maintains our commitment to America's rebuilding program. And I'm grateful that Secretary Weinberger is here to fight for that program with all the determination and ability he has shown in the past.

But my budget does not call for matching these Soviet increases. So one question must be asked: Can we really afford to do less than what I've proposed?

Today we spend a third less of our gross national product on defense than under John Kennedy, yet some in Congress talk of even deeper cuts. Barely six percent of our nation's gross national product—that's all we invest to keep America free, secure and at peace. The Soviets invest more than twice as much. But now strip away spending on salaries, housing, dependents, and the like and compare. The United States invests on actual weapons and research only 2.6 percent of our gross national product, while the Soviet Union invests 11 percent on weapons, more than four times as much. This is the hard, cold reality of our defense deficit.

But it's not just the immense Soviet arsenal that puts us on our guard. The record of Soviet behavior, the long history of Soviet brutality toward those who are weaker, remind us that the only guarantee of peace and freedom is our military strength and our national will. The peoples of Afghanistan and Poland, of Czechoslovakia and Cuba, and so many other captive countries—they understand this.

Some argue that our dialogue with the Soviets means we can treat defense more casually. Nothing could be farther from the truth. It was our seriousness about defense that created the climate in which serious talks could finally begin.

Now that the Soviets are back at the table, we must not undercut our negotiators. Unfortunately, that's exactly what some members of Congress have done. By banning any U.S. tests of antisatellite systems, Congress not only protected a Soviet monopoly, it unilaterally granted the Soviets a concession they could not win at the bargaining table.

Innovation

So, our defense program must rest on these principles. First, we must be smart about what we build. We don't have to copy everything the Soviets do. We don't have to compete on Soviet terms. Our job is to provide for our security by using the strengths of our free society. If we think smart enough, we don't have to think quite so big. We don't have to do the job with large numbers and brute force.

We don't have to increase the size of our forces from two million to their five million as long as our military men and women have the quality tools they need to keep the peace. We don't have to have as many tanks as the Soviets as long as we have sophisticated antitank weapons.

Innovation is our advantage. One example: Advances in making airplanes and cruise missiles almost invisible to Soviet radar could neutralize the vast air defense systems upon which the Soviets and some of their most dangerous client states depend.

But innovation is not enough. We have to follow through. Blueprints alone don't deter aggression. We have to translate our lead in the lab to a lead in the field. But when our budget is cut, we can't do either.

Security Assistance

Second, our security assistance provides as much security for the dollar as our own defense budget. Our friends can perform many tasks more cheaply than we can. And that's why I can't understand proposals in Congress to sharply slash this vital tool. Military assistance to friends in strategic regions strengthens those who share our values and interests. And when they are strong, we're strengthened. It is in our interest to help them meet threats that could ultimately bring harm to us as well.

Third, where defense reform is needed, we will pursue it. The Packard Commission we created will be reporting in two days. We hope they will have ideas for new approaches that give us even better ways to buy our weapons. We're eager for good ideas, for new ideas—America's special genius. Wherever the Commission's recommendations point the way to greater executive effectiveness, I will implement them, even if they run counter to the will of the entrenched bureaucracies and special interests. I will also urge Congress to heed the Commission's report and to remove those obstacles to good management that Congress itself has created over the years.

Reducing the Need for Nuclear Weapons

The fourth element of our strategy for the future is to reduce America's dependence on nuclear weapons.

You've heard me talk about our Strategic Defense Initiative (SDI), the program that could one day free us all from the prison of nuclear terror. It would be pure folly for the United States not to press forward with SDI when the Soviets have already invested up to 20 years on their own program. Let us not forget that the only operational missile defense in the world today guards the capital of the Soviet Union, not the United States.

But while SDI offers hope for the future, we have to consider today's world. For too long, we and our allies have permitted nuclear weapons to be a crutch, a way of not having to face up to real defense needs. We must free ourselves from that crutch. Our goal should be to deter and, if necessary, to repel any aggression without a resort to nuclear arms.

Here again, technology can provide us with the means not only to respond to full scale aggression but to strike back at terrorists without harming innocent civilians.

Today's technology makes it possible to destroy a tank column up to 190 kilometers away without using atomic weapons. This technology may be the first cost-effective conventional defense in postwar history against the giant Red army. When we fail to equip our troops with these modernized systems, we only increase the risk that we may one day have to resort to nuclear weapons.

These are the practical decisions we make when we send a defense budget to Congress. Each generation has to live with the challenges history delivers, and we can't cope with these challenges by evasion.

Building a Secure Peace

If we sustain our efforts now, we have the best chance in decades of building a secure peace. That's why I met with General Secretary Gorbachev last year, and that's why we're talking to the Soviets today, bargaining—if Congress will support us—from strength.

We want to make this a more peaceful world. We want to reduce arms. We want agreements that truly diminish the nuclear danger. We don't just want signing ceremonies and color photographs of leaders toasting each other with champagne. We want more. We want real agreements, agreements that really work, with no cheating. We want an end to state policies of intimidation, threats and the constant quest for domination. We want real peace.

I will never ask for what isn't needed; I will never fight for what isn't necessary. But I need your help.

We've come so far together these last five years; let's not falter now. Let's maintain that crucial level of national strength, unity and purpose that has brought the Soviet Union to the negotiating table and has given us this historic opportunity to achieve real reductions in nuclear weapons and a real chance at lasting peace. That would be the finest legacy we could leave behind for our children and for their children. □

PART IV

The
United States
and
Europe

To Foster the Infrastructure of Democracy

ADDRESS TO THE BRITISH PARLIAMENT

LONDON
JUNE 8, 1982

The journey of which this visit forms a part is a long one. Already it has taken me to two great cities of the West, Rome and Paris, and to the Economic Summit at Versailles. And there, once again, our sister democracies have proved that even in a time of severe economic strain, free peoples can work together freely and voluntarily to address problems as serious as inflation, unemployment, trade and economic development in a spirit of cooperation and solidarity.

Other milestones lie ahead. Later this week, in Germany, we and our NATO allies will discuss measures for our joint defense and America's latest initiatives for a more peaceful, secure world through arms reductions.

Democracy and Oppression

Each stop of this trip is important, but among them all, this moment occupies a special place in my heart and in the hearts of my country-men—a moment of kinship and homecoming in these hallowed halls. Speaking for all Americans, I want to say how very much at home we feel in your house. Every American would, because this is one of democracy's shrines. Here the rights of free people and the processes of repre-sentation have been debated and refined.

It has been said that an institution is the lengthening shadow of a man. This institution is the lengthening shadow of all the men and women who have sat here, and all those who have voted to send representatives here.

This is my second visit to Great Britain as President of the United States. My first opportunity to stand on British soil occurred almost a year-and-a-half ago, when your Prime Minister graciously hosted a diplomatic dinner at the British Embassy in Washington. Mrs. Thatcher said then that she hoped I was not distressed to find, staring down at me from the grand staircase, a portrait of His Royal Majesty, King George III. She suggested it was best to let bygones be bygones, and, in view of our two countries' remarkable friendship in succeeding years, she added that most Englishmen today would agree with Thomas Jefferson that "a little rebellion now and then is a very good thing."

From here I will go to Bonn and then Berlin, where there stands a grim symbol of power untamed. The Berlin Wall, that dreadful gray gash across the city, is in its third decade. It is the fitting signature of the regime that built it.

And a few hundred kilometers behind the Berlin Wall, there is another symbol. In the center of Warsaw, there is a sign that notes the distances to two capitals. In one direction it points toward Moscow. In the other it points toward Brussels, headquarters of Western Europe's tangible unity. The marker says that the distances from Warsaw to Moscow and Warsaw to Brussels are equal. The sign makes this point: Poland is not East or West. Poland is at the center of European civilization. It has contributed mightily to that civilization. It is doing so today by being magnificently unreconciled to oppression.

Poland's struggle to be Poland and to secure the basic rights we often take for granted demonstrates why we dare not take those rights for granted. Gladstone*, defending the Reform Bill of 1866, declared, "You cannot fight against the future. Time is on our side." It was easier to believe in the march of democracy in Gladstone's day—in that high noon of Victorian optimism.

We're approaching the end of a bloody century plagued by a terrible political invention—totalitarianism. Optimism comes less easily today, not because democracy is less vigorous, but because democracy's enemies have refined their instruments of repression. Yet optimism is in order, because day by day democracy is proving itself to be a not-at-all fragile flower. From Stettin on the Baltic to Varna on the Black Sea, the regimes planted by totalitarianism have had more than 30 years to establish their legitimacy. But none—not one regime—has yet been able to risk free elections. Regimes planted by bayonets do not take root.

The strength of the Solidarity movement in Poland demonstrates the truth told in an underground joke in the Soviet Union. It is that the Soviet Union would remain a one-party nation even if an opposition party were permitted, because everyone would join the opposition party.

*1809-1898 Leading British statesman

America's time as a player on the stage of world history has been brief. I think understanding this fact has always made you [the British] patient with your younger cousins—well, not always patient. Sir Winston Churchill said in exasperation about one of our diplomats: "He is the only case I know of a bull who carries his china shop with him."

But witty as Sir Winston was, he also had that special attribute of great statesmen—the gift of vision, the willingness to see the future based on the experience of the past. It is this sense of history, this understanding of the past that I want to talk with you about today, for it is in remembering what we share of the past that our two nations can make common cause for the future.

Threats to Freedom

We have not inherited an easy world. If developments like the Industrial Revolution, which began in England, and the gifts of science and technology have made life much easier for us, they have also made it more dangerous. There are threats now to our freedom, indeed to our very existence, that other generations could never even have imagined.

There is first the threat of global war. No president, no congress, no prime minister, no parliament can spend a day entirely free of this threat. And I don't have to tell you that in today's world the existence of nuclear weapons could mean, if not the extinction of mankind, then surely the end of civilization as we know it. That's why negotiations on intermediate-range nuclear forces now underway in Europe and the START talks—Strategic Arms Reduction Talks—which will begin later this month, are not just critical to American or Western policy; they are critical to mankind. Our commitment to early success in these negotiations is firm and unshakable, and our purpose is clear: reducing the risk of war by reducing the means of waging war on both sides.

At the same time there is a threat posed to human freedom by the enormous power of the modern state. History teaches the dangers of government that overreaches—political control taking precedence over free economic growth, secret police, mindless bureaucracy, all combining to stifle individual excellence and personal freedom.

Now I'm aware that among us here, and throughout Europe, there is legitimate disagreement over the extent to which the public sector should play a role in a nation's economy and life. But on one point all of us are united—our abhorrence of dictatorship in all its forms, but most particularly totalitarianism and the terrible inhumanities it has caused in our time—the great purge, Auschwitz and Dachau, the Gulag and Cambodia.

Historians looking back at our time will note the consistent restraint and peaceful intentions of the West. They will note that it was the democracies who refused to use the threat of their nuclear monopoly in the 1940s and 1950s for territorial or imperial gain. Had that nuclear monopoly been in the hands of the communist world, the map of Europe—indeed, the world—would look very different today. And certainly they will note it was not the democracies that invaded Afghanistan or suppressed Polish Solidarity or used chemical and toxin warfare in Afghanistan and Southeast Asia.

Lessons of History

If history teaches anything, it teaches self-delusion in the face of unpleasant facts is folly. We see around us today the marks of our terrible dilemma—predictions of doomsday, antinuclear demonstrations, an arms race in which the West must, for its own protection, be an unwilling participant. At the same time, we see totalitarian forces in the world who seek subversion and conflict around the globe to further their barbarous assault on the human spirit. What, then, is our course? Must civilization perish in a hail of fiery atoms? Must freedom wither in a quiet, deadening accommodation with totalitarian evil?

Sir Winston Churchill refused to accept the inevitability of war or even that it was imminent. He said, "I do not believe that Soviet Russia desires war. What they desire is the fruits of war and the indefinite expansion of their power and doctrines. But what we have to consider here today, while time remains, is the permanent prevention of war and the establishment of conditions of freedom and democracy as rapidly as possible in all countries."

Well, this is precisely our mission today: to preserve freedom as well as peace. It may not be easy to see; but I believe we live now at a turning point.

Rejection of Collectivism

In an ironic sense Karl Marx was right. We are witnessing today a great revolutionary crisis where the demands of the economic order are conflicting directly with those of the political order. But the crisis is happening not in the free, non-Marxist West, but in the home of Marxism-Leninism, the Soviet Union. It is the Soviet Union that runs against the tide of history by denying human freedom and human dignity to its citizens.

It [the Soviet Union] also is in deep economic difficulty. The rate of growth in the national product has been steadily declining since the 1950s and is less than half of what it was then. The dimensions of this failure are astounding: A country which employs one-fifth of its population in agriculture is unable to feed its own people. Were it not for the private sector, the tiny private sector tolerated in Soviet agriculture, the country might be on the brink of famine. These private plots occupy a bare three percent of the arable land but account for nearly one-quarter of Soviet farm output and nearly one-third of meat products and vegetables.

Overcentralized, with little or no incentives, year after year the Soviet system pours its best resource into the making of instruments of

-175-

destruction. The constant shrinkage of economic growth combined with the growth of military production is putting a heavy strain on the Soviet people. What we see here is a political structure that no longer corresponds to its economic base, a society where productive forces are hampered by political ones.

The decay of the Soviet experiment should come as no surprise to us. Wherever the comparisons have been made between free and closed societies—West Germany and East Germany, Austria and Czechoslovakia, Malaysia and Vietnam—it is the democratic countries that are prosperous and responsive to the needs of their people. And one of the simple but overwhelming facts of our time is this: Of all the millions of refugees we've seen in the modern world, their flight is always away from, not toward, the communist world. Today on the NATO line, our military forces face east to prevent a possible invasion. On the other side of the line, the Soviet forces also face east to prevent their people from leaving.

The hard evidence of totalitarian rule has caused in mankind an uprising of the intellect and will. Whether it is the growth of the new schools of economics in America or England or the appearance of the so-called new philosophers in France, there is one unifying thread running through the intellectual work of these groups—rejection of the arbitrary power of the state, the refusal to subordinate the rights of the individual to the superstate, the realization that collectivism stifles all the best human impulses.

Since the exodus from Egypt, historians have written of those who sacrificed and struggled for freedom—the stand at Thermopylae, the revolt of Spartacus, the storming of the Bastille, the Warsaw uprising in World War II.

El Salvador

More recently we've seen evidence of this same human impulse in one of the developing nations in Central America. For months and months the world news media covered the fighting in El Salvador. Day after day we were treated to stories and film slanted toward the brave freedom fighters battling oppressive government forces on behalf of the silent, suffering people of that tortured country.

And then one day those silent, suffering people were offered a chance to vote, to choose the kind of government they wanted. Suddenly the freedom fighters in the hills were exposed for what they really are—Cuban-backed guerrillas who want power for themselves and their backers, not democracy for the people. They threatened death to any who voted, and destroyed hundreds of buses and trucks to keep the people from getting to the polling places. But on election day, the people of El Salvador, an unprecedented 1.4 million of them, braved ambush and gunfire, and trudged for miles to vote for freedom. They stood for hours in the hot sun waiting for their turn to vote.

Members of our Congress who went there as observers told me of a woman who was wounded by rifle fire on the way to the polls, who refused to leave the line to have her wound treated until after she had voted. A grandmother, who had been told by the guerrillas she would be killed when she returned from the polls, told the guerrillas, "You can kill me, you can kill my family, kill my neighbors, but you can't kill us all." The real freedom fighters of El Salvador turned out to be the people of that country.

Strange, but in my own country there's been little if any news coverage of that war since the election. Now, perhaps they'll say it's because there are newer struggles.

Conflict and Progress

On distant islands in the South Atlantic* young men are fighting for Britain. And, yes, voices have been raised protesting their sacrifice for lumps of rock and earth so far away. But those young men aren't fighting for mere real estate. They fight for a cause—for the belief that armed aggression must not be allowed to succeed, and the people must participate in the decisions of government—the decisions of government under the rule of law. If there had been firmer support for that principle some 45 years ago, perhaps our generation wouldn't have suffered the bloodletting of World War II.

In the Middle East, the guns sound once more, this time in Lebanon, a country that for too long has had to endure the tragedy of civil war, terrorism, and foreign intervention and occupation. The fighting in Lebanon must stop. But this is not enough. We must all work to stamp out the scourge of terrorism that in the Middle East makes war an ever-present threat.

But beyond the trouble spots lies a deeper, more positive pattern. Around the world today, the democratic revolution is gathering new strength. In India, a critical test has been passed with the peaceful change of governing political parties. In Africa, Nigeria is moving in remarkable and unmistakable ways to build and strengthen its democratic institutions. In the Caribbean and Central America, 16 of 24 countries have freely elected governments. And in the United Nations, eight of the 10 developing nations which have joined that body in the past five years are democracies.

In the communist world as well, man's instinctive desire for freedom and self-determination surfaces again and again. To be sure, there are grim reminders of how brutally the police state attempts to snuff out this quest for self-rule—1953 in East Germany, 1956 in Hungary, 1968 in Czechoslovakia, 1981 in Poland. But the struggle continues in Poland. And we know that there are even those who strive and suffer for freedom within the confines of the Soviet Union itself. How we conduct ourselves here in the Western democracies will determine whether this trend continues.

* Falklands

No, democracy is not a fragile flower. Still it needs cultivating. If the rest of this century is to witness the gradual growth of freedom and democratic ideals, we must take actions to assist the campaign for democracy.

Some argue that we should encourage democratic change in right-wing dictatorships, but not in communist regimes. Well, to accept this preposterous notion—as some well-meaning people have—is to invite the argument that once countries achieve a nuclear capability, they should be allowed an undisturbed reign of terror over their own citizens. We reject this course.

As for the Soviet view, President Brezhnev repeatedly has stressed that the competition of ideas and systems must continue and that this is entirely consistent with relaxation of tensions and peace.

Well, we ask only that these systems begin by living up to their own constitutions, abiding by their own laws, and complying with the international obligations they have undertaken. We ask only for a process, a direction, a basic code of decency, not for an instant transformation.

We cannot ignore the fact that, even without our encouragement, there has been and will continue to be repeated explosions against repression and dictatorships. The Soviet Union itself is not immune to this reality. Any system is inherently unstable that has no peaceful means to legitimize its leaders. In such cases, the very repressiveness of the state ultimately drives people to resist it, if necessary by force.

While we must be cautious about forcing the pace of change, we must not hesitate to declare our ultimate objectives and to take concrete actions to move toward them. We must be staunch in our conviction that freedom is not the sole prerogative of a lucky few, but the inalienable and universal right of all human beings. So states the United Nations Universal Declaration of Human Rights, which, among other things, guarantees free elections.

The objective I propose is quite simple to state: to foster the infrastructure of democracy—the system of a free press, unions, political parties, universities—which allows a people to choose their own way, to develop their own culture, to reconcile their own differences through peaceful means.

This is not cultural imperialism; it is providing the means for genuine self-determination and protection for diversity. Democracy already flourishes in countries with very different cultures and historical experiences. It would be cultural condescension, or worse, to say that any people prefer dictatorship to democracy. Who would voluntarily choose not to have the right to vote, decide to purchase government propaganda handouts instead of independent newspapers, prefer government to worker-controlled unions, opt for land to be owned by the state instead of those who till it, want government repression of religious liberty, a single political party instead of a free choice, a rigid cultural orthodoxy instead of democratic tolerance and diversity?

Since 1917 the Soviet Union has given covert political training and assistance to Marxist-Leninists in many countries. Of course, it also has promoted the use of violence and subversion by these same forces. Over the past several decades, West European and other Social Democrats, Christian Democrats and leaders have offered open assistance to fraternal, political and social institutions to bring about peaceful and democratic progress. Appropriately, for a vigorous new democracy, the Federal Republic of Germany's political foundations have become a major force in this effort.

Campaign for Democracy

We in America now intend to take additional steps, as many of our allies have already done, toward realizing this same goal. The chairmen and other leaders of the national Republican and Democratic Party organizations are initiating a study with a bipartisan American political foundation to determine how the United States can best contribute as a nation to the global campaign for democracy now gathering force. They will have the cooperation of congressional leaders of both parties, along with representatives of business, labor and other major institutions in our society. I look forward to receiving their recommendations and to working with these institutions and the Congress in the common task of strengthening democracy throughout the world. It is time that we committed ourselves as a nation—in both the public and private sectors—to assisting democratic development.

We plan to consult with leaders of other nations as well. There is a proposal before the Council of Europe to invite parliamentarians from democratic countries to a meeting next year in Strasbourg, France. That prestigious gathering could consider ways to help democratic political movements.

This November in Washington, there will take place an international meeting on free elections. And next spring there will be a conference of world authorities on constitutionalism and self-government hosted by the Chief Justice of the United States. Authorities from a number of developing and developed countries—judges, philosophers, and politicians with practical experience—have agreed to explore how to turn principle into practice and further the rule of law.

Competition of Ideas, Values

At the same time, we invite the Soviet Union to consider with us how the competition of ideas and values—which it is committed to support—can be conducted on a peaceful and reciprocal basis. For example, I am prepared to offer President Brezhnev an opportunity to speak to the American people on our television if he will allow me the same opportunity with the Soviet people. We also suggest that panels of our newsmen periodically appear on each other's television to discuss major events.

Now I don't wish to sound overly optimistic, yet the Soviet Union is not immune from the reality of what is going on in the world. It has happened in the past—a small ruling elite either mistakenly attempts to ease domestic unrest through greater repression and foreign adventure, or it chooses a wiser course. It begins to allow its people a voice in their own destiny. Even if this latter process is not realized soon, I believe the renewed strength of the democratic movement, complemented by a global campaign for freedom, will strengthen the prospects for arms control and a world at peace.

I have discussed on other occasions the elements of Western policies toward the Soviet Union to safeguard our interests and protect the peace. What I am describing now is a plan and a hope for the long term—the march of freedom and democracy which will leave Marxism-Leninism on the ash heap of history, as it has left other tyrannies which stifle the freedom and muzzle the self-expression of the people. And that's why we must continue our efforts to strengthen NATO even as we move forward with our zero-option initiative in the negotiations on intermediate-range forces and our proposal for a one-third reduction in strategic ballistic missile warheads.

Our military strength is a prerequisite to peace, but let it be clear we maintain this strength in the hope it will never be used, for the ultimate determinant in the struggle that's now going on in the world will not be bombs and rockets, but a test of wills and ideas, a trial of spiritual resolve, the values we hold, the beliefs we cherish, the ideals to which we are dedicated.

The British people know that given strong leadership, time and a little bit of hope, the forces of good ultimately rally and triumph over evil. Here among you is the cradle of self-government, the mother of parliaments. Here is the enduring greatness of the British contribution to mankind, the great civilized ideas: individual liberty, representative government, and the rule of law under God.

Crusade for Freedom

I've often wondered about the shyness of some of us in the West about standing for these ideals that have done so much to ease the plight of man and hardships of our imperfect world. This reluctance to use those vast resources at our command reminds me of the elderly lady whose home was bombed in the Blitz. As the rescuers moved about, they found a bottle of brandy she'd stored behind the staircase, which was all that was left standing. And since she was barely conscious, one of the workers pulled the cork to give her a taste of it. She came around immediately and said, "Here now—there now, put it back. That's for emergencies."

Well, the emergency is upon us. Let us be shy no longer. Let us go to our strength. Let us offer hope. Let us tell the world that a new age is not only possible but probable.

During the dark days of the Second World War, when this island was incandescent with courage, Winston Churchill exclaimed about Britain's adversaries, "What kind of a people do they think we are?" Well,

Britain's adversaries found out what extraordinary people the British are. But all the democracies paid a terrible price for allowing the dictators to underestimate us. We dare not make that mistake again. So, let us ask ourselves, "What kind of people do we think we are?" And let us answer, "Free people, worthy of freedom and determined not only to remain so but to help others gain their freedom as well."

Sir Winston led his people to great victory in war and then lost an election just as the fruits of victory were about to be enjoyed. But he left office honorably and, as it turned out, temporarily, knowing that the liberty of his people was more important than the fate of any single leader. History recalls his greatness in ways no dictator will ever know. And he left us a message of hope for the future, as timely now as when he first uttered it, as opposition leader in the Commons nearly 27 years ago. He said: "When we look back on all the perils through which we have passed, and at the mighty foes that we have laid low and all the dark and deadly designs that we have frustrated, why should we fear for our future? We have," he said, "come safely through the worst."

The task I've set forth will long outlive our own generation. But together, we too have come through the worst. Let us now begin a major effort to secure the best—a crusade for freedom that will engage the faith and fortitude of the next generation. For the sake of peace and justice, let us move toward a world in which all people are at last free to determine their own destiny. □

A Forward Strategy for Freedom

ADDRESS TO A JOINT SESSION OF THE NATIONAL PARLIAMENT OF IRELAND

DUBLIN
JUNE 4, 1984

When I stepped off Air Force One at Shannon a few days ago and saw Ireland, beautiful and green, and felt again the warmth of her people, something deep inside began to stir.

Chords of Memory

Who knows but that scientists will someday explain the complex genetic process by which generations seem to transfer across time and even oceans their fondest memories. Until they do, I will have to rely on President Lincoln's words about the "mystic chords of memory," and say to you that during the past few days at every stop here in your country, those chords have been gently and movingly struck. So, I hope you won't think it too bold of me to say that my feelings here this morning can best be summarized by the words "home—home again."

I do want you to know that for Nancy and me these last few days will remain in our hearts forever. From Shannon to Galway, to Ballyporeen to Dublin, you have truly made us feel as welcome as the flowers in May, and for this we'll always be grateful to you and to the Irish people.

Now of course, I didn't exactly expect a chilly reception. As I look around this chamber, I know I can't claim to be a better Irishman than anyone here, but I can perhaps claim to be an Irishman longer than most any of you here. There are those who just refuse to let me forget that. I also have some other credentials. I am the great-grandson of a Tipperary man; I'm the President of a country with the closest possible ties to Ireland; and I was a friend of Barry Fitzgerald.* One Irishman told me he thought I would fit in. "Mr. President," he said, "you love a good story, you love horses, you love politics—the accent we can work on."

But I also came to the land of my forebears to acknowledge two debts: to express gratitude for a light heart and a strong constitution; and to acknowledge that wellspring of so much American political success: the Blarney Stone.** I don't have to tell you how the Blarney Stone works. Many times, for example, I have congratulated Italians on Christopher Columbus' discovery of America, but that's not going to stop me from congratulating all of you on Brendan the navigator.

I think you know, though, that Ireland has been much in our thoughts since the first days in office. I'm proud to say the first Embassy I visited as President was Ireland's, and I'm proud that our administration is blessed by so many Cabinet members of Irish extraction. Indeed, I had to fight them off Air Force One or there wouldn't be anyone tending the store while we're gone. And that's not to mention the number of Irish-Americans who hold extremely important leadership posts today in the United States Congress.

I can assure you that Irish Americans speak with one voice about the importance of the friendship of our two nations and the bonds of affection between us. The American people know how profoundly Ireland has affected our national heritage and our growth into a world power. And I know that they want me to assure you today that your interests are ours and that, in the United States, you have true and fast friends.

Our visit is a joyous moment, and it will remain so. But this should not keep us from serious work or serious words. This afternoon, I want to speak directly on a few points.

Indiscriminate Terrorism

I know many of you recall with sadness the tragic events of last Christmas: the five people killed and 92 injured after a terrorist bomb went off in Harrods |Department Store| of London. Just the day before, a Garda recruit, Gary Sheehan, and Private Patrick Kelly, a young Irish soldier with four children, were slain by terrorist bullets. These two events, occurring 560 kilometers apart, one in Ireland, one in Britain, demonstrated the pitiless, indiscriminate nature of terrorist violence, a violence evil to its core and contemptible in all its forms. And it showed that the problems of Northern Ireland are taking a toll on the people of both Britain and Ireland, north and south.

Yet, the trouble in the north affects more than just these two great isles. When he was in America in March, your Prime Minister outrageously denounced the support that a tiny number of misguided

*Irish-American actor
**Stone in Blarney Castle, near Cork, Ireland, that, according to legend, bestows skill in flattery on those who kiss it

-183-

Americans give to these terrorist groups. I joined him in that denunciation, as did the vast majority of Irish Americans.

I repeat today, there is no place for the crude, cowardly violence of terrorism—not in Britain, not in Ireland, not in Northern Ireland. All sides should have one goal before them, and let us state it simply and directly: to end the violence, to end it completely and to end it now.

The terrorism, the sense of crisis that has existed in Northern Ireland, has been costly to all. But let us not overlook legitimate cause for hope in the events of the last few months. As you know, active dialogue between the governments—here in Dublin, and in London—is continuing. There's also the constructive work of the New Ireland Forum. The Forum's recent report has been praised. It's also been criticized. But the important thing is that men of peace are being heard and their message of reconciliation discussed.

The position of the United States in all of this is clear: We must not and will not interfere in Irish matters nor prescribe to you solutions or formulas. But I want you to know that we pledge to you our good will and support, and we're with you as you work toward peace.

Freedom and Prosperity

I'm not being overly optimistic when I say today that I believe you will work out a peaceful and democratic reconciliation of Ireland's two different traditions and communities. Besides being a land whose concern for freedom and self-determination is legendary, Ireland is also a land synonymous with hope. It is this sense of hope that saw you through famine and war, that sent so many Irish men and women abroad to seek new lives and to build new nations, that gave the world the saints and scholars who preserved Western culture, the missionaries and soldiers who spoke of human dignity and freedom, and put much of the spark to my own country's quest for independence and that of other nations.

You are still that land of hope. It's nowhere more obvious than in the economic changes being wrought here. I know Ireland faces a serious challenge to create jobs for your population, but you've made striking gains, attracting the most advanced technology and industries in the world, and improving the standard of living of your people. And you've done all of this while maintaining your traditional values and religious heritage, renewing your culture and language, and continuing to play a key role in the world community.

Based on Ireland's traditional neutrality in international affairs, you can be proud of your contribution to the search for peace. Irish soldiers have been part of eight United Nations peacekeeping operations since you joined that organization.

In the economic sphere, we Americans, too, are proud that our businesses have been permitted to prosper in Ireland's new economic environment. As you know, there are more than 300 American businesses here providing between 35,000 and 40,000 jobs. We're continuing to encourage this investment. And I assure you today that we will encourage even greater investment for the future.

I think part of the explanation for the economic progress you are making here in Ireland can be found in your nation's historic regard for personal freedom. Too often the link between prosperity and freedom is overlooked. In fact, it's as tight as ever. And it provides a firm basis for increasing cooperation, not only between our two countries but among all countries of the globe that recognize it.

Men and women everywhere in our shrinking world are having the same experience. For most of mankind the oceans are no longer the fearful distances they were when my great-grandfather, Michael Reagan, took weeks to reach America. Some men and women still set out with their children in small boats fleeing tyranny and deprivation. For most of us, though, the oceans and airways are now peaceful avenues, thronged with ideas, people and goods going in every direction. They draw us together. Slowly but surely, more and more people share the values of peace, prosperity and freedom which unite Ireland and America.

In the last year, I've made two visits to America's neighbors across the Pacific in Asia. This century has brought the Pacific nations many hardships, and many difficulties and differences remain. But what I found everywhere was energy, optimism and excitement. Some nations in Asia have produced astounding economic growth rates by providing incentives that reward initiative by unleashing freedom. More and more, there is a sense of common destiny and possibility for all the peoples of this great region. The vast Pacific has become smaller, but the future of those who live around it is larger than ever before.

Coming to Ireland, I sensed the same stirring, the same optimism toward a better future.

Protecting Peace, Preserving Human Life

I believe that great opportunities do lie ahead to overcome the age-old menaces of disease and hunger and want. But moments of great progress can also be moments of great testing. President Kennedy noted, when he was here, that we live in a "most climactic period" but also, he said, "in the most difficult and dangerous struggle in the history of the world." He was talking about our century's struggle between the forces of freedom and totalitarianism—a struggle overshadowed, we all know too well, by weapons of awful destruction on both sides.

Believe me, to hold the office that I now hold is to understand, each waking moment of the day, the awesome responsibility of protecting peace and preserving human life. The responsibility cannot be met with halfway wishes; it can be met only by a determined effort to consolidate peace with all the strength America can bring to bear.

This is my deepest commitment: to achieve stable peace, not just by being prepared to deter aggression, but also by assuring that economic strength helps to lead the way to greater stability through growth and human progress—being prepared with the strength of our commitment to pursue all possible avenues for arms reduction; and being prepared with the greatest strength of all, the spiritual strength and self-confidence that enables us to reach out to our adversaries. To them, and to all of you who have always been our dear and trusted friends, I tell you today from my heart, America is prepared for peace.

What we're doing now in American foreign policy is bringing an enduring steadiness, particularly in the search for arms reduction. Too often in the past, we sought to achieve grandiose objectives and sweeping agreements overnight. At other times, we set our sights so low that the agreements, when they were made, permitted the numbers and categories of weapons to soar. For example, one nation from the time of the signing of the SALT II agreement until the present has added 3,950 warheads to its arsenal. That might be arms limitation; it certainly isn't arms reduction. Through all of this, I'm afraid, differing proposals and shifting policies have sometimes left both friends and adversaries confused or disconcerted.

And that's why we've put forward, methodically, one of the most extensive arms control programs in history. We believe there can be only one policy, for all nations, if we are to preserve civilization in this modern age: A nuclear war cannot be won and must never be fought.

Reducing the Nuclear Threat

In five areas, we have proposed substantive initiatives. In Vienna, the Western side put forward new proposals on reducing the levels of conventional military forces in Europe. In the same week in Geneva, Vice President George Bush put forward a draft agreement for a worldwide ban on chemical weapons, the gases that have been used in Afghanistan and in Cambodia. In Stockholm, we're pursuing at the Conference on Disarmament in Europe a series of proposals that will help reduce the possibility of conflict. And in Geneva—as most of you are aware—we have been participating, until recently, in arms reduction talks on two fronts: the START (Strategic Arms Reduction Talks) talks on reducing intercontinental nuclear forces, and the INF (Intermediate-Range Nuclear Forces) talks. In addition, we're working to prevent the spread of nuclear weapons and to require comprehensive safeguards on all nuclear exports.

During the months the START and INF talks were underway, the United States proposed seven different initiatives. None of these were offered on a take-it or leave-it basis. Indeed, we made a number of adjustments to respond to the stated concerns of the Soviet side. While Soviet flexibility did not match our own, the Soviets also made some steps of the kind required in any serious negotiations. But then, after the first deployment of intermediate-range missiles here in Europe, the Soviets quit the bargaining table.

Now this deployment was not something we welcomed. It has

been my hope, and that of the European leaders, that negotiations would make the deployments unnecessary. Unfortunately, the Soviet stance in those talks left us no alternative. Since 1977, while we were not deploying, but urging the Soviets to negotiate, they were deploying some 370 SS-20 missiles, capable of reaching every city in every country in Europe. We and our allies could not ignore this threat forever.

But I believe today it is still possible to reach an agreement. Let me assure you that in both the START and INF talks, we want to hear Soviet proposals; we want them to hear our own. I'm prepared to halt, and even reverse, the deployment of our intermediate-range missiles from Europe as the outcome of a verifiable and equitable agreement. But for such an outcome to be possible, we need to have the Soviets return to the bargaining table. And before this body, and the people of Europe, I call on them to do so. Indeed, I believe we must not be satisfied—we dare not rest, until the day we've banished these terrible weapons of war from the face of the Earth forever.

My deepest hope and dream has been that if once we can, together, start down the road of reduction, we will inevitably see the common sense of going all the way, so that our children and grandchildren will not have to live with that threat hanging over the world.

Guarding Against Misunderstanding

In addition to the arms control negotiations, I want to stress today that the United States seeks greater dialogue in two other critical areas of East-West relations. Just as we seek to reduce the burden of armaments, we want to find, also, ways to limit their use in troublesome or potentially difficult regional situations. So, we seek serious discussions with the Soviets to guard against miscalculation or misunderstanding in troubled or strategically sensitive areas of the world. I want to stress again today the serious commitment of the United States to such a process.

In the Stockholm conference I mentioned a moment ago, the United States and 34 other nations are negotiating measures to lessen East-West tensions and reduce uncertainties arising from military activities in Europe, the area with the greatest concentration of armed forces in the world. The 16 nations of the Atlantic Alliance have advanced concrete proposals which would make conflict in Europe less likely. The Soviet Union has not accepted these proposals, but has focused upon a declaration of the non-use of force.

Mere restatement of a principle all nations have agreed to in the U.N. Charter and elsewhere would be an inadequate conclusion to a conference whose mandate calls for much more. We must translate the idea into actions which build effective barriers against the use of force in Europe. If the Soviet Union will agree to such concrete actions, which other countries in the Stockholm conference already seem prepared to accept, this would be an important step forward in creating a more peaceful world.

If discussions on reaffirming the principle not to use force, a principle in which we believe so deeply, will bring the Soviet Union to negotiate agreements which will give concrete, new meaning to that principle, we will gladly enter into such discussions. I urge the Soviet Union now to join all other countries in the Stockholm conference to move promptly to take these steps which will help ensure peace and stability in Europe.

We seek to build confidence and trust with the Soviets in areas of mutual interest by moving forward in our bilateral relations on a broad front. In the economic field, we're taking a number of steps to increase exchanges in non-strategic goods. In other areas, we have, for example, extended our very useful incidents-at-sea agreement for another term. And we've proposed discussions for specific steps to expand and multiply contacts of benefit to our people. I might add here that the democracies have a strong mutual obligation to work for progress in the area of human rights. And positive Soviet steps in this area would be considered by the United States a significant signal.

In summary then, we're seeking increased discussion and negotiation to reduce armaments, solve regional problems and improve bilateral relations. Progress on these fronts would enhance peace and security for people everywhere.

I'm afraid the Soviet response has been disappointing. Rather than join us in our efforts to calm tensions and achieve agreements, the Soviets appear to have chosen to withdraw and to try to achieve their objective through propaganda, rather than negotiations.

The Soviets seek to place the blame on the Americans for this self-imposed isolation. But they have not taken these steps by our choice. We remain ready for them to join with us and the rest of the world community to build a more peaceful world. In solidarity with our allies, confident of our strength, we threaten no nation. Peace and prosperity are in the Soviet interest as well as in ours. So, let us move forward.

Crusading for Freedom

Steadiness in pursuing our arms reduction initiatives and bettering East-West relations will eventually bear fruit. But steadiness is also needed in sustaining the cause of human freedom.

When I was last in Europe, I spoke about a crusade for freedom, about the ways the democracies could inaugurate a program promoting the growth of democratic institutions throughout the world. And now it is underway. And this can have an impact in many ways in many places and be a force for good.

Some, of course, focusing on the nations that have lost their freedom in the postwar era, argue that a crusade for democratic values is impractical or unachievable. But we must take the long view. At the start of this century, there were but few democracies. Today, there are more than 50, comprising one-third of the world's population. And it is no coincidence—showing once again the link between political [and] economic freedom and material progress—that these nations enjoy the highest standards of living.

History is the work of free men and women, not unalterable laws. It is never inevitable, but it does have directions and trends; and one trend is clear—democracies are not only increasing in number, they're growing in strength. Today they're strong enough to give the cause of freedom growing room and breathing space, and that's all that freedom ever really needs. "The mass of mankind has not been born with saddles on their backs." Thomas Jefferson said that. Freedom is the flagship of the future and the flashfire of the future. Its spark ignites the deepest and noblest aspirations of the human soul.

Those who think the Western democracies are trying to roll back history are missing the point. History is moving in the direction of self-government and the human dignity that it institutionalizes, and the future belongs to the free.

On this point of democratic development, I think it is vital to appreciate what has been happening in the Western Hemisphere, particularly Latin America. Great strides have been made in recent years. In fact, 26 of 33 Latin American countries today are democracies or are striving to become democracies. I think it is also vital to understand that the United States' current program of assistance to several Central American countries is designed precisely to assist this spread of democratic self-rule.

Now I know that some see the United States, a large and powerful nation, involved in the affairs of smaller nations to the south and conclude that our mission there must be self-seeking or interventionist. Well, the Irish people, of all people, know Americans well. We strive to avoid violence or conflict. History is our witness on this point.

For a number of years at the end of the last war, the United States had a monopoly on nuclear weapons. We did not exploit this monopoly for territorial or imperial gain. We sought to do all in our power to encourage prosperity and peace and democracy in Europe. One can imagine if some other countries had had these weapons instead of the United States, would the world have been as much at peace in the last 40 years as it has been?

In a few days in France, I will stand near the only land in Europe that is occupied by the United States—those mounds of earth marked with crosses and Stars of David, the graves of Americans who never came home, who gave their lives that others might live in freedom and peace. It is freedom and peace that the people of Central America seek today.

El Salvador

Three times in little more than two years, the people of El Salvador have voted in free elections. Each time they had to brave the threats of the guerrillas supported by the Sandinista regime in Nicaragua and by

Cuba and the Soviet Union. These guerrillas use violence to support their threats. Their slogan in each one of those elections has been, "Vote today and die tonight." Yet the people of El Salvador, 1.4 million of them, have braved ambush and gunfire and trudged for miles to vote for freedom and then stood in line for hours waiting their turn to vote.

Some of our observers who went down there—many of them going down convinced that perhaps we were wrong in what we are trying to do there—came home converted. Some of them came home converted by one woman standing in the voting line—who had been there for hours. She had been shot. She suffered from a rifle bullet. She refused to leave the line for medical treatment until she had had her opportunity to vote. They [the observers] came home convinced that the people of El Salvador want democracy.

All the United States is attempting to do—with only 55 military advisers and $474 million in aid, three-fourths of which is earmarked for economic and social development—is give the Salvadorans the chance they want for democratic self-determination, without outside interference. But this the government of Nicaragua has been determined not to permit.

Nicaragua

By their own admission, they've been supplying and training the Salvadoran guerrillas. In their own country they have never held elections. They have all but crushed freedom of the press and moved against labor unions, outlawed political freedoms, and even sponsored mob action against Nicaragua's independent human rights commission, imprisoning its director.

Despite this repression, 100,000 Nicaraguan Catholics attended a rally on Good Friday this year to support their church, which has been persecuted by the Sandinistas' communist dictatorship. And the bishop has now written a pastoral letter citing this persecution of the church by that government. And yet, even in our own country we didn't read anything of that demonstration. Somehow word of it didn't get out through the news channels of the world.

In an homily to 4,000 Nicaraguans packed into Don Bosco Church several weeks ago, the head of the Nicaraguan Bishops Conference, Bishop Pablo Antonio Vega, said, "The tragedy of the Nicaraguan people is that we are living with a totalitarian ideology that no one wants in this country." The words of Nicaraguan Archbishop Obando y Bravo echo this feeling. He said, "To those who say that the only course for Central American countries is Marxism-Leninism, we Christians must show another way. That is to follow Christ, whose path is that of truth and liberty."

The vast majority of those now struggling for freedom in Nicaragua—contrary to what the Sandinistas would have the world believe—are good and worthy people who did not like the Somoza dictatorship and who do not want the communist dictatorship. The tragedy is they haven't been given the chance to choose.

The people of Nicaragua and El Salvador have a right to resist the nightmare outside forces want to impose on them, just as they have the right to resist extremist violence from within, whether from the left or right. The United States must not turn its back on the democratic aspirations of the people of Central America.

Democracy and Totalitarianism

Moreover, this is a worldwide struggle. The Irish orator James Philpot Curran once said, "The condition upon which God hath given liberty to man is eternal vigilance." And yes, military strength is indispensable to freedom. I have seen four wars in my lifetime, and none of them came about because the forces of freedom were too strong.

In the moving words used by the Czechoslovak Charter 77 group in reply to supporters of nuclear disarmament in the West: "Unlike you, we have personal experience of other, perhaps less conspicuous, but no less effective means of destroying civilization than those represented by thermonuclear war; some of us, at the very least, prefer the risk involved in maintaining a firm stance against aggression to the certainty of the catastrophic consequences of appeasement."

The struggle between freedom and totalitarianism today is not ultimately a test of arms or missiles, but a test of faith and spirit. And in this spiritual struggle, the Western mind and will is the crucial battleground. We must not hesitate to express our dream of freedom; we must not be reluctant to enunciate the crucial distinctions between right and wrong—between political systems based on freedom and those based on a dreadful denial of the human spirit.

If our adversaries believe that we will diminish our own self-respect by keeping silent or acquiescing in the face of successive crimes against humanity, they're wrong. What we see throughout the world is an uprising of intellect and will. As Lech Walesa said: "Our souls contain exactly the contrary of what they [the Soviet leadership] wanted. They wanted us not to believe in God, and our churches are full. They wanted us to be materialistic and incapable of sacrifice. They wanted us to be afraid of the tanks, of the guns, and instead we don't fear them at all."

Let us not take the counsel of our fears. Let us instead offer the world a politics of hope, a forward strategy for freedom. The words of William Faulkner, at a Nobel prize ceremony more than three decades ago, are an eloquent answer to those who predict nuclear doomsday or the eventual triumph of the superstate. "Man will not merely endure," Faulkner said, "he will prevail...because he will return to the old verities and truths of the heart. He is immortal because, alone among creatures, he has a soul, a spirit capable of compassion and sacrifice and endurance."

Those old verities, those truths of the heart—human freedom under God—are on the march everywhere in the world. All across the world today—in the shipyards of Gdansk, the hills of Nicaragua, the rice paddies of Cambodia, the mountains of Afghanistan—the cry again is liberty. And the cause is the same as that spoken in this chamber more than two decades ago by a young American President, who said, "A future of peace and freedom."

It was toward the end of his visit here that John Fitzgerald Kennedy said, "I am going to come back and see old Shannon's face again." And on his last day in Ireland, he promised, "I certainly will come back in the springtime."

It was a promise left unkept, for a spring that never came. But surely in our hearts there is the memory of a young leader who spoke stirring words about a brighter age for mankind, about a new generation that would hold high the torch of liberty and truly light the world.

This is the task before us: to plead the case of humanity, to move the conscience of the world, to march together—as in olden times—in the cause of freedom.

Thank you for this great honor, and God bless you all.   □

The Men of Normandy

REMARKS TO VETERANS AT POINTE DU HOC

NORMANDY
JUNE 6, 1984

W e're here to mark that day in history when the Allied armies joined in battle to reclaim this continent to liberty. For four long years, much of Europe had been under a terrible shadow. Free nations had fallen, Jews cried out in the camps, millions cried out for liberation. Europe was enslaved, and the world prayed for its rescue. Here in Normandy the rescue began. Here the Allies stood and fought against tyranny in a giant undertaking unparalleled in human history.

Americans At the Cliffs

W e stand on a lonely, windswept point on the northern shore of France. The air is soft, but 40 years ago at this moment, the air was dense with smoke and the cries of men, and the air was filled with the crack of rifle fire and the roar of cannon. At dawn, on the morning of the 6th of June 1944, 225 American Rangers jumped off British landing craft and ran to the bottom of those cliffs. Their mission was one of the most difficult and daring of the invasion: to climb these sheer and desolate cliffs and take out the enemy guns. The Allies had been told that some of the mightiest of these guns were here and they would be trained on the beaches to stop the Allied advance.

The Rangers looked up and saw the enemy soldiers on the edge of the cliffs shooting down at them with machine guns and throwing grenades. And the American Rangers began to climb. They shot rope ladders over the face of these cliffs and began to pull themselves up. When one Ranger fell, another would take his place. When one rope was cut, a Ranger would grab another and begin his climb again. They climbed, shot back, and held their footing. Soon, one by one, the Rangers pulled themselves up, and in seizing the firm land at the top of these cliffs, they began to seize back the continent of Europe.

Two hundred and twenty-five came here. After two days of fighting, only 90 could still bear arms.

Behind me is a memorial that symbolizes the Ranger daggers that were thrust into the top of these cliffs. And before me are the men who put them there.

These are the boys of Pointe du Hoc. These are the men who took the cliffs. These are the champions who helped free a continent. These are the heroes who helped end a war.

Gentlemen, I look at you, and I think of the words of Stephen Spender's poem. You are men who in your "lives fought for life...and left the vivid air signed with your honor."

Highlanders at the Bridge

I think I know what you may be thinking right now: "We were just part of a bigger effort; everyone was brave that day." Well everyone was. Do you remember the story of Bill Millin of the 51st Highlanders? Forty years ago today, British troops were pinned down near a bridge, waiting desperately for help. Suddenly, they heard the sound of bagpipes, and some thought they were dreaming. Well, they weren't. They looked up and saw Bill Millin with his bagpipes, leading the reinforcements and ignoring the smack of the bullets into the ground around him.

Lord Lovat was with him—Lord Lovat of Scotland—who calmly announced when he got to the bridge, "Sorry I'm a few minutes late," as if he'd been delayed by a traffic jam, when in truth he'd just come from the bloody fighting on Sword Beach, which he and his men had just taken.

There was the impossible valor of the Poles who threw themselves between the enemy and the rest of Europe as the invasion took hold, and the unsurpassed courage of the Canadians who had already seen the horrors of war on this coast. They knew what awaited them there, but they would not be deterred. And once they hit Juno Beach, they never looked back.

All of these men were part of a roll call of honor with names that spoke of a pride as bright as the colors they bore: the Royal Winnipeg Rifles, Poland's 24th Lancers, the Royal Scots Fusiliers, the Screaming

Eagles, the Yeomen of England's armored divisions, the forces of Free France, the Coast Guard's "Matchbox Fleet" and you, the American Rangers.

Forty Summers Past

Forty summers have passed since the battle that you fought here. You were young the day you took these cliffs; some of you were hardly more than boys, with the deepest joys of life before you. Yet, you risked everything here. Why? Why did you do it? What impelled you to put aside the instinct for self-preservation and risk your lives to take these cliffs? What inspired all the men of the armies that met here? We look at you, and somehow we know the answer. It was faith and belief; it was loyalty and love.

The men of Normandy had faith that what they were doing was right, faith that they fought for all humanity, faith that a just God would grant them mercy on this beachhead or on the next. It was the deep knowledge—and pray God we have not lost it—that there is a profound, moral difference between the use of force for liberation and the use of force for conquest. You were here to liberate, not to conquer, and so you and those others did not doubt your cause. And you were right not to doubt.

You all know that some things are worth dying for. One's country is worth dying for, and democracy is worth dying for, because it's the most deeply honorable form of government ever devised by man. All of you loved liberty. All of you were willing to fight tyranny, and you knew the people of your countries were behind you.

The Americans who fought here that morning knew word of the invasion was spreading through the darkness back home. They fought—or felt in their hearts, though they couldn't know in fact, that in Georgia they were filling the churches at four a.m., in Kansas they were kneeling on their porches and praying, and in Philadelphia they were ringing the Liberty Bell.

Something else helped the men of D-day: their rock-hard belief that Providence would have a great hand in the events that would unfold here; that God was an ally in this great cause. And so, the night before the invasion, when Colonel Wolverton asked his parachute troops to kneel with him in prayer he told them: "Do not bow your heads, but look up so you can see God and ask His blessing in what we're about to do." Also that night, General Matthew Ridgway on his cot, listening in the darkness for the promise God made to Joshua: "I will not fail thee nor forsake thee."

Reconciliation and Division

These are the things that impelled them; these are the things that shaped the unity of the Allies.

When the war was over, there were lives to be rebuilt and governments to be returned to the people. There were nations to be reborn. Above all, there was a new peace to be assured. These were huge and daunting tasks. But the Allies summoned strength from the faith, belief, loyalty and love of those who fell here. They rebuilt a new Europe together.

There was first a great reconciliation among those who had been enemies, all of whom had suffered so greatly. The United States did its part, creating the Marshall Plan to help rebuild allies and former enemies. The Marshall Plan led to the Atlantic Alliance—a great alliance that serves to this day as our shield for freedom, for prosperity and for peace.

In spite of our great efforts and successes, not all that followed the end of the war was happy or planned. Some liberated countries were lost. The great sadness of this loss echoes down to our own time in the streets of Warsaw, Prague and East Berlin. Soviet troops that came to the center of this continent did not leave when peace came. They're still there, uninvited, unwanted, unyielding, almost 40 years after the war. Because of this, allied forces still stand on this continent. Today, as 40 years ago, our armies are here for only one purpose—to protect and defend democracy. The only territories we hold are memorials like this one and graveyards where our heroes rest.

We in America have learned bitter lessons from two World Wars: It is better to be here ready to protect the peace, than to take blind shelter across the sea, rushing to respond only after freedom is lost. We've learned that isolationism never was and never will be an acceptable response to tyrannical governments with an expansionist intent.

But we try always to be prepared for peace; prepared to deter aggression; prepared to negotiate the reduction of arms; and, yes, prepared to reach out again in the spirit of reconciliation. In truth, there is no reconciliation we would welcome more than a reconciliation with the Soviet Union, so together, we can lessen the risks of war, now and forever.

Borne By Their Memory

It's fitting to remember here the great losses also suffered by the Russian people during World War II: 20 million perished, a terrible price that testifies to all the world the necessity of ending war. I tell you from my heart that we in the United States do not want war. We want to wipe from the face of the Earth the terrible weapons that man now has in his hands. And I tell you, we are ready to seize that beachhead. We look for some sign from the Soviet Union that they are willing to move forward, that they share our desire and love for peace, and that they will give up the ways of conquest. There must be a change there that will allow us to turn our hope into action.

We will pray forever that some day that change will come. But for now, particularly today, it is good and fitting to renew our commitment to each other, to our freedom and to the alliance that protects it.

We are bound today by what bound us 40 years ago, the same loyalties, traditions and beliefs. We're bound by reality. The strength of

America's allies is vital to the United States, and the American security guarantee is essential to the continued freedom of Europe's democracies. We were with you then; we are with you now. Your hopes are our hopes, and your destiny is our destiny.

Here, in this place where the West held together, let us make a vow to our dead. Let us show them by our actions that we understand what they died for. Let our actions say to them the words for which Matthew Ridgway listened: "I will not fail thee nor forsake thee."

Strengthened by their courage, heartened by their valor, and borne by their memory, let us continue to stand for the ideals for which they lived and died.

Thank you very much, and God bless you all.   □

The Legacy of Yalta

STATEMENT ON THE 40th ANNIVERSARY OF THE YALTA CONFERENCE

THE WHITE HOUSE, WASHINGTON, D.C
FEBRUARY 5, 1985

Forty years ago this week, the leaders of the United States, Great Britain and the Soviet Union met at Yalta, to confer on the approaching end of World War II and on the outlines of the postwar world. The agreements they reached, including the Declaration on Liberated Europe, committed all three governments to the reconstruction of a democratic continent.

Yalta's Two Memories

Since that time, Yalta has had a double meaning. It recalls an episode of cooperation between the Soviet Union and free nations in a great common cause. But it also recalls the reasons that this cooperation could not continue—the Soviet promises that were not kept, the elections that were not held, the two halves of Europe that have remained apart.

Why is Yalta important today? Not because we in the West want to reopen old disputes over boundaries; far from it. The reason Yalta remains important is that the freedom of Europe is unfinished business. Those who claim the issue is boundaries or territory are hoping that the real issues—democracy and independence—will somehow go away. They will not.

There is one boundary which Yalta symbolizes that can never be made legitimate, and that is the dividing line between freedom and repression. I do not hesitate to say that we wish to undo this boundary. In so doing, we seek no military advantage for ourselves or for the Western Alliance. We do not deny any nation's legitimate interest in security. But protecting the security of one nation by robbing another of its national independence and national traditions is not legitimate. In the long run, it is not even secure.

Long after Yalta, this much remains clear: The most significant way of making all Europe more secure is to make it more free. Our 40-year pledge is to be the goal of a restored community of free European nations. To this work we recommit ourselves today.   □

Beyond the Pain and Suffering of Time

REMARKS AT A COMMEMORATIVE CEREMONY

BERGEN-BELSEN CONCENTRATION CAMP
MAY 5, 1985

Chancellor Kohl and honored guests, this painful walk into the past has done much more than remind us of the war that consumed the European continent. What we have seen makes unforgettably clear that no one of the rest of us can fully understand the enormity of the feelings carried by the victims of these camps. The survivors carry a memory beyond anything that we can comprehend. The awful evil started by one man, an evil that victimized all the world with its destruction, was uniquely destructive of the millions forced into the grim abyss of these camps.

Holocaust

Here lie people—Jews—whose death was inflicted for no reason other than their very existence. Their pain was borne only because of who they were and because of the God in their prayers. Alongside them lay many Christians—Catholics and Protestants.

For year after year, until that man and his evil were destroyed, hell yawned forth its awful contents. People were brought here for no other purpose but to suffer and die—to go unfed when hungry, uncared for when sick, tortured when the whim struck, and left to have misery consume them when all there was around them was misery.

I'm sure we all share similar first thoughts, and that is: What of the youngsters who died at this dark stalag? All was gone for them forever—not to feel again the warmth of life's sunshine and promise, not the laughter and the splendid ache of growing up, nor the consoling embrace of a family. Try to think of being young and never having a day without searing emotional and physical pain—desolate, unrelieved pain.

Today, we've been grimly reminded why the commandant of this camp was named "the Beast of Belsen." Above all, we're struck by the horror of it all—the monstrous, incomprehensible horror. And that's what we've seen but can never understand as the victims did. Nor with all our compassion can we feel what the survivors feel to this day and will feel as long as they live. What we've felt and are expressing with words cannot convey the suffering that they endured. That is why history will forever brand what happened as the Holocaust.

'Suffer the Children of God'

Here, death ruled, but we've learned something as well. Because of what happened, we found that death cannot rule forever, and that's why we're here today. We're here because humanity refuses to accept that freedom of the spirit of man can ever be extinguished. We're here to commemorate that life triumphed over the tragedy and the death of the Holocaust—overcame the suffering, the sickness, the testing and, yes, the gassings. We're here today to confirm that the horror cannot outlast hope and that, even from the worst of all things, the best may come forth. Therefore, even out of this overwhelming sadness, there must be some purpose, and there is. It comes to us through the transforming love of God.

We learn from the Talmud that: "It was only through suffering that the children of Israel obtained three priceless and coveted gifts: The Torah, the Land of Israel, and the World to Come." Yes, out of this sickness—as crushing and cruel as it was—there was hope for the world as well as for the world to come. Out of the ashes—hope, and from all the pain—promise.

So much of this is symbolized today by the fact that most of the leadership of free Germany is represented here today. Chancellor Kohl, you and your countrymen have made real the renewal that had to happen. Your nation and the German people have been strong and resolute in your willingness to confront and condemn the acts of a hated regime of the past. This reflects the courage of your people and their devotion to freedom and justice since the war. Think how far we've come from that time when despair made these tragic victims wonder if anything could survive.

As we flew here from Hanover, low over the greening farms and the emerging springtime of the lovely German countryside, I reflected that there must have been a time when the prisoners at Bergen-Belsen and those of every other camp must have felt the springtime was gone forever from their lives. Surely we can understand that when we see what is around us—all these children of God under bleak and lifeless mounds, the plainness of which does not even hint at the unspeakable acts that created them. Here they lie, never to hope, never to pray, never to love, never to heal, never to laugh, never to cry.

And too many of them knew that this was their fate, but that was not the end. Through it all was their faith and a spirit that moved their faith.

Anne Frank

Nothing illustrates this better than the story of a young girl who died here at Bergen-Belsen. For more than two years Anne Frank and her family had hidden from the Nazis in a confined annex in Holland where she kept a remarkably profound diary. Betrayed by an informant, Anne and her family were sent by freight car first to Auschwitz and finally here to Bergen-Belsen.

Just three weeks before her capture, young Anne wrote these words: "It's really a wonder that I haven't dropped all my ideals because they seem so absurd and impossible to carry out. Yet I keep them because in spite of everything I still believe that people are good at heart. I simply can't build up my hopes on a foundation consisting of confusion, misery and death. I see the world gradually being turned into a wilderness. I hear the ever approaching thunder which will destroy us too; I can feel the suffering of millions and yet, if I looked up into the heavens I think that it will all come right, that this cruelty too will end and that peace and tranquility will return again." Eight months later, this sparkling young life ended here at Bergen-Belsen. Somewhere here lies Anne Frank.

Never Again

Everywhere here are memories—pulling us, touching us, making us understand that they can never be erased. Such memories take us where God intended His children to go—toward learning, toward healing, and, above all, toward redemption. They beckon us through the endless stretches of our heart to the knowing commitment that the life of each individual can change the world and make it better.

We're all witnesses; we share the glistening hope that rests in every human soul. Hope leads us, if we're prepared to trust it, toward what our American President, Abraham Lincoln called the better angels of our nature. And then, rising above all this cruelty, out of this tragic and nightmarish time, beyond the anguish, the pain and the suffering for all time, we can and must pledge: Never again. □

Reaffirming the Constancy of the American Purpose

ADDRESS TO THE EUROPEAN PARLIAMENT

STRASBOURG
MAY 8, 1985

We mark today the anniversary of the liberation of Europe from tyrants who had seized this continent and plunged it into a terrible war. Forty years ago today, the guns were stilled and peace began—a peace that has become the longest of this century.

May 1945

On this day 40 years ago, they swarmed onto the boulevards of Paris, rallied under the Arc de Triomphe and sang the "Marseillaise." They were out there in the free and open air. On this day 40 years ago, Winston Churchill walked out onto a balcony in Whitehall and said to the people of Britain, "This is your victory." And the crowd yelled back, in an unforgettable moment of love and gratitude, "No—it is yours." Londoners tore the blackout curtains from their windows and put floodlights on the great symbols of English history. And for the first time in nearly six years, Big Ben, Buckingham Palace and St. Paul's Cathedral were illuminated against the sky.

Across the ocean, a half million New Yorkers flooded Times Square and laughed and posed for the cameras. In Washington, our new President, Harry Truman, called reporters into his office and said, "The flags of freedom fly all over Europe."

On that day 40 years ago, I was at my post at an Army Air Corps installation in Culver City, California. Passing a radio, I heard the words,

"Ladies and gentlemen, the war in Europe is over." I felt a chill, as if a gust of cold wind had just swept past, and—even though, for America, there was still a war on the Pacific front—I realized I would never forget that moment.

This day can't help but be emotional, for in it we feel the long tug of memory; we are reminded of shared joy and shared pain. A few weeks ago in California, an old soldier with tears in his eyes said, "It was such a different world then. It's almost impossible to describe it to someone who wasn't there. But when they finally turned the lights on in the cities again, it was like being reborn."

If it is hard to communicate the happiness of those days, it is even harder to communicate, to those who did not share it, the depth of Europe's agony. So much of it lay in ruins. Whole cities had been destroyed. Children played in the rubble and begged for food.

Remembering

By this day 40 years ago, over 40 million lay dead, and the survivors—they composed a continent of victims. And to this day, we wonder: How did this happen? How did civilization take such a terrible turn? After all the books and the documentaries, after all the histories and studies, we still wonder: How?

Hannah Arendt spoke of "the banality of evil"—the banality of the little men who did the terrible deeds. We know they were totalitarians who used the state, which they had elevated to the level of a "God," to inflict war on peaceful nations and genocide on innocent peoples. We know of the existence of evil in the human heart, and we know that in Nazi Germany that evil was institutionalized—given power and direction by the state and those who did its bidding. We also know that early attempts to placate the totalitarians did not save us from war. They didn't save us from war; in fact, they guaranteed war. There are lessons to be learned in this and never forgotten.

But there is a lesson, too, in another thing we saw in those days and perhaps we can call it "the commonness of virtue." The common men and women who somehow dug greatness from within their souls, the people who sang to the children during the Blitz, who joined the resistance and said "no" to tyranny, the people who had the courage to hide and save the Jews and the dissidents, the people who became, for a moment, the repositories of all the courage of the West—from a child named Anne Frank to a hero named Raoul Wallenberg. These names shine. They give us heart forever. The glow of their memories lit Europe in her darkest days.

Who can forget the hard days after the war? We can't help but look back and think: Life was so vivid then. There was the sense of purpose, the joy of shared effort and, later, the impossible joy of our triumph. Those were the days when the West rolled up its sleeves and repaired the damage that had been done, the days when Europe rose in glory from the ruins. Old enemies were reconciled with the European family. Together, America and Western Europe created and put into place the Marshall Plan to rebuild from the rubble. Together, we created an Atlantic Alliance, which proceeded not from transient interests of state, but from shared ideals. Together, we created the North Atlantic Treaty Organization (NATO), a partnership aimed at seeing that the kind of tyrants that had tormented Europe would never torment her again.

Choosing Freedom

NATO was a triumph of organization and effort, but it was also something very new and very different. For NATO derived its strength directly from the moral values of the people it represented, from their high ideals, their love of liberty and their commitment to peace. But perhaps the greatest triumph of all was not in the realm of a sound defense or material achievement. No, the greatest triumph after the war was that in spite of all the chaos, poverty, sickness and misfortune that plagued this continent, the people of Western Europe resisted the call of new tyrants and the lure of their seductive ideologies. Your nations did not become the breeding ground for new extremist philosophies. You resisted the totalitarian temptation. Your people embraced democracy, the dream the fascists could not kill. They chose freedom.

Today, we celebrate the leaders who led the way—Churchill and Monnet, Adenauer and Schuman, De Gasperi and Spaak, Truman and Marshall. And we celebrate, too, the free political parties that contributed their share of greatness: the Liberals and the Christian Democrats, the Social Democrats and Labor and the Conservatives. Together they tugged at the same oar, and the great and mighty ship of Europe moved on.

If any doubt their success, let them look at you. In this room are those who fought on opposite sides 40 years ago, and their sons and daughters. Now you work together to lead Europe democratically; you buried animosity and hatred in the rubble. There is no greater testament to reconciliation and to the peaceful unity of Europe than the men and women in this chamber.

In the decades after the war, Europe knew great growth and power, amazing vitality in every area of life—from fine arts to fashion, from manufacturing to science to the world of ideas. Europe was robust and alive, and none of this was an accident. It was the natural result of freedom, the natural fruit of the democratic ideal. We in America looked at Europe and called her what she was: an economic miracle.

And we could hardly be surprised. When we Americans think about our European heritage, we tend to think of your cultural influences and the rich ethnic heritage you gave us. But the Industrial Revolution that transformed the American economy came from Europe. The guiding intellectual lights of our democratic system—Locke, Montesquieu and Adam Smith—came from Europe. And the geniuses who ushered in the modern industrial-technological age camefrom—well, I think you know, but two examples will suffice: Alexander Graham Bell, whose great invention maddens every American parent whose child insists on phoning his European pen pal rather than writing to him. He was a Scotsman. And Guglielmo Marconi, who invented the radio, thereby providing a living for a young man from Dixon, Illinois, who later went into politics. I guess I should explain: That's me. Blame Marconi. And Marconi, as you know was born in Italy.

Tomorrow will mark the 35th anniversary of the Schuman Plan, which led to the European Coal and Steel Community, the first block in the creation of a United Europe. The purpose was to tie French and German—and European—industrial production so tightly together that war between them "becomes not merely unthinkable but materially impossible." Those are the words of Robert Schuman; the Coal and Steel Community was the child of his genius. If he were here today, I believe he would say: "We have only just begun!"

American Loyalty

I'm here to tell you that America remains, as she was 40 years ago, dedicated to the unity of Europe. We continue to see a strong and unified Europe not as a rival but as an even stronger partner. Indeed, John F. Kennedy, in his ringing "declaration of interdependence" in the Freedom Bell city of Philadelphia 23 years ago, explicitly made this objective a key tenet of postwar American policy; that policy saw the New World and the Old as twin pillars of a larger democratic community. We Americans still see European unity as a vital force in that historic process. We favor the expansion of the European Community; we welcome the entrance of Spain and Portugal into that Community, for their presence makes for a stronger Europe, and a stronger Europe is a stronger West.

Yet despite Europe's economic miracle, which brought so much prosperity to so many, despite the visionary ideas of the European leaders, despite the enlargement of democracy's frontiers within the European Community itself, I'm told that a more doubting mood is upon Europe today. I hear words like "Europessimism" and "Europaralysis." I'm told that Europe seems to have lost that sense of confidence that dominated that postwar era. If there is something of a "lost" quality these days, is it connected to the fact that some, in the past few years, have begun to question the ideals and philosophies that have guided the West for centuries? That some have even come to question the moral and intellectual worth of the West?

I wish to speak, in part, to that questioning today. And there is no better place to do it than Strasbourg—where Goethe studied, where Pasteur taught, where Hugo knew inspiration. This has been a lucky city for questioning and finding valid answers. It is also a city for which some of us feel a very sweet affection. You know that our Statue of Liberty was a gift from France, and its sculptor, Auguste Bartholdi, was a son of France. I don't know if you've ever studied the face of the statue, but immigrants entering New York Harbor used to strain to see it, as if it would tell them something about their new world. It is a strong, kind face. It is the face of Bartholdi's mother, a woman of Alsace. And so, among the many things we Americans thank you for, we thank you for her.

The Statue of Liberty—made in Europe, erected in America—helps remind us not only of past ties but present realities. It is to those realities we must look in order to dispel whatever doubts may exist about the course of history and the place of free men and women within it. We live in a complex, dangerous, divided world, yet a world which can provide all of the good things we require, spiritual and material, if we but have the confidence and courage to face history's challenge.

Deterrence

We in the West have much to be thankful for—peace, prosperity and freedom. If we are to preserve these for our children, and for theirs, today's leaders must demonstrate the same resolve and sense of vision which inspired Churchill, Adenauer, De Gasperi and Schuman. The challenge was to rebuild a democratic Europe under the shadow of Soviet power. Our task, in some ways even more daunting, is to keep the peace with an ever more powerful Soviet Union, to introduce greater stability in our relationship with it, and to live together in a world in which our values can prosper.

The leaders and people of postwar Europe had learned the lessons of their history from the failures of their predecessors. They learned that aggression feeds on appeasement and that weakness itself can be provocative. We, for our part, can learn from the success of our predecessors. We know that both conflict and aggression can be deterred, that democratic nations are capable of the resolve, the sacrifices and the consistency of policy needed to sustain such deterrence.

From the creation of NATO in 1949 through the early 1970s, Soviet aggression was effectively deterred. The strength of Western economies, the vitality of our societies, the wisdom of our diplomacy, all contributed to Soviet restraint. But certainly the decisive factor must have been the countervailing power—ultimately, military and, above all, nuclear power—which the West was capable of bringing to bear in the defense of its interests.

Strategic Balance

It was in the early 1970s that the United States lost that superiority over the Soviet Union in strategic nuclear weapons which had characterized the postwar era. In Europe, the effect of this loss was not quickly perceptible but, seen globally, Soviet conduct changed markedly and dangerously. First in Angola in 1975, then, when the West failed to respond in Ethiopia, in South Yemen, in Cambodia and ultimately in Afghanistan, the Soviet Union began courting more risks, and expanding its influence through the indirect and direct application of military power. Today, we see similar Soviet efforts to profit from and stimulate regional conflicts in Central America.

The ineffectual Western response to Soviet adventurism of the late 1970s had many roots, not least the crisis of self-confidence within the American body politic wrought by the Vietnam experience. But just as Soviet decision-making in the earlier postwar era had taken place against a background of overwhelming American strategic power, so the decisions of the late '70s were taken in Moscow, as in Washington and throughout Europe, against a background of growing Soviet and stagnating Western nuclear strength.

One might draw the conclusion from these events that the West should reassert that nuclear superiority over the Soviet Union upon which our security and our strategy rested through the postwar era. That is not my view. We cannot and should not seek to build our peace and freedom perpetually upon the basis of expanding nuclear arsenals.

In the short run, we have no alternative but to compete with the Soviet Union in this field, not in the pursuit of superiority, but merely of balance. It is thus essential that the United States maintain a modern and survivable nuclear capability in each leg of the strategic triad—sea-, land- and air-based. It is similarly important that France and Britain maintain and modernize their independent strategic capabilities.

Now the Soviet Union, however, does not share our view of what constitutes a stable nuclear balance. It has chosen, instead, to build nuclear forces clearly designed to strike first, and thus disarm their adversary. The Soviet Union is now moving toward deployment of new mobile MIRVed missiles which have these capabilities, plus the potential to avoid detection, monitoring or arms control verification. In doing this, the Soviet Union is undermining stability and the basis for mutual deterrence.

One can imagine several possible responses to the continued Soviet buildup of nuclear forces. On the one hand, we can ask the Soviet Union to reduce its offensive systems through equitable, verifiable arms control measures. We are pressing that case in Geneva. Thus far, however, we have heard nothing new from the other side.

A second possibility would be for the West to step up our current modernization effort to keep up with constantly accelerating Soviet deployments, not to regain superiority, but merely to keep up with Soviet deployments. But is this really an acceptable alternative? Even if this course could be sustained by the West, it would produce a less stable strategic balance than the one we have today. Must we accept an endless process of nuclear arms competition? I don't think so. We need a better guarantee of peace than that.

Fortunately, there is a third possibility. It is to offset the continued Soviet offensive buildup in destabilizing weapons by developing defenses against these weapons. In 1983 I launched a new research program—the Strategic Defense Initiative (SDI).

The state of modern technology may soon make possible, for the first time, the ability to use non-nuclear systems to defeat ballistic missiles. The Soviets themselves have long recognized the value of defensive systems and have invested heavily in them. Indeed, they have spent as much on defensive systems as they have on offensive systems for more than 20 years.

Now this research program will take time. As we proceed with it, we will remain within existing treaty constraints. We will also consult in the closest possible fashion with our allies. And when the time for decisions on the possible production and deployment of such systems comes, we must and will discuss and negotiate these issues with the Soviet Union.

Higher Aspirations

Both for the short and long term, I'm confident that the West can maintain effective military deterrence. But surely we can aspire to more than maintaining a state of highly armed truce in international politics.

During the 1970s, we went to great lengths to restrain unilaterally our strategic weapons programs out of the conviction that the Soviet Union would adhere to certain rules in its conduct—rules such as neither side seeking to gain unilateral advantage at the expense of the other. Those efforts of the early 1970s resulted in some improvements in Europe, the Berlin Quadripartite Agreement being the best example. But the hopes for a broader and lasting moderation of the East-West competition foundered in Angola, Ethiopia, Afghanistan and Nicaragua.

The question before us today is whether we have learned from those mistakes, and can we undertake a stable and peaceful relationship with the Soviet Union based upon effective deterrence and the reduction of tensions. I believe we can. I believe we've learned that fruitful cooperation with the Soviet Union must be accompanied by successful competition in areas—particularly Third World areas—where the Soviets are not yet prepared to act with restraint.

U.S. Policy Toward the Soviet Union

Let me talk about the reflections which have molded our policy toward the Soviet Union. That policy embodies the following basic elements:

— While we maintain deterrence to preserve the peace, the United States will make a steady, sustained effort to reduce tensions and solve problems in its relations with the Soviet Union.

— The United States is prepared to conclude fair, equitable, verifiable agreements for arms reduction, above all with regard to offensive nuclear weapons.

— The United States will insist upon compliance with past agreements, both for their own sake and to strengthen confidence in the possibility of future accords.

— The United States seeks no unilateral advantages and, of course, can accept none on the Soviet side.

— The United States will proceed in full consultation with its allies, recognizing that our fates are intertwined, and we must act in unity.

— The United States does not seek to undermine or change the Soviet system nor to impinge upon the security of the Soviet Union. At the same time it will resist attempts by the Soviet Union to use or threaten force against others, or to impose its system on others by force.

Ultimately, I hope the leaders of the Soviet Union will come to understand that they have nothing to gain from attempts to achieve military superiority or to spread their dominance by force, but have much to gain from joining the West in mutual arms reduction and expanding cooperation.

I have directed the Secretary of State to engage with the Soviet Union on an extended agenda of problem solving. Yet even as we embark upon new efforts to sustain a productive dialogue with the Soviet Union, we're reminded of the obstacles posed by our so fundamentally different concepts of humanity, of human rights, of the value of a human life. The murder of Major Nicholson by a Soviet soldier in East Germany, and the Soviet Union's refusal to accept responsibility for this act, is only the latest reminder.

If we're to succeed in reducing East-West tensions, we must find means to ensure against the arbitrary use of lethal force in the future— whether against individuals like Major Nicholson, or against groups, such as the passengers on a jumbo jet.*

Practical Steps

It is for that reason that I would like to outline for you today what I believe would be a useful way to proceed. I propose that the United States and the Soviet Union take four practical steps.

First, that our two countries make a regular practice of exchanging military observers at military exercises and locations. We now follow this practice with many other nations, to the equal benefit of all parties.

Second, as I believe it is desirable for the leaders of the United States and the Soviet Union to meet and tackle problems, I am also convinced that the military leaders of our nations could benefit from more contact. I therefore propose that we institute regular, high-level contacts between Soviet and American military leaders, to develop better understanding and to prevent potential tragedies from occurring.

Third, I urge that the Conference on Disarmament in Europe act promptly and agree on the concrete confidence-building measures proposed by the NATO countries. The United States is prepared to discuss the Soviet proposal on non-use of force in the context of Soviet agreement to concrete confidence-building measures.

Fourth, I believe a permanent military-to-military communications link could serve a useful purpose in this important area of our relationship. It could be the channel for exchanging notifications and other information regarding routine military activities, thereby reducing

* The shooting down of South Korean Airlines Flight 007 by a Soviet interceptor on September 1, 1983

the chances of misunderstanding and misinterpretation. Over time, it might evolve into a "risk-reduction" mechanism for rapid communication and exchange of data in times of crisis.

These proposals are not cure-alls for our current problems and will not compensate for the deaths which have occurred. But as terrible as past events have been, it would be more tragic if we were to make no attempt to prevent even larger tragedies from occurring through lack of contact and communication.

Western Unity

We in the West have much to do—and we must do it together. We must remain unified in the face of attempts to divide us and strong in spite of attempts to weaken us. And we must remember that our unity and strength are not a mere impulse of like-minded allies, but the natural result of our shared love for liberty.

Surely we have no illusions that convergence of the communist system and the free societies of the West is likely. We're in for an extended period of competition of ideas. It is up to us in the West to answer whether or not we will make available the resources, ideas and assistance necessary to compete with the Soviet Union in the Third World. We have much in our favor, not least the experience of those states which have tried Marxism and are looking for an alternative.

We do not aspire to impose our system on anyone, nor do we have pat answers for all the world's ills. But our ideals of freedom and democracy and our economic systems have proven their ability to meet the needs of our people. Our adversaries can offer their people only economic stagnation and the corrupt hand of a state and party bureaucracy, which ultimately satisfy neither material nor spiritual needs.

I want to reaffirm to the people of Europe the constancy of the American purpose. We were at your side through two great wars. We have been at your side through 40 years of a sometimes painful peace. We're at your side today because, like you, we have not veered from the ideals of the West—the ideals of freedom, liberty and peace. Let no one—no one—doubt our purpose.

The United States is committed not only to the security of Europe—we are committed to the re-creation of a larger and more genuinely European Europe. The United States is committed not only to a partnership with Europe—the United States is committed to an end to the artificial division of Europe.

We do not deny any nation's legitimate interest in security. We share the basic aspirations of all of the peoples of Europe—freedom, prosperity and peace. But when families are divided, and people are not allowed to maintain normal human and cultural contacts, this creates international tension. Only in a system in which all feel secure and sovereign can there be a lasting and secure peace.

For this reason we support and will encourage movement toward the social, humanitarian and democratic ideals shared in Europe. The issue is not one of state boundaries, but of insuring the right of all nations to conduct their affairs as their peoples desire. The problem of a divided Europe, like others, must be solved by peaceful means. Let us rededicate ourselves to the full implementation of the Helsinki Final Act in all its aspects.

Encouraging Democracy

As we seek to encourage democracy, we must remember that each country must struggle for democracy within its own culture. Emerging democracies have special problems and require special help. Those nations whose democratic institutions are newly emerged and whose confidence in the process is not yet deeply rooted need our help. They should have an established community of their peers, other democratic countries to whom they can turn for support or just advice.

In my address to the British Parliament in 1982, I spoke of the need for democratic governments to spread the message of democracy throughout the world. I expressed my support for the Council of Europe's effort to bring together delegates from many nations for this purpose. I am encouraged by the product of that conference, the "Strasbourg Initiative."

We in our country have launched a major effort to strengthen and promote democratic ideals and institutions. Following a pattern first started in the Federal Republic of Germany, the United States Congress approved the National Endowment for Democracy. This organization subsequently established institutes of labor, business and political parties dedicated to programs of cooperation with democratic forces around the world. I hope other democracies will join in this effort and contribute their wisdom and talents to this cause.

One Europe

Here in Western Europe, you have created a multinational democratic community in which there is a free flow of people, of information, of goods and of culture. West Europeans move frequently and freely in all directions, sharing and partaking of each other's ideas and culture. It is my hope that in the 21st century—which is only 15 years away—all Europeans, from Moscow to Lisbon, will be able to travel without a passport and the free flow of people and ideas will include the other half of Europe. It is my fervent wish that in the next century there will be one free Europe.

I do not believe those who say the people of Europe today are paralyzed and pessimistic. And I would say to those who think this: Europe, beloved Europe, you are greater than you know. You are the treasury of centuries of Western thought and Western culture; you are the father of Western ideals and the mother of Western faith. Europe, you have been the power and the glory of the West, and you are a moral success. In the horrors after World War II, you rejected totalitarianism; you rejected the lure of the new "superman" and a "new communist man." You proved that you were—and are—a moral triumph.

You in the West are a Europe without illusions, a Europe firmly grounded in the ideals and traditions that made her greatness, a Europe unbound and unfettered by a bankrupt ideology. You are, today, a new Europe on the brink of a new century—a democratic community with much to be proud of.

We have so much to do. The work ahead is not unlike the building of a great cathedral. The work is slow, complicated and painstaking. It's passed on with pride from generation to generation. It is the work not only of leaders but of ordinary people. The cathedral evolves as it is created, with each generation adding its own vision. But the initial ideal remains constant, and the faith that drives the vision persists. The results may be slow to see, but our children and their children will trace in the air the emerging arches and spires and know the faith and dedication and love that produced them. My friends, Europe is the cathedral, and it is illuminated still.

And if you doubt your will, and your spirit, and your strength to stand for something, think of those people 40 years ago—who wept in the rubble, who laughed in the streets, who paraded across Europe, who cheered Churchill with love and devotion and who sang the "Marseillaise" down the boulevards. Spirit like that does not disappear. It cannot perish; it will not go away. There's too much left unsung within it....　　　□

A New Age of Freedom

TELEVISED ADDRESS TO WESTERN EUROPE

VENICE
JUNE 5, 1987

Good afternoon. I am speaking to you today from Venice, Italy, over the satellite channels of Worldnet. I have come here to meet with the leaders of Japan, France, Canada, Italy, the United Kingdom and the Federal Republic of Germany for the 13th Economic Summit. Our task: to determine what we must do as a community to prepare for the challenge of a new century.

Our sights are in the future, and that is why, in these next few minutes, I would like to address my remarks especially to the young people of Europe. As someone whose life has spanned most of this century, permit me to offer some observations about the next, about a future of expanding hope and possibility where dreams can come alive if only we have the courage to pursue them.

Not so long ago, in the last decade, it was fashionable to talk about the age of limits. The world, we were told, was running out of resources, winding down, growing poorer. It was a time of diminishing expectations, when people would simply have to learn to make do with less.

The West in those years experienced what can only be described as a crisis of confidence in our fundamental values. We increasingly heard talk about the so-called convergence of the free world and the communist bloc. Some said our freedoms were a luxury we could no longer afford. Faced with the rigid necessities of a shrinking world, the free nations would have to sacrifice more and more of their economic and political freedoms and accept increasing government control.

I want to talk to you today about how and why the opposite happened, how the "age of limits" was swept away by a resurgence of political and economic freedom, how our economies are entering a new era in which they are transcending the limits of physical resources. Now, instead of "convergence," the contrast between the free and the unfree has become ever sharper, while the totalitarian states have come to talk of "openness" and liberalization, recognizing that, if only as a matter of survival, they must allow some freedom into societies.

And I want to talk to you today about how this divergence between democratic and totalitarian nations can only increase if the totalitarians don't reform, how the only course for the world as we approach the 21st century is to choose freedom and free societies that liberate mankind's full human potential.

The world and its economy are in the midst of a profound transformation. Sometimes that change is so rapid it's hard to keep track, but let me offer just a few examples from the technological revolution, examples that will serve as a kind of measuring rod of how far we've come and a kind of pointer showing us where we are heading.

Superconductivity

Recently, the headlines have been full of a term called "superconductivity," as papers struggle to keep up with the seemingly daily breakthroughs in the lab. Only half a year ago, superconductivity was considered a scientific backwater, a phenomenon with little practical purpose; now scientists are saying it may change our lives. "It shows all the dreams we have had can come true," said one theorist. "The sky is the limit."

Scientists talk of high-speed trains that will float above their tracks. Automobile companies are already planning for electric cars. Some think that solar energy may become competitive. Anything that uses electricity—motors, generators, wires, magnets—could suddenly become astonishingly more efficient. That means diminishing dependence on foreign oil, less pollution, and a cleaner environment. It will be like a shot of adrenalin in the world economy, spurring growth and job creation and improving the quality of life for all.

Computer Chips

Superconductivity will accelerate another revolution: the daily revolution that is taking place in the computer industry. One recent advance is the speciality semiconductor chip. On specific tasks, a handful of these chips, costing about two dollars apiece, may outperform yesterday's multimillion dollar supercomputers. If automotive technology had progressed as fast as semiconductor technology has in the past 20 years, a Rolls Royce would now cost less than three dollars, get three million miles to the gallon, deliver enough power to drive an ocean liner; and six of them would fit on the head of a pin.

This is more than simply a productivity explosion. Operating in the mysterious world of quantum physics, today's computers signal a quantum leap in the world's economy. We are moving from the economy of the Industrial Revolution, an economy feeding on and tied to the Earth's physical and natural resources, to, as one economist titled his book, *The Economy in Mind*, where human imagination, creativity and courage are the most precious commodities.

Think of that little computer chip. Those chips are the driving force of the modern economy, but they are made from the silicon in sand, one of the most common substances on Earth. Their value doesn't come from the material that makes them up, but from the microscopic architecture designed into them by ingenious human minds. Or take this Worldnet telecast, which is transmitted by a satellite hookup. That satellite, the product of human invention, replaces thousands of tons of copper dug from the Earth and molded into wire. We're moving from an age of things to an age of thoughts, of mind over matter. It is the mind of man, free to invent, free to experiment, free to dream, that will shape the economy and the world of the future.

A World Economy in Transformation

Now this is bad news for statism. The centrally planned state can dig metals out of the ground or pump oil. Though less productively than a free economy, it can run huge factories and assembly lines. But it cannot fabricate the spirit of enterprise. It cannot imitate the trial and error of free markets, the riot of experiment that produces knowledge and progress. No government can manufacture the entrepreneur, or light that spark of invention; all they can do is let their people go, give them freedom of mind and spirit.

Some believe that government planning is more efficient, so they rely on tax breaks and other subsidies to those businesses that already exist. But that never works. In America it is estimated that some 70 percent of the nearly 14 million new jobs that we've created have come from new, small and growing firms. One of the most successful computer firms in America was started by two college students in the garage behind their house.*

*Apple Computer, Inc

The most fertile and rapidly growing sector of any economy is that part that exists right now only as a dream in someone's head or an inspiration in his heart. No one can ever predict where the change will come from or foresee the industries of the future. No government would have ever targeted those two young men working through the night making dreams come true in their garage.

So, as we hold the Economic Summit in Venice this year, we see around us a world economy that is in rapid transformation, and it is a transformation that demands freedom. What can governments do? What our summit partners have begun to do: starting with policies that promote opportunity and economic growth—low tax rates, privatization and deregulation. They must also move to dismantle trade-distorting subsidies and labor laws that promote unemployment.

The Venice Agenda

Also high on our agenda in Venice will be ways in which we can improve cooperation between our nations. Agricultural subsidies, for instance, have been some of the worst culprits behind our growing trade frictions. Let's jointly diffuse this expensive farms race by setting a goal of a subsidy-free world for the year 2000. Meanwhile, we must make good our commitment to reduce instability in exchange rates and promote economic growth. The economy is slowing in Germany, and that slows growth across Western Europe. It is essential that Germany follow up on its commitment to revive its sluggish economy. Japan, too, could help right the imbalance in the world economy by righting the imbalance of its own economy. It's time for the Japanese to let free the pent-up consumer demand in their nation, allow the Japanese people to enjoy more of the benefits of the remarkable economy they have worked so hard to build. I know Prime Minister Nakasone recognizes this and has recently submitted a program for action to the Japanese Diet. The Japanese promise to extend more than $20,000 million in financial support to the developing world to ease their enormous debt.

Regarding the U.S. budget deficit, we've made real progress, but we must do more. In the months ahead, I will be going directly to the American people on tax reform. I'm going to say we've got the special interests out of our tax code—it's time to get them out of the budget. It's time to demand real budget reform.

Last but not least, all nations must resist calls for protectionism. So-called protectionism is like the evil of drugs: It will end up destroying all those who use it. And that's why I call it "destructionism," because all it does is slow growth, wipe out jobs and close the door on progress.

A New Age of Freedom and Prosperity

But as we approach the beginning of a new century, the problems that confront us are far outweighed by the possibilities. We look around the world and we see freedom is rising. As free markets energize Asia, free elections spread across Central and South America. In Africa many leaders have agreed that freedom is the key to development. In China reform means the first taste of freedom for over 1,000 million people.

Still, we cannot forget that there is an implacable reality that today stands against this freedom tide. Next week I'll be addressing the people of West Berlin. I will stand in front of the wall that runs like an open wound through the heart of Europe, the wall that represents all that is most hostile to our democratic values of freedom and human rights. A regime that so fears its own people it must imprison them behind a wall is a regime that will always be a source of tension in Europe. It will always be at odds with free people everywhere.

As it happens, this day, June 5th, marks the 40th anniversary of the inauguration of the Marshall Plan. Those were days of great generosity and courage, when the countries of Europe rose from the ashes of war, put away their centuries-old animosities, and together with America built a new age of freedom and prosperity.

In the spirit of the time, America offered the benefits of the Marshall Plan to all the nations of Europe, East and West, including the Soviet Union. The ground rules were simple: openness and good faith. All countries had to open their books, and no country would be allowed to manipulate the plan for political profit. Some nations under Soviet control hoped to join the plan, but Stalin ordered their representatives home. The Soviets would not let them open their books, or their countries, to the fresh air of freedom and enterprise.

We've heard a lot about the Soviet desire to participate in the world economy, to no longer be the odd man out. The ground rules remain the same as they were 40 years ago. No playing the spoiler. No manipulation of world organizations for political gain. Open your economy. Open your political system. Open your borders. Let your people go. Let them travel where they wish, live where they want to. Let them bathe in the light of freedom. And one thing further: leave your weapons at home. Quit Afghanistan; you have no business there. Dismantle your weapons pointed at Europe. Then we will gladly welcome you as a constructive partner in our 21st-century enterprise.

Commitment to Europe

When I last participated in an economic summit in Europe, there were many young people who came out to demonstrate. They wanted to end nuclear weapons, they said. How I wanted to let them know that my heart was with them, that I, too, yearned for a day when mankind could live free of the terror of nuclear annihilation. But the task wasn't as easy as simply signing a treaty. The wall that divides Europe, put up in violation of Soviet promises and every human decency, showed us that much. We could not stake our freedom and our lives on such flimsy security. A treaty, in order to be worth anything at all, must be verified with on-site inspections. It must dramatically reduce the total number of weapons on both sides rather than simply codify a buildup, as treaties so often have in the past. Most important, it can't leave either side outmatched and vulnerable.

Our persistence and steadfastness could now pay off in an agreement very much in our interest and on our terms. We're not there yet, of course; some hard questions remain. But the prospects are good.

It's important to emphasize: the INF (Intermediate-Range Nuclear Forces) treaty we are now negotiating will not be the end but the beginning of the arms reduction effort. Our top priority remains deep, equitable and verifiable reductions in intercontinental nuclear arms. And as long as the Soviet Union stockpiles chemical weapons and maintains massive conventional forces poised in attack positions on its own territory and in Eastern Europe, the free nations of Europe must remain strong and ready. Indeed, given the Soviet superiority in these forces, we must improve our conventional defense capabilities, difficult and expensive as that might be. The United States will not waver in its commitment to the defense of Europe. We will sustain the credibility of NATO's doctrine of flexible response, which has served us well and remains the center of alliance strategy.

At the same time, our ultimate goal remains not just to reduce and confine nuclear weapons but to make them forever obsolete, to construct a high-tech defense that will destroy nuclear weapons before they can destroy people. The technological breakthroughs I mentioned earlier, superconductivity and supercomputers on a chip, could both speed along that day when man will no longer have to fear terror in the skies, when we can breathe free, confident, secure and peaceful.

History Is on the Side of the Free

If I can leave the young people of Europe with one message it is this: History is on the side of the free. Hope and an unshakable belief in our basic values of freedom and human rights—these are the only guides we need as we travel into not only the 21st century but the third millennium. The crisis of confidence in the West a decade ago has been replaced by strength and assurance. Now it is the East which talks of openness, of *glasnost.* We hope that the first few tokens of change in the Soviet Union signal a real desire to open up that closed society.

The choice is theirs: They can either participate in the advance of history or fall farther and farther behind into economic irrelevance. We can look forward to the day when technology may eliminate the threat of mutual nuclear terror, when simply amassing huge stockpiles of nuclear weapons does not make a nation a superpower. Then the Soviet Union will appear as it truly is: a country that has sacrificed individual liberty for an antiquated 19th-century materialist philosophy and an unworkable economic system, an example to the world of how not to run a country. The contrast between totalitarianism and freedom will grow ever more stark.

Today as we celebrate the 40th anniversary of the Marshall Plan, we can be proud of what we together have created: a new age of freedom, a new age of hope and prosperity unrivaled in human history, a model to all the world of what free men can accomplish.

It is a different world today from 40 years ago. The younger generations of Europe, those of you born since the war, have not had to suffer the destruction and heartache of your parents' time. But your challenge is no less great; it is nothing less than to embrace the promise of the future and to extend the lessons of our freedom to a waiting world.

Thank you all and God bless you. □

One Berlin

WEST BERLIN
JUNE 12, 1987

Twenty-four years ago, President John F. Kennedy visited Berlin, speaking to the people of this city and the world. Since then two other presidents have come, each in his turn, to Berlin. And today I make my second visit to your city.

"Es Gibt Nur Ein Berlin"

We come to Berlin, we American presidents, because it's our duty to speak, in this place of freedom. But I must confess, we're drawn here by other things as well: by the feeling of history in this city, more than 500 years older than our own nation; by the beauty of the Grunewald and the Tiergartern; most of all, by your courage and determination.

Perhaps the composer, Paul Lincke, understood something about American presidents. You see, like so many presidents before me, I come here today because wherever I go, whatever I do: *Ich hab noch einen koffer in Berlin.* (I still have a suitcase in Berlin.)

Our gathering today is being broadcast throughout Western Europe and North America. I understand that it is being seen and heard as well in the East. To those listening thoughout Eastern Europe, I extend my warmest greetings and the good will of the American people. To those listening in East Berlin, a special word: Although I cannot be with you, I address my remarks to you just as surely as to those standing here before me. For I join you, as I join your fellow countrymen in the West, in this firm, this unalterable belief: *Es gibt nur ein Berlin.* (There is only one Berlin.)

-221-

The Wall

Behind me stands a wall that encircles the free sectors of this city, part of a vast system of barriers that divides the entire continent of Europe. From the Baltic in the south, those barriers cut across Germany in a gash of barbed wire, concrete, dog runs, and guard towers. Farther south, there may be no visible, no obvious wall. But there remain armed guards and checkpoints all the same—still a restriction on the right to travel, still an instrument to impose upon ordinary men and women the will of a totalitarian state. Yet it is here in Berlin where the wall emerges most clearly; here, cutting across your city, where the news photo and the television screen have imprinted this brutal division of a continent upon the mind of the world. Standing before the Brandenburg Gate, every man is a German, separated from his fellow men. Every man is a Berliner, forced to look upon a scar.

President von Weizsacker has said: "The German question is open as long as the Brandenburg Gate is closed." Today I say: As long as this gate is closed, as long as this scar of a wall is permitted to stand, it is not the German question alone that remains open, but the question of freedom for all mankind. Yet I do not come here to lament. For I find in Berlin a message of hope, even in the shadow of this wall, a message of triumph.

From Ruin to Freedom

In this season of spring in 1945, the people of Berlin emerged from their air raid shelters to find devastation. Thousands of miles away, the people of the United States reached out to help. And in 1947 U.S. Secretary of State George Marshall announced the creation of what would become known as the Marshall Plan. Speaking precisely 40 years ago this month, he said: "Our policy is directed not against any country or doctrine, but against hunger, poverty, desperation and chaos."

In the Reichstag a few moments ago, I saw a display commemorating this 40th anniversary of the Marshall Plan. I was struck by the sign on a burnt-out, gutted structure that was being rebuilt. I understand that Berliners of my own generation can remember seeing signs like it dotted throughout the western sectors of the city. The sign read simply: "The Marshall Plan is helping here to strengthen the free world." A strong, free world in the West—that dream became real. Japan rose from ruin to become an economic giant. Italy, France, Belgium—virtually every nation in Western Europe saw political and economic rebirth; the European Community was founded.

In West Germany and here in Berlin, there took place an economic miracle, the *Wirtschaftswunder*. Adenauer, Erhard, Reuter, and other leaders understood the practical importance of liberty—that just as truth can flourish only when the journalist is given freedom of speech, so prosperity can come about only when the farmer and businessmen enjoy economic freedom. The German leaders reduced tariffs, expanded free trade, lowered taxes. From 1950 to 1960 alone, the standard of living in West Germany and Berlin doubled.

Where four decades ago there was rubble, today in West Berlin there is the greatest industrial output of any city in Germany—busy office blocks, fine homes and apartments, proud avenues and the spreading lawns of park land. Where a city's culture seemed to have been destroyed, today there are two great universities, orchestras and an opera, countless theaters and museums. Where there was want, today there's abundance—food, clothing, automobiles—the wonderful goods of the *Ku'damm*. From devastation, from utter ruin, you Berliners have, in freedom, rebuilt a city that once again ranks as one of the greatest on Earth. The Soviets may have had other plans. But, my friends, there were a few things the Soviets didn't count on—*Berliner herz, Berliner humor, ja, und Berliner schnauze.* (Berliner heart, Berliner humor, yes, and a Berliner schnauze.)

Profound Changes or Token Gestures?

In the 1950's, Khrushchev predicted: "We will bury you." But in the West today, we see a free world that has achieved a level of prosperity and well-being unprecedented in all human history. In the communist world, we see failure, technological backwardness, declining standards of health, even want of the most basic kind—too little food. Even today, the Soviet Union still cannot feed itself. After these four decades, then, there stands before the entire world one great and inescapable conclusion: Freedom leads to prosperity. Freedom replaces the ancient hatreds among the nations with comity and peace. Freedom is the victor.

And now the Soviets themselves may, in a limited way, be coming to understand the importance of freedom. We hear much from Moscow about a new policy of reform and openness. Some political prisoners have been released. Certain foreign news broadcasts are no longer being jammed. Some economic enterprises have been permitted to operate with greater freedom from state control.

Are these the beginnings of profound changes in the Soviet state? Or are they token gestures, intended to raise false hopes in the West, or to strengthen the Soviet system without changing it? We welcome change and openness; for we believe that freedom and security go together, that the advance of human liberty can only strengthen the cause of world peace. There is one sign the Soviets can make that would be unmistakable, that would advance dramatically the cause of freedom and peace.

General Secretary Gorbachev, if you seek peace, if you seek prosperity for the Soviet Union and Eastern Europe, if you seek liberalization: Come here to this gate! Mr. Gorbachev, open this gate! Mr. Gorbachev, tear down this wall!

I understand the fear of war and the pain of division that afflict this continent—and I pledge to you my country's efforts to help overcome these burdens. To be sure, we in the West must resist Soviet expansion. So we must maintain defenses of unassailable strength. Yet we seek peace; so we must strive to reduce arms on both sides.

Beginning 10 years ago, the Soviets challenged the Western Alliance with a grave new threat, hundreds of new and more deadly SS-20 nuclear missiles, capable of striking every capital in Europe. The Western Alliance responded by committing itself to a counter-deployment unless the Soviets agreed to negotiate a better solution; namely, the elimination of such weapons on both sides. For many months, the Soviets refused to bargain in earnestness. As the Alliance, in turn, prepared to go forward with its counter-deployment, there were difficult days—days of protests like those during my 1982 visit to this city—and the Soviets later walked away from the table.

But through it all, the Alliance held firm. And I invite those who protested then—I invite those who protest today—to mark this fact: Because we remained strong, the Soviets came back to the table. And because we remained strong, today we have within reach the possibility, not merely of limiting the growth of arms, but of eliminating, for the first time, an entire class of nuclear weapons from the face of the Earth.

As I speak, NATO ministers are meeting in Iceland to review the progress of our proposals for eliminating these weapons. At the talks in Geneva, we have also proposed deep cuts in strategic offensive weapons. And the Western allies have likewise made far-reaching proposals to reduce the danger of conventional war and to place a total ban on chemical weapons.

While we pursue these arms reductions, I pledge to you that we will maintain the capacity to deter Soviet aggression at any level at which it might occur. And in cooperation with many of our allies, the United States is pursuing the Strategic Defense Initiative—research to base deterrence not on the threat of offensive retaliation, but on defenses that truly defend; on systems, in short, that will not target populations, but shield them. By these means we seek to increase the safety of Europe and all the world. But we must remember a crucial fact: East and West do not mistrust each other because we are armed; we are armed because we mistrust each other. And our differences are not about weapons but about liberty. When President Kennedy spoke at the City Hall those 24 years ago, freedom was encircled, Berlin was under siege. And today, despite all the pressures upon this city, Berlin stands secure in its liberty. And freedom itself is transforming the globe.

In the Philippines, in South and Central America, democracy has been given a rebirth. Throughout the Pacific, free markets are working miracle after miracle of economic growth. In the industrialized nations, a technological revolution is taking place—a revolution marked by rapid, dramatic advances in computers and telecommunications.

In Europe, only one nation and those it controls refuse to join the community of freedom. Yet in this age of redoubled economic growth, of information and innovation, the Soviet Union faces a choice: It must make fundamental changes, or it will become obsolete.

Creating A Safer, Freer World

Today thus represents a moment of hope. We in the West stand ready to cooperate with the East to promote true openness, to break down barriers that separate people, to create a safer, freer world. And surely there is no better place than Berlin—the meeting place of East and West—to make a start. Free people of Berlin: Today, as in the past, the United States stands for the strict observance and full implementation of all parts of the Four Power Agreement of 1971. Let us use this occasion, the 750th anniversary of this city, to usher in a new era, to seek a still fuller, richer life for the Berlin of the future. Together, let us maintain and develop the ties between the Federal Republic and the Western sectors of Berlin, which is permitted by the 1971 agreement.

And I invite Mr. Gorbachev: Let us work to bring the Eastern and Western parts of the city closer together, so that all the inhabitants of all Berlin can enjoy the benefits that come with life in one of the great cities of the world.

To open Berlin still further to all Europe, East and West, let us expand the vital air access to this city, finding ways of making commercial air service to Berlin more comfortable, and more economical. We look to the day when West Berlin can become one of the chief aviation hubs in all central Europe.

With our French and British partners, the United States is prepared to help bring international meetings to Berlin. It would be only fitting for Berlin to serve as the site of United Nations meetings, or world conferences on human rights and arms control or other issues that call for international cooperation.

There is no better way to establish hope for the future than to enlighten young minds, and we would be honored to sponsor summer youth exchanges, cultural events and other programs for young Berliners from the East. Our French and British friends, I'm certain, will do the same. And it's my hope that an authority can be found in East Berlin to sponsor visits from young people of the Western sectors.

One final proposal, one close to my heart: Sport represents a source of enjoyment and ennoblement, and you many have noted that the Republic of Korea—South Korea—has offered to permit certain events of the 1988 Olympics to take place in the North. International sports competitions of all kinds could take place in both parts of this city. And what better way to demonstrate to the world the openness of this city than to offer in some future year to hold the Olympic games here in Berlin, East and West?

"This Wall Will Fall"

In these four decades, as I have said, you Berliners have built a great city. You've done so in spite of threats—the Soviet attempts to impose the East-mark, the blockade. Today the city thrives in spite of the challenges implicit in the very presence of this wall. What keeps you here? Certainly there's a great deal to be said for your fortitude, for your defiant courage. But I believe there's something deeper, something that involves Berlin's whole look and feel and way of life—not mere sentiment. No one could live long in Berlin without being completely disabused of illusions. Something instead, that has seen the difficulties of life in Berlin but chose to accept them, that continues to build this good and proud city in contrast to a surrounding totalitarian presence that refuses to release the human energies or aspirations. Something that speaks with a powerful voice of affirmation, that says yes to this city, yes to the future, yes to freedom. In a word, I would submit that what keeps you in Berlin is love—love both profound and abiding.

Perhaps this gets to the root of the matter, to the most fundamental distinction of all between East and West. The totalitarian world produces backwardness because it does such violence to the spirit, thwarting the human impulse to create, to enjoy, to worship. The totalitarian world finds even symbols of love and of worship an affront. Years ago, before the East Germans began rebuilding their churches, they erected a secular structure: the television tower at Alexander Platz. Virtually ever since, the authorities have been working to correct what they view as the tower's one major flaw, treating the glass sphere at the top with paints and chemicals of every kind. Yet even today when the sun strikes that sphere—that sphere that towers over all Berlin—the light makes the sign of the cross. There in Berlin, like the city itself, symbols of love, symbols of worship, cannot be suppressed.

As I looked out a moment ago from the Reichstag, that embodiment of German unity, I noticed words crudely spray-painted upon the wall, perhaps by a young Berliner, "This wall will fall. Beliefs become reality." Yes, across Europe, this wall will fall. For it cannot withstand faith; it cannot withstand truth. The wall cannot withstand freedom.

And I would like, before I close, to say one word. I have read, and I have been questioned since I've been here, about certain demonstrations against my coming. And I would like to say just one thing to those who demonstrate. I wonder if they have ever asked themselves that if they should have the kind of government they apparently seek, no one would ever be able to do what they're doing again.

Thank you and God bless you all. □

The Family of Free People

TELEVISED WORLDNET ADDRESS TO EUROPE

THE WHITE HOUSE, WASHINGTON, D C.
NOVEMBER 4, 1987

I am speaking with you from here in Washington via the satellite channels of Worldnet and Voice of America. This is but another demonstration of the dramatic effect technology is having on our lives. Science is shrinking distances, overcoming obstacles and opening borders. Today, individuals in distant lands are working, trading and even playing together on a global scale. We are, as would never have been thought possible a century ago, truly becoming a community—perhaps even a family—of free people, united by humane values and democratic ideals, and sharing in a prosperity that is closely linked to the trade and commerce between us.

A Common Purpose

Earlier in this century, during a time when fascism and communism were on the rise, there were those who believed that the light of democracy might well be extinguished. It was feared that the era of representative government, of political and economic freedom, would prove to be a short interlude of history and would disappear just as the democracy of Greece and the Roman Republic had vanished.

Well, our cause may have seemed precariously perched, fragile and without the power projected by strutting troops and mass political spectacles. But it should be clear now that the courage and resilience of free people are too easily underestimated, as is our resolve to cooperate, to see a common purpose and to act together in our own defense.

Victor Hugo once wrote, "People do not lack strength; they lack will." In my life, I have time and again seen evidence that gives me great confidence that those who live in freedom do indeed have the will to remain free, even under enormous pressure, even against great odds. Those of us who lived through the Second World War saw that in the British people, whose indomitable spirit never broke under heavy bombardment. We saw it in the French troops and resistance fighters who battled to free their homeland; in Polish home army soldiers who rose in Warsaw; in the moral heroes throughout the continent, including within Germany itself, who resisted Nazism, often at the cost of their own lives; and others who risked all to save Jews—sometimes perfect strangers—from the death camps. We saw it in Normandy where Americans joined with people from all over Europe to breach the Atlantic wall and head inland, joined together in one mighty crusade to rid the continent of Hitler's national socialism and all the horrors that went with it.

Yes, and in the four decades since the end of the Second World War, the free peoples of the world have continued to prove their courage and, just as important, as never before to demonstrate their solidarity with one another. The North Atlantic Alliance, a lasting triumph of unity and cooperation among free peoples, has maintained peace on the European continent for four decades. It has been the shield of democracy and the greatest deterrent to war in history.

Four decades of European peace have been no accident. They have been earned by those in uniform who stood guard, and paid for by all of us whose taxes kept our allied forces manned, equipped and armed with the conventional and nuclear weapons needed to deter aggression. We've all had to do our part or it would not have worked. But it has worked. The Alliance has been prepared to meet any challenge. The message to anyone who would threaten the peace has been simple and direct: "Don't even think about it."

Unflagging Solidarity

And when our will has been tested, we have come together as allies, as people whose destinies are inextricably linked, and have acted in unison to meet the challenge. It has not been easy, yet we have done what was necessary to keep our countries free and to preserve the peace. That certainly was true of the Alliance's response to the vast expansion of Soviet military power in the late 1970s, especially their introduction of the new SS-20 intermediate-range missiles.

It was in 1977 when the Soviet Union deployed its first SS-20s. This triple-warhead weapon could hit anywhere in Western Europe and much of Asia. Though NATO had no comparable missile to counter this new threat, by August 1982, the number of Soviet INF missiles had climbed to over 300, with more than 900 warheads.

What we were witnessing was an attempt to tip the military balance of power in Europe and erode the security bond between Europe and the United States. It tested our cohesion and could well have had serious, even catastrophic, long-term consequences had the Alliance not acted with resolve.

But we did act. In December of 1979, Western leaders made the decision to move forward on a "two-track" approach:

First, the United States would negotiate with the Soviets in an attempt to convince them to withdraw their new missiles.

Second, as long as the Soviets continued on their course and kept their missiles in place, NATO would deploy in Europe a limited number of Pershing II and ground-launched cruise missiles. What the Alliance sought, however, were fewer missiles, not more.

Our plan depended upon unflagging solidarity and steadfastness of purpose, even under immense pressure. And the pressure was put on. Had the nuclear freeze and unilateral disarmament protestors won, Europe would now be condemned to live under the shadow of Soviet, nuclear-armed INF missiles. To democracy's credit, the political courage of far-sighted European leaders carried the day. That resolve has now made it possible to achieve an historic agreement—an agreement that will eliminate a whole class of U.S. and Soviet INF missiles from the face of the planet.

Zero Option

The agreement we are now nearing is based upon the proposal that the United States, in full consultation with allied leaders, put forward in 1981—"the zero option." The plan will require the Soviets to remove four times as many nuclear warheads as the United States. Not only will the entire Soviet force of SS-20s and SS-4s be destroyed, but also the shorter-range SS-12s and SS-23s. It will be the first mutual reduction of the world's nuclear arsenals in history.

And more than that, the shorter-range Soviet missiles that will be eliminated are capable of carrying not just nuclear but also chemical and conventional warheads. Thus, we will be making a promising start in cutting back these threats to Europe as well.

Achievements like this are not the result of wishful thinking, nor are they made more likely by loud proclamations of a desire for peace. Lasting progress derives from hard-nosed realism, strenuous effort and firmness of principle. I can assure you that any treaty I sign will be realistic and in the long-term interest of all the members of the Alliance, or no agreement will be signed.

The Soviet Union, for example, has a poor record of compliance with past arms control agreements. So any new treaty will contain iron-clad provisions for effective verification, including on-site inspection of facilities before and during reductions, and short-notice inspections afterwards. The verification regime we have put forward is the most

-229-

stringent in the history of arms control negotiations. None of us in the Alliance can settle for anything less.

Arms reduction—if done with care to ensure the continuing credibility of our deterrent, both nuclear and conventional—is in the interest of all Western countries. And any INF agreement should be viewed not as the end of the process, but the beginning, a first big step.

Strategic Arms

We and the Soviets have also been negotiating possible reductions in our strategic arsenals, which for us is a high priority. Again, it's an American proposal that is the centerpiece of the negotiation—a dramatic proposition to cut our strategic arsenals in half. Considerable progress has been made, and further movement can be expected if Soviet flexibility is evident.

What is totally unacceptable, however, is the Soviet tactic of holding these offensive reductions hostage to measures that would cripple our Strategic Defense Initiative (SDI). We won't bargain away SDI, which offers the promise of a safer world in which both sides would rely more on defenses—which threaten no one—than on offensive forces. It shouldn't escape our attention that the Soviets themselves have been spending thousands of millions on a strategic defense program of their own.

Glasnost

Much has been heard of late about reforms being instituted within the Soviet Union. *Glasnost*, we are told, is ushering in a new era. Well, who cannot but hope these reports are true, that the optimism is justified? Good sense, however, dictates that we look for tangible changes in behavior—for action, not words—in deciding what is real or illusionary.

We will, for example, closely watch the condition of human rights within the Soviet Union. It is difficult to imagine that a government that continues to repress freedom in its own country, breaking faith with its own people, can be trusted to keep agreements with others.

Yes, this year some people, including a few very prominent individuals, were permitted to leave the Soviet Union. It is better than the record of recent years, yet many more emigration and divided-family cases remain. And let us remember, denial of the right to emigrate is only a small part of the problem of the repressive Soviet system. A recognition of freedom of speech, religion and press, a release of all prisoners of conscience, an ending of the practice of sending perfectly sane political dissidents to psychiatric hospitals, tolerance of real opposition, and freedom of political choice: These things—which we in the United States take for granted—would signal that a true turning point has been reached and would offer hope of positive changes in the international arena as well. If there is one observation that rings true in today's changing world, it is that freedom and peace go hand in hand.

The further the Soviet leadership opens their system and frees their people, the more likely it will be that the tensions between East and West will lessen.

Regional Issues

Reflecting this, we also hope to see changes in Soviet foreign policy. The Soviet occupation of Afghanistan is most certainly a dreadful quagmire. The Afghan people have proven themselves the bravest of the brave. They will continue to have the sympathy and support of free nations in their struggle for independence. Soviet leaders can win accolades from people of goodwill everywhere and free their country from a no-win situation by grounding their helicopter gunships, promptly withdrawing their troops and permitting the Afghan people to choose their own destiny. Such actions would be viewed, not as a retreat, but as a courageous and positive step.

Another sign to look for—this one closer to home for you on your side of the Atlantic—would be a loosening of the Soviet hold over Eastern Europe. Why should the peoples of Europe remain divided as they are with barbed wire, watch towers and machine guns? Why shouldn't all Europeans be free to travel, to visit one another or to conduct business with each other? Shouldn't the Brezhnev Doctrine finally be renounced? Four decades after the war, why should 17 million Germans be treated like prisoners in their own land? A true opening-up and recognition of their sovereign independence would be welcomed by all the peoples of Eastern and Central Europe, and it would not threaten the security of the Soviet Union or anyone else.

A few months ago, I visited Berlin. I stood there alongside the cruel wall that symbolizes so powerfully the scar that divides the European continent. It is time for that wound to heal and that scar to disappear. Wouldn't it be a wonderful sight for the world to see, if someday General Secretary Gorbachev and I could meet in Berlin and together take down the first bricks of that wall—and continue taking down walls until the distrust between our peoples and the scars of the past are forgotten.

Peace Through Strength

A few moments ago, I recalled the valiant fight, 40 years ago, to liberate the European continent. Who cannot help but appreciate that, in that epic struggle, the peoples of the Soviet Union fought bravely and sacrificed so immensely to defeat the common enemy. After the war, we became adversaries, at times bitter adversaries. Yet this need not have happened and need not continue. Any philosophy or leader suggesting that there is a predetermined course of history, and that conflict between our peoples and systems is inevitable, is wrong. We are not condemned by forces beyond our control. We—all peoples in every land—can shape the world in which we live and determine the future. We in the Western democracies have been doing just that. Together we've built a freer and more prosperous way of life, a community of free people. I'm certain you agree with me that the door is open to all who would join with us.

German literary figure Heinrich Heine has written, "Do not mock our dreamers. Their words become the seeds of freedom." Well, today our vision, not only of a more peaceful world, but of a world of freedom in which democratic rights are enjoyed in every land, seems ever more in focus, almost as if it is within reach. We will continue to watch and to be hopeful, yet we must also remain vigilant. The strength and viability of the Alliance remains essential, even as an agreement between the United States and the Soviet Union opens new opportunities for peace. It is just such strength as NATO has demonstrated that is a precondition to such progress. Weakness, vulnerability and wishful thinking can undo what has been accomplished by standing firm.

This, nevertheless, can be a time of great change. As you are likely aware, General Secretary Gorbachev has accepted my invitation to come to Washington for a summit in early December. We'll be discussing face to face the wide spectrum of issues I've spoken to you about today. I, in fact, expect we'll sign that agreement concerning U.S. and Soviet INF missiles during the time of our meetings.

For our part, the commitment of the United States to the Alliance and to the security of Europe—INF treaty or no INF treaty—remains unshakable. Over 300,000 American servicemen with you on the continent, and our steadfast nuclear guarantee, underscore this pledge. Those who worry that we will somehow drift apart or that deterrence has been weakened are mistaken on both counts.

Partners in Peace

Our ties will be strengthened, not diminished, by this success. Such an historic reduction in nuclear weapons will be a resounding vindication of the unity, strength and determination of the Alliance.

As far as our ability to keep the peace, the NATO strategy of flexible response will continue to ensure that aggression, at any level, is blocked. A viable deterrent force of nuclear weapons of many types, including ground-based systems, as well as those carried by aircraft and submarines, still protects Europe and remains in place. And we have agreed with our allies that the existing imbalances in conventional forces and chemical weapons must be redressed prior to any further nuclear reductions in Europe.

The Alliance has had underway for some time a program of modernizing our forces so that a credible deterrent is maintained over the long term. That is why major initiatives are moving forward to upgrade NATO's conventional strength. And, after 18 years of unilaterally refraining from any production of chemical weapons, improvements are being made in our modest chemical weapon inventory. The Soviet Union, of course, possesses what is by far the world's most extensive chemical weapon stockpile.

But just as we are doing in our INF talks, we are also seeking through negotiation to correct the disparities we face in both the chemical and conventional areas. In fact, in 1984 the United States, with allied support, proposed an effective global ban on chemical weapons.

As far as conventional forces, the Alliance stands ready—if the East meets us halfway—to make reductions in Central Europe through mutual balanced forced reductions, or MBFR, as they are called. At the same time, in Vienna, an agreement between East and West is being sought that would mandate new negotiations on conventional stability from the Atlantic Ocean to the Ural Mountains.

Our common security agenda, as you can see, is broad and ambitious. An INF agreement is an important first step, but only the first one, toward our greater goal.

And let there be no doubt, the citizens of the United States fully understand and appreciate that we are partners for peace with you, the peoples of our fellow Western democracies. That is why we applaud what we see as a new willingness, even eagerness, on the part of some of our allies to increase the level of cooperation and coordination among themselves in European defense. The growing cooperation between France and Germany is a positive sign, as is the modernization of the British and French independent nuclear deterrents, which are both vital components of the Western security system. Last week, the foreign and defense ministers of the Western European Union issued an impressive declaration. It reaffirmed the importance of maintaining our nuclear and conventional deterrents and affirmed a positive Western European identity in the field of defense within the framework of the Atlantic Alliance. We welcome these developments.

Over these last four decades, all too often the United States has been viewed as the senior partner of the Alliance. Today, when the economic strength of Western Europe and the United States are fully comparable, the time has long since come when we will view ourselves as equal partners. And a more equal relationship should not diminish our bonds, but strengthen them. It should not limit our potential, but expand it.

Freedom—Right of All

Goethe, the soul of German literature, once wrote, "If you would create something, you must be something." Well, in these last four decades the people of the United States and Europe have been a force for progress and freedom on this planet. And, only a few short years from now, as mankind literally enters into a new millennium, we will have laid the foundation for a prosperous and free future. We've proven wrong—dead wrong—those doubters and despots who, earlier in this century, thought democracy was soon to be extinct. We have ensured that, in the centuries ahead, it is free people who will dominate the affairs of mankind. And let me predict that, someday, the realm of liberty and justice will encompass the planet. Freedom is not just the birthright of the few, it is the God-given right of all His children, in every country. It won't come by conquest. It will come because freedom is right and freedom works. It will come because cooperation and goodwill among free people will carry the day.

There is a story that was brought to my attention a few years ago about an elderly couple who live in the small town of Marstal on the Island of Aero in Denmark—Natalia and Nels Mortensen. For the last 40 years they have tended the grave of a young man they never met. They dig the weeds and place flowers, and always there is a small American flag. When it becomes worn, they replace it with another.

They are watching over the final resting place of U.S. Air Force Sergeant Jack Wagner, who died when his plane was shot down on June 20, 1944, near Aero, which was then occupied territory. Jack Wagner's body washed up on shore a few days later, and the word quickly spread through the tiny community. When the Nazi occupation troops came to bury the young American they found nearly the whole town of 2,000 had been waiting by the grave since early in the morning to pay tribute to the young flyer. The path had been lined with flowers. And when the troops laid young Jack Wagner in his grave, the townspeople conducted a funeral service and placed red, white and blue flowers on his grave, along with a banner that read, "Thank you for what you have done."

Jack was a 19-year-old American from Snyder County, Pennsylvania. The Danish townspeople had never met him, but they knew this young man had given his life for them. He cared enough for people he'd never met to make the supreme sacrifice for their freedom. The Mortensens never forgot this. They still care for that grave as if he was a member of their family. And, in a way he was. Just as we are—all part of the family of free people.

Many young people, from all of our countries, have died to preserve the freedom we now enjoy. Many of our children still serve. They stand together on the ramparts of freedom. We care about each and every one of them as if he or she was our own. Let us be as brave as they are brave; as proud as they are proud.

Thank you for letting me share these moments with you. God bless you.   □

PART V

The United States and the Soviet Union

Laying the Foundation for Enduring Peace

ADDRESS BEFORE THE 40TH SESSION OF THE UNITED NATIONS GENERAL ASSEMBLY

NEW YORK CITY
OCTOBER 24, 1985

F orty years ago, the world awoke daring to believe hatred's unyielding grip had finally been broken, daring to believe the torch of peace would be protected in liberty's firm grasp. Forty years ago, the world yearned to dream again innocent dreams, to believe in ideals with innocent trust. Dreams of trust are worthy, but in these 40 years too many dreams have been shattered, too many promises have been broken, too many lives have been lost. The painful truth is that the use of violence to take, to exercise and to preserve power remains a persistent reality in much of the world.

The vision of the U.N. Charter—to spare succeeding generations this scourge of war—remains real. It still stirs our souls and warms our hearts. But it also demands of us a realism that is rock-hard, clear-eyed, steady and sure, a realism that understands the nations of the United Nations are not united.

I come before you this morning preoccupied with peace, with ensuring that the differences between some of us not be permitted to degenerate into open conflict. And I come offering for my own country a new commitment, a fresh start.

Star of Freedom

On this U.N. anniversary, we acknowledge its successes: the decisive action during the Korean War; negotiation of the non-proliferation treaty; strong support for decolonization; and the laudable achievements by the United Nations High Commissioner for Refugees. Nor must we close our eyes to this organization's disappointments: its failure to deal with real security issues, the total inversion of morality in the infamous "Zionism is Racism" resolution, the politicization of too many agencies, the misuse of too many resources.

The U.N. is a political institution and politics requires compromise. We recognize that. But let us remember, from those first days, one guiding star was supposed to light our path toward the U.N. vision of peace and progress—a star of freedom.

What kind of people will we be 40 years from today? May we answer: free people, worthy of freedom and firm in the conviction that freedom is not the sole prerogative of a chosen few, but the universal right of all God's children.

This is the Universal Declaration of Human Rights set forth in 1948, and this is the affirming flame the United States has held high to a watching world. We champion freedom not only because it is practical and beneficial, but because it is morally right and just.

Free people, whose governments rest upon the consent of the governed, do not wage war on their neighbors. Free people, blessed by economic opportunity and protected by laws that respect the dignity of the individual, are not driven toward the domination of others.

America's Efforts Toward Peace

We readily acknowledge that the United States is far from perfect. Yet we have endeavored earnestly to carry out our responsibilities to the Charter these past 40 years, and we take national pride in our contributions to peace. We take pride in 40 years of helping avert a new world war and pride in our alliances that protect and preserve us and our friends from aggression. We take pride in the Camp David agreements and our efforts for peace in the Middle East rooted in Resolutions 242 and 338; in supporting Pakistan, target of outside intimidation; in assisting El Salvador's struggle to carry forward its democratic revolution; in answering the appeal of our Caribbean friends in Grenada; in seeing Grenada's representative here today, voting the will of its own people. And we take pride in our proposals to reduce the weapons of war.

We submit this history as evidence of our sincerity of purpose. But today it is more important to speak to you about what my country proposes to do, in these closing years of the 20th century, to bring about a safer, a more peaceful, a more civilized world.

Let us begin with candor—with words that rest on plain and simple facts. The differences between America and the Soviet Union are deep and abiding.

The United States is a democratic nation. Here the people rule. We build no walls to keep them in, nor organize any system of police to keep them mute. We occupy no country. The only land abroad we occupy is beneath the graves where our heroes rest. What is called the West is a voluntary association of free nations, all of whom fiercely value their independence and their sovereignty. And as deeply as we cherish our beliefs, we do not seek to compel others to share them.

When we enjoy these vast freedoms as we do, it's difficult for us to understand the restrictions of dictatorships which seek to control each institution and every facet of people's lives—the expression of their beliefs, their movements and their contacts with the outside world. It's difficult for us to understand the ideological premise that force is an acceptable way to expand a political system.

U.S.-Soviet Difference

We Americans do not accept that any government has the right to command and order the lives of its people, that any nation has an historic right to use force to export its ideology. This belief—regarding the nature of man and the limitations of government—is at the core of our deep and abiding differences with the Soviet Union, differences that put us into natural conflict—and competition—with one another.

Now, we would welcome enthusiastically a true competition of ideas, welcome a competition of economic strength and scientific and artistic creativity, and, yes, welcome a competition for the good will of the world's people. But we cannot accommodate ourselves to the use of force and subversion to consolidate and expand the reach of totalitarianism.

When Mr. Gorbachev and I meet in Geneva next month, I look to a fresh start in the relationship of our two nations. We can and should meet in the spirit that we can deal with our differences peacefully. And that is what we expect.

The only way to resolve differences is to understand them. We must have candid and complete discussions of where dangers exist and where peace is being disrupted. Make no mistake: Our policy of open and vigorous competition rests on a realistic view of the world. And therefore, at Geneva we must review the reasons for the current level of mistrust.

For example, in 1972 the international community negotiated in good faith a ban on biological and toxin weapons; in 1975 we negotiated the Helsinki Accords on human rights and freedoms; and during the decade just past, the United States and the Soviet Union negotiated several agreements on strategic weapons. Yet, we feel it will be necessary at Geneva to discuss with the Soviet Union what we believe are their violations of a number of the provisions in all of these agreements.

Indeed, this is why it is important that we have this opportunity to air our differences through face-to-face meetings—to let frank talk substitute for anger and tension.

Reducing the Nuclear Threat

The United States has never sought treaties merely to paper over differences. We continue to believe that a nuclear war is one that cannot be won and must never be fought. That is why we have sought for nearly 10 years, still seek, and will discuss in Geneva radical, equitable, verifiable reductions in these vast arsenals of offensive nuclear weapons....

The United States is also seeking to discuss with the Soviet Union in Geneva the vital relationship between offensive and defensive systems, including the possibility of moving toward a more stable and secure world in which defenses play a growing role.

The ballistic missile is the most awesome, threatening and destructive weapon in the history of man. Thus, I welcome the interest of the new Soviet leadership in the reduction of offensive strategic forces. Ultimately, we must remove this menace—once and for all—from the face of this earth.

Until that day, the United States seeks to escape the prison of mutual terror by research and testing that could, in time, enable us to neutralize the threat of these ballistic missiles and, ultimately, render them obsolete.

How is Moscow threatened—if the capitals of other nations are protected? We do not ask that the Soviet leaders, whose country has suffered so much from war, leave their people defenseless against foreign attack. Why then do they insist that we remain undefended? Who is threatened if Western research and Soviet research, that is itself well-advanced, should develop a non-nuclear system which would threaten not human beings, but only ballistic missiles?

Surely, the world will sleep more securely when these missiles have been rendered useless, militarily and politically, when the sword of Damocles that has hung over our planet for too many decades is lifted by Western and Russian scientists working to shield their cities and their citizens and one day shut down space as an avenue for weapons of mass destruction.

If we are destined by history to compete militarily to keep the peace, then let us compete in systems that defend our societies rather than weapons which can destroy us both, and much of God's creation along with us.

Some 18 years ago, then Premier Aleksei Kosygin was asked about a moratorium on the development of an anti-missile defense system. The official news agency, TASS, reported that he replied with these words: "I believe the defensive systems, which prevent attack, are not the cause of the arms race, but constitute a factor preventing the death of people. Maybe an anti-missile system is more expensive than an offensive system, but it is designed not to kill people, but to preserver human lives."

Defining Peace

Preserving lives—no peace is more fundamental than that. Great obstacles lie ahead, but they should not deter us. Peace is God's commandment. Peace is the holy shadow cast by men treading on the path of virtue.

But just as we all know what peace is, we certainly know what peace is not. Peace based on repression cannot be true peace and is secure only when individuals are free to direct their own governments.

Peace based on partition cannot be true peace. Put simply: Nothing can justify the continuing and permanent division of the European continent. Walls of partition and distrust must give way to greater communication for an open world. Before leaving for Geneva, I shall make major new proposals to achieve this goal.

Peace based on mutual fear cannot be true peace because staking our future on a precarious balance of terror is not good enough. The world needs a balance of safety.

And finally, a peace based on averting our eyes from trouble cannot be true peace. The consequences of conflict are every bit as tragic when the destruction is contained within one country.

Regional Conflicts

Real peace is what we seek, and that is why today the United States is presenting an initiative that addresses what will be a central issue in Geneva—the resolution of regional conflicts in Africa, Asia and Central America.

Our own position is clear: As the oldest nation of the new world, as the first anticolonial power, the United States rejoiced when decolonization gave birth to so many new nations after World War II. We have always supported the right of the people of each nation to define their own destiny. We have given $300,000 million since 1945 to help people of other countries. And we have tried to help friendly governments defend against aggression, subversion and terror.

We have noted with great interest similar expressions of peaceful intent by leaders of the Soviet Union. I am not here to challenge the good faith of what they say. But isn't it important for us to weigh the record, as well?
— In Afghanistan, there are 118,000 Soviet troops prosecuting war against the Afghan people.
— In Cambodia, 140,000 Soviet-backed Vietnamese soldiers wage a war of occupation.
— In Ethiopia, 1,700 Soviet advisers are involved in military planning and support operations along with 2,500 Cuban combat troops.

— In Angola, 1,200 Soviet military advisers are involved in planning and supervising combat operations, along with 35,000 Cuban troops.

— In Nicaragua, there are some 8,000 Soviet bloc and Cuban personnel, including about 3,500 military and secret police personnel.

All of these conflicts—some of them underway for a decade—originate in local disputes, but they share a common characteristic: They are the consequence of an ideology imposed from without, dividing nations and creating regimes that are, almost from the day they take power, at war with their own people. And in each case, Marxism-Leninism's war with the people becomes war with their neighbors.

These wars are exacting a staggering human toll and threaten to spill across national boundaries and trigger dangerous confrontations. Where is it more appropriate than right here at the United Nations to call attention to Article Two of our Charter, which instructs members to refrain "from the threat or use of force against the territorial integrity or political independence of any state...."?

Three-Level Peace Process

During the past decade these wars played a large role in building suspicions and tensions in my country over the purpose of Soviet policy. This gives us an extra reason to address them seriously today.

Last year I proposed from this podium that the United States and Soviet Union hold discussions on some of these issues, and we have done so. But I believe these problems need more than talk. For that reason, we are proposing, and are fully committed to support, a regional peace process that seeks progress on three levels.

First, we believe the starting point must be a process of negotiation among the warring parties in each country I've mentioned—which, in the case of Afghanistan, includes the Soviet Union. The form of these talks may and should vary, but negotiations—and an improvement of internal political conditions—are essential to achieving an end to violence, the withdrawal of foreign troops and national reconciliation.

There is a second level: Once negotiations take hold and the parties directly involved are making real progress, representatives of the United States and the Soviet Union should sit down together. It is not for us to impose any solutions in this separate set of talks. Such solutions would not last. But the issue we should address is how best to support the ongoing talks among the warring parties. In some cases, it might well be appropriate to consider guarantees for any agreements already reached. But in every case the primary task is to promote this goal: verified elimination of the foreign military presence and restraint on the flow of outside arms.

Finally, if these first two steps are successful, we could move on to the third: welcoming each country back into the world economy so its citizens can share in the dynamic growth that other developing countries—countries that are at peace—enjoy. Despite past differences with these regimes, the United States would respond generously to their democratic reconciliation with their own people, their respect for human rights, and their return to the family of free nations.

Of course, until such time as these negotiations result in definitive progress, America's support for struggling democratic resistance forces must not and shall not cease.

This plan is bold. And it is realistic. It is not a substitute for existing peacemaking efforts; it complements them. We are not trying to solve every conflict in every region of the globe, and we recognize that each conflict has its own character. Naturally other regional problems will require different approaches. But we believe that the recurrent pattern of conflict that we see in these five cases ought to be broken as soon as possible.

Freedom Works

We must begin somewhere, so let us begin where there is great need and great hope. This will be a clear step forward to help people choose their future more freely. Moreover, this is an extraordinary opportunity for the Soviet side to make a contribution to regional peace which in turn can promote future dialogue and negotiations on other critical issues.

With hard work and imagination, there is no limit to what, working together, our nations can achieve. Gaining a peaceful resolution of these conflicts will open whole new vistas of peace and progress—the discovery that the promise of the future lies not in measures of military defense or the control of weapons, but in the expansion of individual freedom and human rights.

Only when the human spirit can worship, create and build, only when people are given a personal stake in determining their own destiny and benefiting from their own risks do societies become prosperous, progressive, dynamic and free.

We need only open our eyes to the economic evidence all around us. Nations that deny their people opportunity—in Eastern Europe, Indochina, southern Africa and Latin America—without exception are dropping further behind in the race for the future.

But where we see enlightened leaders who understand that economic freedom and personal incentive are key to development, we see economies striding forward. Singapore, Taiwan and South Korea—India, Botswana and China. These are among the current and emerging success stories because they have the courage to give economic incentives a chance.

Let us all heed the simple eloquence in Andrei Sakharov's Nobel Peace Prize message: "International trust, mutual understanding, disarmament and international security are inconceivable without an open society with freedom of information, freedom of conscience, the right to publish and the right to travel and choose the country in which one wishes to live."

At the core, this is an eternal truth; freedom works. That is the promise of the open world and awaits only our collective grasp. Forty years ago, hope came alive again for a world that hungered for hope. I believe fervently that hope is still alive.

Enduring Peace

The United States has spoken with candor and conviction today, but that does not lessen these strong feelings held by every American. It's in the nature of Americans to hate war and its destructiveness. We would rather wage our struggle to rebuild and renew, not to tear down. We would rather fight against hunger, disease and catastrophe. We would rather engage our adversaries in the battle of ideals and ideas for the future.

These principles emerge from the innate openness and good character of our people—and from our long struggle and sacrifice for our liberties and the liberties of others. Americans always yearn for peace. They have a passion for life. They carry in their hearts a deep capacity for reconciliation.

Last year at this General Assembly, I indicated there was every reason for the United States and the Soviet Union to shorten the distance between us. In Geneva, the first meeting between our heads of government in more than six years, Mr. Gorbachev and I will have that opportunity.

So, yes, let us go to Geneva with both sides committed to dialogue. Let both sides go committed to a world with fewer nuclear weapons—and some day with none. Let both sides go committed to walk together on a safer path into the 21st century and to lay the foundation for enduring peace.

It is time, indeed, to do more than just talk of a better world. It is time to act. And we will act when nations cease to try to impose their ways upon others. And we will act when they realize that we, for whom the achievement of freedom has come dear, will do what we must to preserve it from assault.

America is committed to the world because so much of the world is inside America. After all, only a few miles from this very room is our Statue of Liberty, past which life began anew for millions, where the peoples from nearly every country in this hall joined to build these United States. The blood of each nation courses through the American vein and feeds the spirit that compels us to involve ourselves in the fate of this good Earth. It is the same spirit that warms our heart in concern to help ease the desperate hunger that grips proud people on the African continent.

It is the internationalist spirit that came together last month when our neighbor Mexico was struck suddenly by an earthquake. Even as the Mexican nation moved vigorously into action, there were heartwarming offers by other nations offering to help and glimpses of people working together, without concern for national self-interest or gain.

And if there was any meaning to salvage out of that tragedy, it was found one day in a huge mound of rubble that was once the Juarez Hospital in Mexico City. A week after that terrible event, and as another day of despair unfolded, a team of workers heard a faint sound coming from somewhere in the heart of the crushed concrete. Hoping beyond hope, they quickly burrowed toward it. And as the late afternoon light faded, and racing against time, they found what they had heard, the first of three baby girls—newborn infants emerged to the safety of the rescue team. And let me tell you the scene through the eyes of one who was there: "Everything was so quiet when they lowered that little baby down in a basket covered with blankets. The baby didn't make a sound either. But the minute they put her in the Red Cross ambulance, everybody just got up and cheered." Well, amidst all that hopelessness and debris came a timely and timeless lesson for us all. We witnessed the miracle of life.

It is on this that I believe our nations can make a renewed commitment. The miracle of life is given by one greater than ourselves, but once given, each life is ours to nurture and preserve, to foster, not only for today's world but for a better one to come.

There is no purpose more noble than for us to sustain and celebrate life in a turbulent world. That is what we must do now. We have no higher duty, no greater cause as humans. Life—and the preservation of freedom to live it in dignity—is what we are on this earth to do.

Everything we work to achieve must seek that end so that some day our prime ministers, our premiers, our presidents and our general secretaries will talk not of war and peace—but only of peace.

We've had 40 years to begin. Let us not waste one more moment to give back to the world all that we can in return for this miracle of life.

Thank you all. God bless you all. □

Peace as Our Goal and Freedom as Our Guide

REPORT TO THE U.S. CONGRESS ON THE GENEVA SUMMIT

WASHINGTON, D.C.,
NOVEMBER 21, 1985

I have just come from Geneva and talks with General Secretary Gorbachev. In the past few days, we spent over 15 hours in various meetings with the General Secretary and the members of his official party. Approximately five of those hours were talks between Mr. Gorbachev and myself, just one-on-one. That was the best part—our fireside summit.

There will be, I know, a great deal of commentary and opinion as to what the meetings produced and what they were like. There were over 3,000 reporters in Geneva, so it's possible there will be 3,000 opinions on what happened. So, maybe it's the old broadcaster in me but I decided to file my own report directly to you.

We met, as we had to meet. I had called for a fresh start—and we made that start. I can't claim we had a meeting of the minds on such fundamentals as ideology or national purpose—but we understand each other better. That's key to peace. I gained a better perspective; I feel he did, too.

It was a constructive meeting. So constructive, in fact, that I look forward to welcoming Mr. Gorbachev to the United States next year. And I have accepted his invitation to go to Moscow the following year. We arranged that out in the parking lot.

I found Mr. Gorbachev to be an energetic defender of Soviet policy. He was an eloquent speaker and a good listener. Our subject matter was shaped by the facts of this century.

Peaceful Competition

These past 40 years have not been an easy time for the West or the world. You know the facts; there is no need to recite the historical record. Suffice it to say that the United States cannot afford illusions about the nature of the U.S.S.R. We cannot assume that their ideology and purpose will change; this implies enduring competition. Our task is to ensure that this competition remains peaceful. With all that divides us, we cannot afford to let confusion complicate things further. We must be clear with each other and direct. We must pay each other the tribute of candor.

When I took the oath of office for the first time, we began dealing with the Soviet Union in a way that was more realistic than in the recent past. And so, in a very real sense, preparations for the summit started not months ago but five years ago when—with the help of Congress— we began strengthening our economy, restoring our national will, and rebuilding our defenses and alliances. America is once again strong— and our strength has given us the ability to speak with confidence and see that no true opportunity to advance freedom and peace is lost. We must not now abandon policies that work. I need your continued support to keep America strong.

That is the history behind the Geneva Summit, that is the context in which it occurred. And may I add that we were especially eager that our meetings give a push to important talks already under way on reducing nuclear weapons. On this subject it would be foolish not to go the extra mile—or in this case the extra 4,000 miles.

We discussed the great issues of our time. I made clear before the first meeting that no question would be swept aside, no issue buried, just because either side found it uncomfortable or inconvenient. I brought these questions to the summit and put them before Mr. Gorbachev.

Reduction of Nuclear Arms

We discussed nuclear arms and how to reduce them. I explained our proposals for equitable, verifiable and deep reductions. I outlined my conviction that our proposals would make not just for a world that feels safer, but one that is really safer.

I am pleased to report tonight that General Secretary Gorbachev and I did make a measure of progress here. We have a long way to go, but we're still heading in the right direction. We moved arms control forward from where we were last January, when the Soviets returned to the table. We are both instructing our negotiators to hasten their vital work. The world is waiting for results.

Specifically, we agreed in Geneva that each side should move to cut offensive nuclear arms by 50 percent in appropriate categories. In our joint statement we called for early progress on this, turning the talks toward our chief goal—offensive reductions. We called for an interim accord on intermediate-range nuclear forces, leading, I hope, to the complete elimination of this class of missiles. All this with tough verification.

We also made progress in combatting together the spread of nuclear weapons, an arms control area in which we've cooperated effectively over the years. We are also opening a dialogue on combatting the spread and use of chemical weapons, while moving to ban them altogether. Other arms control dialogues—in Vienna on conventional forces, and in Stockholm on lessening the chances for surprise attack in Europe—also received a boost. And finally, we agreed to begin work on risk reduction centers....

Strategic Defense Initiative

I described our Strategic Defense Initiative (SDI)—our research effort that envisions the possibility of defensive systems which could ultimately protect all nations against the danger of nuclear war. This discussion produced a very direct exchange of views.

Mr. Gorbachev insisted that we might use a strategic defense system to put offensive weapons into space and establish nuclear superiority. I made it clear that SDI has nothing to do with offensive weapons; that, instead, we are investigating non-nuclear defensive systems that would only threaten offensive missiles, not people. If our research succeeds, it will bring much closer the safer, more stable world that we seek. Nations could defend themselves against missile attack, and mankind, at long last, escape the prison of mutual terror—this is my dream.

So, I welcomed the chance to tell Mr. Gorbachev that we are a nation that defends, rather than attacks; that our alliances are defensive, not offensive. We don't seek nuclear superiority. We do not seek a first-strike advantage over the Soviet Union. Indeed, one of my fundamental arms control objectives is to get rid of first-strike weapons altogether. This is why we have proposed a 50-percent reduction in the most threatening nuclear weapons, especially those that could carry out a first strike.

Cooperation on SDI

I went further in expressing our peaceful intentions. I described our proposal in the Geneva negotiations for a reciprocal program of open laboratories in strategic defense research. We are offering to permit Soviet experts to see firsthand that SDI does not involve offensive weapons. American scientists would be allowed to visit comparable facilities of the Soviet strategic defense program, which, in fact, has involved much more than research for many years.

Finally, I reassured Mr. Gorbachev on another point. I promised that if our research reveals that a defense against nuclear missiles is possible, we would sit down with our allies and the Soviet Union to see how together we could replace all strategic ballistic missiles with such a defense, which threatens no one.

Peace and Human Rights

We discussed threats to the peace in several regions of the world. I explained my proposals for a peace process to stop the wars in Afghanistan, Nicaragua, Ethiopia, Angola and Cambodia—those places where insurgencies that speak for the people are pitted against regimes which obviously do not represent the will or the approval of the people. I tried to be very clear about where our sympathies lie; I believe I succeeded.

We discussed human rights. We Americans believe that history teaches no clearer lesson than this: Those countries which respect the rights of their own people tend, inevitably, to respect the rights of their neighbors. Human rights, therefore, is not an abstract moral issue—it is a peace issue.

People-to-People Contact

Finally, we discussed the barriers to communication between our societies, and I elaborated on my proposals for real people-to-people contacts on a wide scale. Americans should know the people of the Soviet Union—their hopes and fears and the facts of their lives. And citizens of the Soviet Union need to know of America's deep desire for peace and our unwavering attachment to freedom.

As you can see, our talks were wide ranging. Let me at this point tell you what we agreed upon and what we didn't.

We remain far apart on a number of issues, as had to be expected. However, we reached agreement on a number of matters, and, as I mentioned, we agreed to continue meeting, and this is important and very good. There's always room for movement, action and progress when people are talking to each other instead of about each other.

We have concluded a new agreement designed to bring the best of America's artists and academics to the Soviet Union. The exhibits that will be included in this exchange are one of the most effective ways for the average Soviet citizen to learn about our way of life. This agreement will also expand the opportunities for Americans to experience the Soviet people's rich cultural heritage—because their artists and academics will be coming here.

We have also decided to go forward with a number of people-to-people initiatives that will go beyond greater contact, not only between the political leaders of our two countries, but our respective students, teachers and others as well. We have emphasized youth exchanges. This will help break down stereotypes, build friendships and, frankly, provide an alternative to propaganda.

Bilateral Agreements

We have agreed to establish a new Soviet consulate in New York and a new American consulate in Kiev. This will bring a permanent U.S. presence to the Ukraine for the first time in decades.

We have also, together with the government of Japan, concluded a

Pacific Air Safety Agreement with the Soviet Union. This is designed to set up cooperative measures to improve civil air safety in that region of the Pacific. What happened before must never be allowed to happen again.*

As a potential way of dealing with the energy needs of the world of the future, we have also advocated international cooperation to explore the feasibility of developing fusion energy.

All of these steps are part of a long-term effort to build a more stable relationship with the Soviet Union. No one ever said it would be easy. But we've come a long way.

Steady As We Go

As for Soviet expansionism in a number of regions of the world—while there is little chance of immediate change—we will continue to support the heroic efforts of those who fight for freedom. But we have also agreed to continue—and to intensify—our meetings with the Soviets on this and other regional conflicts and to work toward political solutions.

We know the limits as well as the promise of summit meetings. This is, after all, the 11th summit of the postwar era—and still the differences endure. But we believe continued meetings between the leaders of the United States and the Soviet Union can help bridge those differences.

The fact is, every new day begins with possibilities; it's up to us to fill it with the things that move us toward progress and peace. Hope, therefore, is a realistic attitude—and despair an uninteresting little vice.

And so: Was our journey worthwhile?

Well, 30 years ago, when Ike, President Eisenhower, had just returned from a summit in Geneva, he said, "...the wide gulf that separates so far East and West is wide and deep." Today, three decades later, that is still true.

But, yes, this meeting was worthwhile for both sides. A new realism spawned the summit; the summit itself was a good start; and now our byword must be: Steady as we go.

I am, as you are, impatient for results. But good will and good hopes do not always yield lasting results. Quick fixes don't fix big problems.

Just as we must avoid illusions on our side, so we must dispel them on the Soviet side. I have made it clear to Mr. Gorbachev that we must reduce the mistrust and suspicions between us if we are to do such things as reduce arms, and this will take deeds, not words alone. I believe he is in agreement.

Real Peace

Where do we go from here? Well, our desire for improved relations is strong. We're ready and eager for step-by-step progress. We know that peace is not just the absence of war. We don't want a phony peace or a frail peace. We did not go in pursuit of some kind of illusory detente. We

*The shooting down of South Korean Airlines Flight 007 by a Soviet interceptor on September 1, 1983

can't be satisfied with cosmetic improvements that won't stand the test of time. We want real peace.

As I flew back this evening, I had many thoughts. In just a few days families across America will gather to celebrate Thanksgiving. And again, as our forefathers who voyaged to America, we traveled to Geneva with peace as our goal and freedom as our guide. For there can be no greater good than the quest for peace—and no finer purpose than the preservation of freedom.

It is 350 years since the first Thanksgiving, when Pilgrims and Indians huddled together on the edge of an unknown continent. And now here we are gathered together on the edge of an unknown future—but, like our forefathers, really not so much afraid, but full of hope and trusting in God, as ever. □

A Time for Reflection and Hope

TELEVISED NEW YEAR'S DAY ADDRESS TO THE SOVIET PEOPLE

JANUARY 1, 1986

Good evening. This is Ronald Reagan, President of the United States. I am pleased to speak to you on the occasion of the New Year. This is a time for reflection—and for hope. As we look back on the year just concluded, and on the year that is to come, I want to share with you my hopes for the New Year, hopes for peace, prosperity and good will that the American and Soviet people share.

A Fresh Start

Just over a month ago, General Secretary Gorbachev and I met for the first time in Geneva. Our purpose was to begin a fresh chapter in the relations between our two countries and to try to reduce the suspicions and mistrust between us.

I think we made a good beginning. Mr. Gorbachev and I spent many hours together, speaking frankly and seriously about the most important issues of our time: reducing the massive nuclear arsenals on

-253-

both sides, resolving regional conflicts, ensuring respect for human rights as guaranteed under international agreements and other questions of mutual interest.

As the elected representative of the American people, I told Mr. Gorbachev of our deep desire for peace and that the American people do not wish the Soviet people any harm.

While there were many areas where we did not agree—which was to be expected—we left Geneva with a better understanding of one another and of the goals we each have. We are determined to build on that understanding in the coming months and years.

Common Ground

One of the most important things on which we agreed was the need to reduce the massive nuclear arsenals on both sides. As I have said many times, a nuclear war cannot be won and must never be fought. Therefore, we agreed to accelerate negotiations, where there is common ground, to reduce and eventually eliminate the means of nuclear destruction.

Our negotiators will soon be returning to the Geneva talks on nuclear and space arms where Mr. Gorbachev and I agreed we will seek agreements on the principle of 50-percent reductions in offensive nuclear arms and an interim agreement on intermediate-range nuclear systems. And it is my hope that one day we will be able to eliminate these weapons altogether, and rely increasingly for our security on defense systems that threaten no one.

Both the United States and Soviet Union are doing research on the possibilities of applying new technologies to the cause of defense. If these technologies become a reality, it is my dream to one day free us all from the threat of nuclear destruction.

Mutual Understanding

One of the best ways to build mutual understanding is to allow the American and Soviet peoples to get to know one another better. In Geneva, we signed a new agreement to exchange our most accomplished artists and academics. We also agreed to expand the contacts between our peoples so that students, teachers and young people can get to know each other directly. If people in both countries can visit, study and work together, too, then we will strengthen the bonds of understanding and build a true foundation for lasting peace.

I also discussed the American people's strong interest in humanitarian issues. Our democratic system is founded on the belief in the sanctity of human life and the rights of the individual—rights such as freedom of speech, of assembly, of movement and of worship. It is a sacred truth to us that every individual is a unique creation of God, with his or her own special talents, abilities, hopes and dreams. Respect for all people is essential to peace. And as we agreed in Geneva, progress in resolving humanitarian issues in a spirit of cooperation would go a long way to making 1986 a better year for all of us.

Year of Peace

A safe and lasting peace also requires finding peaceful settlements to armed conflicts, which cause so much human suffering in many parts of the world. I have proposed several concrete steps to help resolve such conflicts. It is my hope that in 1986 we will make progress toward this end. I see a busy year ahead in building on the foundations laid in Geneva. There is much work to be done. Mr. Gorbachev will visit the United States later this year, and I look forward to showing him our country. In 1987 I plan to visit your country, and hope to meet many of you.

On behalf of the American people, I wish you all a happy and healthy New Year. Let's work together to make it a year of peace. There is no better goal for 1986, or for any year. Let us look forward to a future of *chistoye nyebo*, blue skies, for all mankind. Thank you. □

A Time of Peace

ADDRESS TO THE SOVIET AND AMERICAN PEOPLES FOLLOWING THE SIGNING OF THE INF TREATY

THE WHITE HOUSE, WASHINGTON, D C
DECEMBER 8, 1987

General Secretary Gorbachev and distinguished guests, my fellow Americans and citizens of the Soviet Union.

The American philosopher, Ralph Waldo Emerson, once wrote that "there is properly no history; only biography." He meant by this that it is not enough to talk about history as simply forces and factors. History is ultimately a record of human will, human spirit, human aspirations of Earth's men and women, each with the precious soul and free will that the Lord bestows.

Time and Patience

Today, I, for the United States, and the General Secretary, for the Soviet Union, have signed the first agreement ever to eliminate an entire class of U.S. and Soviet nuclear weapons. We have made history. And yet, many so-called wise men once predicted that this agreement would be impossible to achieve—too many forces and factors stood against it. Well, still we persevered. We kept at it. And I hope the General Secretary will forgive me if I reveal that in some of the bleakest times, when it did truly seem that an agreement would prove impossible, I bucked myself up with the words of a great Russian, Leo Tolstoy, who wrote, "The strongest of all warriors are these two—time and patience."

In the next few days we will discuss further arms reductions and other issues—and again it will take time and patience to reach agreements. But as we begin these talks, let us remember that genuine inter-

national confidence and security are inconceivable without open societies with freedom of information, freedom of conscience, the right to
publish and the right to travel. So, yes, we will address human rights and
regional conflicts, for surely the salvation of all mankind lies only in
making everything the concern of all. With time, patience and willpower,
I believe we will resolve these issues. We must if we are to achieve a true,
secure and enduring peace.

A Time to Live

As different as our systems are, there is a great bond that draws the
American and Soviet peoples together. It is the common dream of
peace. More than 40 years ago we fought in a great war as allies. On the
day that news of the enemy's surrender reached Moscow, crowds gathered in front of the American Embassy. There they cheered the friendship of a nation that had opened a second front and sent food, muni-
tions and trucks to the Soviet peoples as they displayed awesome courage and will in turning the invader back. A young American diplomat
later told of a Soviet soldier in the crowds who shouted over and over,
"Now it is time to live."

Too often in the decades since then the soldier's dream—a time
to live—has been put off, at least as far as it concerned genuine peace
between our two countries. Yet we Americans have never stopped praying for peace. In every part of the world we want this to be a time to live.

Only those who don't know us believe that America is a materialistic land. But the true America is not supermarkets filled with meats,
milk and goods of all descriptions. It is not highways filled with cars. No,
true America is a land of faith and family. You can find it in our churches,
synagogues and mosques—in our homes and schools. As one of our
great writers put it: America is a willingness of the heart—the universal,
human heart—for Americans come from every part of Earth, including
the Soviet Union. We want a peace that fulfills the dream of all peoples
to raise their families in freedom and safety. And I believe that if both of
our countries have courage and the patience, we will build such a peace.

In the next two months, people throughout the world will take
part in two great festivals of faith—Hanukkah and Christmas. One is a
celebration of freedom, the other of peace on Earth, good will toward
men. My great hope is that the biographies of our times will record that
we had the will to make this the right season for this summit.

Thank you and God bless you.   □

www.ingramcontent.com/pod-product-compliance
Lightning Source LLC
Chambersburg PA
CBHW030534030726
47495CB00004B/985